The Irish war on drugs

MANCHESTER
1824

Manchester University Press

The Irish war on drugs

The seductive folly of prohibition

Paul O'Mahony

Manchester University Press
Manchester and New York

distributed exclusively in the USA by Palgrave

The right of Paul O'Mahony to be identified as the author of this work has been asserted by him in accordance with the Copyright, Designs and Patents Act 1988.

Published by Manchester University Press
Oxford Road, Manchester M13 9NR, UK
and Room 400, 175 Fifth Avenue, New York, NY 10010, USA
www.manchesteruniversitypress.co.uk

Distributed exclusively in the USA by
Palgrave, 175 Fifth Avenue, New York,
NY 10010, USA

Distributed exclusively in Canada by
UBC Press, University of British Columbia, 2029 West Mall,
Vancouver, BC, Canada V6T 1Z2

British Library Cataloguing-in-Publication Data
A catalogue record for this book is available from the British Library

Library of Congress Cataloging-in-Publication Data applied for

ISBN 978 0 7190 7790 6 *hardback*
ISBN 978 0 7190 7902 3 *paperback*

First published 2008

17 16 15 14 13 12 11 10 09 08   10 9 8 7 6 5 4 3 2

Typeset in Caslon
by Koinonia, Manchester
Printed in Great Britain
by CPI Antony Rowe, Chippenham, Wiltshire

Contents

Tables and figures

Tables

Figures

Acknowledgements

Without in any way implying that they endorse the arguments of this book, the author would like to gratefully acknowledge the helpful advice of Sean Cassin OFM, Johnny Connolly and Tony Geoghegan on various sections of the manuscript. I would especially like to thank Peter McVerry SJ for his encouragement and Tim Murphy for his constructive and erudite criticism of the whole manuscript. Needless to say, any errors are the sole responsibility of the author.

1

Philosophy, politics and rhetoric

The debate on illicit drugs is highly emotive, generating more heat than light and characterised by an endless, futile rehearsal of old arguments. Political, academic and popular arguments about drugs are frequently overburdened with vaguely defined concepts, unresolved contradictions and artificial antinomies. The public debate on drugs, therefore, tends to be obscure, confused and irredeemably sterile – often a mere dialogue of the deaf between prohibitionists and decriminalisers.[1]

Proponents and opponents of prohibition alike often hold ardent moral convictions about illicit drugs and tend to be singularly impervious to counterargument. Consequently, the drugs debate, though it makes copious use of 'evidence', rarely has a secure anchorage in reliable, objectively considered evidence. Prohibitionists in particular can be so convinced that they are right about the evils of drugs and the need to banish them that they entirely ignore the most crucial evidence of all – that, under prohibition, harmful forms of drug use, so far from declining, have greatly increased.

In Ireland, a prohibitionist, 'war on drugs' rhetoric is dominant at the political level and in most media representations of drug issues. This rhetoric has a strong emotional appeal, resonating with people because of the obvious harm that can be caused by drugs. This harm is epitomised by the lives, families and communities devastated by drug use and by the many hundreds of deaths from opiate overdoses and from AIDS and other diseases spread by shared injecting equipment and other drug-related practices. The 'war on drugs' rhetoric also resonates with people because of the violence and ruthlessness associated with the criminal drugs trade and because of the huge amount of property crime committed by some drug users. People fearful of drugs and their ill-effects are easily seduced by a prohibitionist rhetoric, which promises, although it never delivers, crushing defeat for illicit drugs users, traders and producers. The 'war on drugs' rhetoric demonises drugs, drugs dealers and drug users, but exerts a generally pernicious influence by oversimplifying issues, encouraging intolerance and discouraging critical thought.

This book looks behind the rhetoric and examines how the criminal law, as the main and essential instrument of the 'war on drugs', has in reality shaped the Irish (specifically the Republic of Ireland's) response to illicit drug use since the late 1970s. How the Irish 'war on drugs' has been waged over the last 30 years and to what effect are described in some detail. A deeper purpose of the book is to make the case for the abandonment of prohibition in Ireland and, indeed, throughout the world, based on an analysis not just of the ill-effects of prohibition, but also of the positive benefits which could be gained, if society were to recognise a fundamental, though by no means absolute, right to use drugs. In order to do this a number of steps are necessary. The first step (Chapter 1) is to examine the language, meaning and logic of the important national, international and institutional policy statements which guide current drugs policy in Ireland. The second step (Chapter 2) is to describe and carefully define the major alternative perspectives on drugs, which variously underpin prohibition, harm reduction and legalisation policies and approaches. Chapter 3 then examines the general relationship between drugs and crime and outlines the history of this relationship in Ireland. The following three chapters describe the evolution of Irish policy on drugs, since the inception, by way of the Misuse of Drugs Act 1977, of an explicit, fully elaborated system of drugs prohibition in Ireland. Special emphasis is placed on the use of the criminal law against intrinsically drug-related crime, such as possession and supply of drugs, but these chapters also address the harm reductionist movement, which gained considerable momentum after 1996, effectively transforming the nature of the Irish 'war on drugs' and introducing a stronger focus on the alleviation of health and social drug-related problems. The third of these chapters (Chapter 6) evaluates the claim that Ireland now has an appropriately 'balanced' policy on drugs.

Chapter 7 broadens the discussion to the international 'war on drugs' and provides a theoretical explanation, based on contemporary scientific understandings of human nature, for the obvious failure of prohibition to lower the prevalence of drug use, especially destructive and problematic forms of drug use, and for its seeming inability to dissuade a large number of young people from experimenting with or regularly using illicit drugs. Chapter 8 carefully evaluates the Irish evidence on drug-related health, crime and social problems and concludes that prohibition has had very deleterious effects in Ireland and that the new compromise system of prohibition incorporating significant harm reduction measures, which has rapidly developed since 1996, is failing to deliver on its promise and does not provide an adequate response to the underlying problems. Chapter 9 analyses the powerful defences, which allow prohibitionist ideas to continue to dominate across the world. This chapter exposes the logical fallacies, misinterpretations of evidence, moral confusions and emotional manipulation which enable prohibitionists to dismiss the overwhelming evidence for the failure of prohibition and ignore the urgent need for a radically different approach. The final chapter outlines the kind of non-prohibitionist approach which would offer net gains in the reduction of drug harms and also respect the human right to take drugs as long as the rights of others are not thereby infringed.

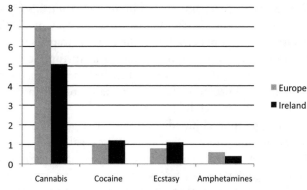

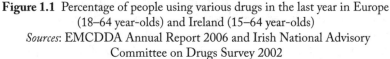

Figure 1.1 Percentage of people using various drugs in the last year in Europe
(18–64 year-olds) and Ireland (15–64 year-olds)
Sources: EMCDDA Annual Report 2006 and Irish National Advisory
Committee on Drugs Survey 2002

The book is premised on the belief that the evidence for and against prohibition must be described in concrete, practical as well as abstract, theoretical terms. A purely theoretical analysis is of limited value unless it is accompanied by an examination of the actual implementation of prohibitionist policies and the real effects of these policies. It is valid and useful to evaluate prohibition only within the context of a specific society and jurisdiction. Local laws, customs, values, policies and practices characterise and differentiate local forms of prohibition. But these local forms of prohibition, such as Irish prohibition, contain and give shape to a universal philosophy of prohibition, which transcends jurisdictional boundaries and is embedded in and promoted by international law. Systems of prohibition are always a combination of local character and certain key, universal ideas and principles. This book will pay special attention to the specific Irish formulation of prohibition and its recent history and will analyse universal theoretical and practical aspects mainly through the prism of Irish prohibition.

The 30-year history of drugs prohibition in Ireland is of intrinsic interest. Ironically, it represents a trajectory of dramatic transformation from an era when the use of drugs and drug-related problems were negligible, to the current era when drug use is widespread throughout Irish society and very troubling. Figure 1.1 indicates that use of cannabis and stimulants in Ireland is similar to or greater than that found in other European countries. Although similar comparative figures are not available for opiates, according to the European Monitoring Centre for Drugs and Drug Addiction,[2] the Irish prevalence of problematic use of opiates is one of the highest in Europe at about 8 cases per 1,000 adults. According to a recent survey of 15 and 16 year old schoolchildren across Europe, the percentages of Irish children reporting that various drugs were fairly easily or very easily available to them were among the highest in Europe.[3] They were the highest for inhalants (77%), ecstasy (34%), cocaine (22%) and crack (18%) and second highest for cannabis (60%), magic mushrooms (25%) and heroin (17%). While these are only perceptions, they reflect the pervasiveness and penetration of the drugs culture in Ireland. Today drug-related crime, violence, illness, death and social disruption are major ills that seriously threaten the quality of life of all Irish citizens. This transition has coincided with and is connected to Ireland's metamorphosis into an affluent, progressive, economically successful country.

Ireland is a small, peripheral jurisdiction with its legal roots in the British common law system and the habit of importing legal innovations, such as ASBOs[4] and Drug Courts, from larger jurisdictions – mainly Britain but more recently also the U.S. Ireland is not a drug-producing nor a drug trend-setting country. Instead it is a country that imports drugs and tends to follow the drug fashions established elsewhere. Nonetheless, Ireland provides a useful case study for the analysis of the underlying, universal issues of prohibition.

While Ireland is a small country with a short history of serious drug problems, it is now one of the most globalised and economically successful countries in the world and a notable exemplar of the many problems that afflict wealthy developed nations, including drug use.[5] Ireland's short history with drug problems is reasonably easy to encapsulate and provides valuable insights into the country's transition from backwater tranquillity to troubled modernity and affluence. Ireland's history with drugs has been short but intense and bitter and has exposed the country to most of the difficulties and issues, which many far larger countries face. These problems arise both from drug use itself and from the international system of prohibition. Ireland's small size is in fact an analytical advantage since it allows for the kind of detailed and comprehensive overview of the reality of drug problems and the state's response to them that would be impossible with a much larger jurisdiction or a federal nation such as the U.S.

Ireland, although not specially progressive in its policies, is also a useful case study of the problems of prohibition, both because, for a long period, it adopted an unreflective, rather crude prohibitionist approach and because, in recent years, it has considerably softened its hard-line approach and made a very substantial investment in a diversity of more constructive approaches to drug problems.

This book will make the case that the stern, unnuanced form of prohibition which existed in Ireland before 1996 did far more harm than good and that it is increasingly obvious that the more enlightened form of prohibition, which has emerged since 1996 and promotes harm reduction approaches, is failing to deliver the expected gains. In this specific Irish context, this book will argue that the time is now ripe to consider the abolition of prohibition. However, it is obvious that the project of abandoning prohibition, although it can be the legitimate aspiration of a single small jurisdiction, makes little sense as a unilateral project or an isolated experiment. The overall success of such a project clearly requires a high degree of international consensus and a major paradigm shift in global values and thinking and, most obviously, in international law. It is difficult to see how this will come about, since the many published critiques of prohibition, which enumerate prohibition's failures and disastrous costs, have had so little impact. This book, however, will argue that a sea-change in thinking on illicit drugs is possible, but only if the critics of prohibition pay particular attention to understanding and overcoming the intrinsic rhetorical and political advantages of prohibition. These largely unnoticed and unchallenged advantages are so powerful and influential in Ireland and elsewhere that they effectively preclude any serious discussion of more hopeful, alternative approaches, despite what almost everyone agrees are the obvious failures of prohibition.

This book focuses mainly on the role of criminal justice, because the criminal law and its manner of implementation through law enforcement define prohibition and are at the heart of the present system. In fact, the Irish response to drugs is first and last a matter of criminal justice policy, though this fact is frequently forgotten. Some people, who work to ameliorate drugs problems in the areas of public health, harm reduction and social inclusion, tend to forget or minimise the powerful, defining role of the criminal law – as long as it does not actively impinge on their work. This is a serious mistake and this book will begin by analysing and parsing official drugs policy in Ireland and the EU in order to elucidate the inexorable, dominant role of criminal justice within Irish social policy on drugs. The paramount influence of the criminal law in drugs policy is the enduring reality, which ensures that Ireland remains resolutely prohibitionist despite all its concessions to harm reduction.

The tangled web of policy

Despite its central importance, it is an impossible task to characterise Irish criminal justice policy on drugs and drug-related crime in a simple formula. There are a number of reasons for this. First, it is very difficult to disentangle health, social, economic and criminal justice policies on drugs because there is enormous overlap and interaction both in terms of the intention of such policies, their implementation and their planned and unplanned effects. So, health-directed actions often impact on the criminal justice system and criminal justice initiatives and practices often impact on health outcomes. In addition, these policies are not always coherent and indeed are sometimes conflicting.

Second, the definitive statement of criminal justice policy on drugs and drug-related crime is to be found in legislation, but legislation itself is sometimes little more than aspirational and sometimes represents an impracticable compromise position between conflicting viewpoints and approaches. While law is of overriding importance and, arguably, has the final say, any ambiguities in the law or unrealistic aspirations of the law will lead to uncertainties and anomalies in practice. These uncertainties and anomalies are part of the reality of policy as it is implemented and obviously confound the task of interpretation of the policy implications of the law.

Third, while legislation is the major vehicle for the expression of the democratic will of the government and the people's representatives, there are many other powerful, relatively independent, decision-makers in the criminal justice system. The system is complex and allows very significant discretion to the judiciary, who are constitutionally independent, the Garda,[6] and all those professionals, such as probation officers and general practitioners, who are empowered by the system to implement sanctions and treatments with drug offenders. This discretion is not infrequently used in ways that deliberately or inadvertently undermine the explicit or implicit intentions of legislation.

Fourth, because of the rapid advances in communications/information technology, we have entered a new political era, in which there is irresistible pressure on governments and their associated agencies to provide overarching policy statements and long-term strategy documents on issues such as drugs and crime. Some of this pressure results from membership of the EU and the UN and other international bodies, which seek international cooperation and coordination on illicit drugs issues. There is a general expectation that such statements will provide the blueprint for a comprehensive, constructive, coherent and effective policy. Furthermore, government policy statements are expected to be evidence-based, transparent and accountable. These statements often purport to come from an ideologically neutral, pragmatic, benevolent and 'progressive' stance.

The cynical view is that these strategies and policy statements are often merely rhetorical devices that create the mirage of integrated policy, when in reality they put a gloss and public relations spin on a variety of actions that are driven by other, often contradictory, ideologically inspired policies. Statements, such as the National Drugs Strategy,[7] which now typically give equal weight to demand reduction, supply reduction and harm reduction, have the politically useful appearance of being all things to all men. These statements seem to satisfy the main demands of at least two of the major perspectives on how to handle the drugs issue. However, they usually achieve this by resorting to ambiguous language or simplistic slogans and by simply asserting the compatibility of potentially opposed strategies, such as demand reduction, supply reduction and harm reduction, without actually resolving or even examining key underlying dilemmas and profound conflicts between these strategies.

Fifth, while the law is paramount, the National Drugs Strategy in a sense takes political precedence, since it signals the government's most recent and still evolving, official thinking on the drugs problem. It is quite plausible, perhaps even to be expected, that there will be tensions between the National Drugs Strategy and the criminal law, which at some future date might be remedied by legislative change. This is particularly the case since the National Drugs Strategy is not focused solely or even chiefly on criminal justice aspects, but also encompasses health, social welfare and other issues, and since it deliberately sets out to conjoin the disparate strategies of demand reduction, supply reduction and harm reduction. It is quite likely that practices that result from the attempt to implement the National Drugs Strategy, including practices which represent newly forged compromises between the goals of demand reduction, supply reduction and harm reduction, will be inconsistent with current law and will eventually provoke legislative change.

Sixth and finally, if legislation and strategy statements represent the official, formal framework of policy on crime and drugs, there is a whole other level of informal political engagement with the issues through everyday discourse, which strongly influences both policy itself and the way policy is implemented. The media and the public play an important role in this informal policy-making process. Exaggerated and scare-mongering media coverage, vociferous and impassioned public complaint (often justified) and even single sensational events can trigger knee-jerk political responses aimed mainly at immediate personal and party political, electoral advantage rather than long-lasting solutions. On criminal justice matters, politicians often legislate in a rushed manner[8] so as to create a public perception that the government takes the matter seriously and has effective solutions. This perception is usually short-lived and is gained at the cost of failing to establish a more integrated and long-term approach to the issues.

It can also be argued that the hyperbole, sensationalism and mindless dogmatism of much media coverage of drugs issues have helped promote the dominance of condemnatory, repressive and punitive attitudes in public and political discourse. It is certainly the case that the tenor and substance of media coverage of drugs issues have perpetuated a restricted, stereotypic public and political debate. Demonisation of drugs and drug users and the narrowing of the parameters of debate have in turn encouraged the exploitation of the area for political purposes and contributed to the failure to depoliticise the crucially important issue of drugs and crime.[9]

The confused rhetoric of official statements

The EU Action Plans

In order to illustrate some of these problems of interpretation and definition, especially difficulties in delineating the relationship between the goals and methods of demand reduction, supply reduction and harm reduction, it may be useful to examine some key statements from policy documents relevant to Ireland. The *EU Action Plan 2000–2004*,[10] for example, outlines a fundamental need to continue the 'balanced approach to the fight against drugs, in which supply and demand reduction are seen as mutually reinforcing elements'.

It should first be noted that there is a clear and unequivocal commitment in this statement to a *fight* against drugs. The view that those drugs that are currently categorised as illicit, are inherently bad and harmful is here given the status of a consensual, common sense assumption. But there is also a concern expressed in the statement that supply and demand reduction should be *seen* as mutually reinforcing. This is tacit recognition of the fact that supply and demand reduction are sometimes seen as, and actually have a major potential to be, mutually opposed strategies. It is reasonable to assume that the EU are in fact urging the various drugs policy actors not merely to create the perception of mutual reinforcement but also to implement supply and demand reduction strategies in a balanced way so that they are as mutually reinforcing as possible. How this is to be done, however, is not spelled out.

In reality, while it is easy to envisage situations where the two strategies are mutually reinforcing – for instance, if successful supply reduction increases the retail cost of drugs, it may be easier to dissuade people from their use – there are many ways in which supply reduction and demand reduction inevitably counteract each other. So, for example, the highly symbolic, illegal, forbidden status of drugs, which in large part derives from prohibition laws and supply reduction approaches, is, paradoxically, a key component of the psychological attraction and negative glamour of drugs, especially for rebellious teenagers and marginalised people who are antipathetic to authority. Some people are excited by and attracted to drugs partly because they are forbidden. Moreover, the scarcity, which results from effective supply reduction, of any commodity, including drugs, not only increases the economic price of the commodity but also adds to its perceived value and desirability. Most obviously, there is tension between supply and demand reduction objectives because prohibitionist law enforcement tends to discourage drug users from accessing treatment and rehabilitation opportunities and services. As Cohen and Csete state, 'the reality of the drug user being driven 'underground' by fear of arrest and not seeking services is familiar to HIV/AIDS and public health experts'.[11]

The more recent *EU Action Plan 2005–2008*[12] states that 'the ultimate aim of the Action Plan is to significantly reduce the prevalence of drug use among the population and to reduce the social harm and health damage caused by the use of and trade in illicit drugs. It aims to provide a framework for a balanced approach to reducing both supply and demand through a number of specific actions.' Five separate areas for action are specified: 1) coordination, which focuses on the coordination of drugs policy within Member States and at the EU level; 2) information, research and evaluation; 3) international cooperation; 4) supply reduction; and 5) demand reduction. Action on supply reduction is intended to achieve a 'measurable improvement in the effectiveness, efficiency and knowledge base of law enforcement interventions by the EU and its Member States targeting production, trafficking of drugs, the diversion of precursors, including the diversion of synthetic drug precursors imported into the EU, drug trafficking and the financing of terrorism, and money laundering in relation to drug crime. This is to be achieved by focusing on drug-related organised crime … and looking for ways of intensifying preventive action in relation to drug-related crime'. Action on demand reduction is intended to achieve a 'measurable reduction of the use of drugs, of dependence and of drug-related health and social risks through the development and improvement of an effective and integrated comprehensive knowledge-based demand reduction system including prevention, early intervention, treatment, harm reduction, rehabilitation and social reintegration measures within the EU Member States'.

The most recent EU Action Plan, then, does not address the compatibility of supply and demand reduction approaches nor does it use the terminology of a fight against drugs. However, there is no question of a weakening of resolve or of a change in policy in this regard. Illicit drugs are still clearly perceived as inherently bad and the grounding purpose of policy is to reduce their use and the social and health-related harms associated with them, including harms related to the involvement of organised crime in the supply of drugs. Two points are worthy of note.

First, there is the dual use of the concept of harm reduction. Harm reduction is, on the one hand, the fundamental purpose and justification for EU drugs policy. At this level the concept of harm reduction underpins both supply reduction and demand reduction. The fundamental aim of both approaches is to reduce harm. In other words, at this broad level, supply and demand reduction are actually harm reduction measures. On the other hand, the concept of harm reduction is listed in the Action Plan as one of a series of demand reduction interventions, along with treatment, prevention and others. This is a very different 'micro level' use of the concept and refers to services, such as needle exchange and safe injecting rooms, epitomising the operationalisation of harm reduction as a specific policy strategy. This specific, 'micro level' policy strategy is in fact distinct from both supply reduction and demand reduction and may even be seen as opposed to these approaches. The operation of these kind of 'micro level' harm reduction approaches often requires special dispensations from the law. Furthermore, 'micro level' harm reduction interventions, such as needle exchange and safe injecting rooms, are not truly demand reduction measures since they countenance continued use. 'Micro level' harm reduction approaches clearly place certain constraints on the operation of punitive, prohibitionist, law enforcement action in both the supply and demand reduction domains.

It is a weakness of the EU Action Plan that it pays so little attention to harm reduction and that it confusingly subsumes a particularly narrow conception of harm reduction under the heading of demand reduction. This is especially unhelpful in the context of enlargement, when, as Chatwin has recently pointed out:

> In the areas of drug trafficking and production and the exchange of information between member states some concrete policy measures have been almost directly transferable to new member states, largely due to the high degree of co-operation between existing member states in these areas. However, in the more controver-

sial areas of harm reduction and dealing with drug use and drug users there are
no concrete EU guidelines in place and policy is left up to the national governments of individual countries. In this important area many existing EU member
states have adopted important measures designed to reduce the harm of official
drug policy but these practices are not proving to be so easily transferable to new
Member States.[13]

This potential confusion in terminology illustrates the slippery nature of
slogans such as demand reduction, supply reduction and harm reduction. In
fact, the meanings of the terms frequently differ from person to person and
from context to context. Obviously, if confusion is to be avoided, these are
concepts that require explication in terms of their intended connotations in
each specific context of use. However, these key concepts rarely receive this
kind of attention.

In fact, 'micro level' harm reduction approaches are explicitly motivated by
a philosophy of harm reduction, which differs significantly from the broad
harm reduction concept that, according to the Action Plan, is the ulterior
motive force behind both supply and demand reduction. This suggests that
it is important to distinguish at least three different usages of the term harm
reduction: 1) as a description of specific interventions, 2) as the underlying
philosophy behind such interventions (harm reduction not requiring elimination of drug use) and 3) as the wider philosophy that motivates and justifies
both supply reduction and demand reduction (harm reduction calling for the
elimination of drug use). The term harm reduction, then, can refer to two
superficially similar philosophies, which are in fact diametrically opposed in at
least some of their core implications. A loose, shrewd or disingenuous use of
the term can permit advocates of one of these philosophies to masquerade as
or be mistaken for an advocate of the other philosophy as the occasion suits. In
this book, harm reduction not requiring elimination of drug use will be termed
harm reductionism or the *harm reductionist* perspective in order to distinguish
it from the broad harm reduction concept, which sees the elimination of drug
use as the chief means of harm reduction.

Second, it is noteworthy that the Action Plan appears to view the role of the
criminal law as confined to supply control and is almost totally silent on the
whole area of the criminalisation of possession and use of drugs at the level of
the individual user. Perhaps the EU is avoiding this somewhat contentious area
because it is mindful of the diversity of approaches to the issues of possession
and use in the criminal law of Member States. However, the criminalisation of
possession and use is a key legal process of relevance to both supply reduction
and demand reduction. The use of the criminal law against individuals who use
drugs is a crucial facet of the prohibition approach, which in the Action Plan is
associated with the aim of supply reduction, but not with the aim of demand
reduction. However, it appears most logical to classify this kind of preventive
use of the criminal law as a demand reduction technique. In Ireland, people
can be and are frequently arrested, charged, tried and punished because they

use drugs, i.e. for the possession of small amounts of a drug for personal use. This criminal and penal process is intended to be a serious deterrent, scaring people, who use or are contemplating using, off drugs through fear of the legal consequences, if they should be caught.

In short, the law enforcement process is coercively deployed in demand reduction as well as in supply reduction. There is, then, despite what the Action Plan suggests, no neat separation of fields of operation, with law enforcement restricted to supply reduction and public health and education to demand reduction. Indeed, the role of law enforcement in demand reduction is critical and substantial. It is, in fact, far too significant to have been ignored in this way by the Action Plan.

The Irish National Drugs Strategy

The overall strategic objective in the *Irish National Drugs Strategy 2001–2008*,[14] like the most recent EU Action Plan, eschews the language of 'war on' or 'fight against' drugs and underpins the whole strategy with a harm reduction purpose. It states that 'the objective is to significantly reduce the harm caused to individuals and society by the misuse of drugs through a concerted focus on supply reduction, prevention, treatment and research'. In essence this statement echoes the main objectives of the EU Action Plan 2005–2008. The terminology of demand reduction has been replaced in the statement with that of prevention and treatment. It is clear that the Irish National Drugs Strategy like the Action Plan ignores and fails to comprehend the important fact that law enforcement is also centrally involved in demand reduction.

However, the phrase 'reduce the harm caused to individuals and society by the misuse of drugs', which is clearly central in the overall strategic objective, can be construed as suggesting a somewhat different perspective to that of the EU. While the EU Action Plan straightforwardly aims 'to reduce the prevalence of (illicit) drug use', the Irish use of the phrase *misuse of drugs* qualifies and complicates matters. This phrase contains more than a hint of the philosophy of harm reduction not requiring the elimination of drug use. By specifying *misuse,* the possibility is raised that there may be acceptable, that is not harmful or only trivially harmful, forms of use of illicit drugs – that there may be problem and non-problem drug users who should be treated differently. Thus, the at-first-glance, seemingly straightforward, strategic objective turns out to be pregnant with divergent meanings, which are likely to have conflicting implications for policy. Furthermore, this key strategy statement also tends to obscure rather than clarify matters by coupling individual and societal harm reduction in the one objective, a manoeuvre, which papers over the very considerable potential for serious clashes between individual and societal views of what is harmful.

Garda Drug Policy

Current Garda Drug Policy[15] is 'to enforce the laws relating to drugs'. This is one of six major policing goals and, in their policy statement, the Garda note that the Public Attitudes Survey of 1999[16] 'placed enforcing the laws relating to drugs number one in order of importance'. The statement continues: 'central to our policy is the rigorous enforcement of all drug legislation reducing the supply of drugs within society … the organisation [Garda Síochána] makes no distinction in terms of criminality with either the physical and or psychological effects of specific drugs of abuse … [but] … demand reduction [also] forms an integral part of our policing strategy … [involving] commitment to education and prevention programmes as a means of reducing the demand for drugs … and supporting treatment provision facilities delivered at a local level'.

In other words, the Garda statement, like the overall strategy objective of the Irish National Drugs Strategy 2001–2008, defines demand reduction so as to exclude the most obvious role of the Garda in demand reduction that is through law enforcement against the possession of drugs for personal use. This is a very significant omission because it allows the Garda to endorse demand reduction as if this had no implications for their own practice of enforcing 'the laws relating to drugs'. In reality many demand reduction approaches of the treatment type and especially 'micro level' harm reduction interventions require the Garda to show considerable restraint in terms of enforcing drug laws.

The firm focus of the Garda Drug Policy is on law enforcement. There is a strength and clarity to the unequivocal Garda commitment to the rigorous enforcement of all drug laws without regard to differences between drugs. It is, however, questionable whether Garda operations realise this aim. Whether or not the Garda rigorously enforce all drug laws without reference to the type of drug or the type of user is a matter of fact requiring examination of the empirical evidence. It is clear that the Garda claim faithful adherence to an undifferentiated prohibitionist policy and that this policy is inspired by the philosophy of harm reduction requiring elimination of illicit drugs. When the Garda speak of 'drugs of abuse' they are referring to all drugs that are classified as illegal and they specifically rule out taking any account of differences in the way such drugs might be used.

There are, therefore, very significant differences between Garda policy and the policy expressed in the overall strategic objective of the National Drugs Strategy. As we have seen, the latter appears to draw distinctions between the use and misuse of drugs and so between problem users and non-problem users and appears to contain an implicit commitment to a philosophy of harm reduction not requiring the elimination of illicit drugs. Garda policy ignores these nuances and claims only to be concerned with the eradication of the use of illegal substances. There would, then, appear to be considerable potential for conflict between the Garda policy and National Drugs Strategy policy.

A concrete example of conflict

A statement by the former Minister for Justice, Michael McDowell, provides a useful example of the limitations and ambiguities of broad policy statements and the questionable nature of any simple assertion that supply reduction, demand reduction and harm reduction approaches are compatible. In a Dail Debate (8 December 2004) the Minister stated his opposition to needle exchange programmes in the Irish prison system, despite the fact that such programmes have been found to be useful, 'micro level', harm reduction measures in some other jurisdictions.[17] He stated: 'needle exchange schemes would subvert and run contrary to increasing staff vigilance in searching for drugs and preventing them from being smuggled into prisons. I remain committed to pursuing government policy to end the use of heroin in Irish prisons. It would be a contradiction of this stated government aim for the Irish Prison Service to tolerate continuing intravenous drug use involving a needle exchange programme. Ending of all heroin use must mean just that.'

This situation provides a concrete example, which illustrates the fact that the ambiguities I have described surrounding harm reduction principles are not merely semantic quibbles. Indeed, this situation is a classic exemplar of the inherent conflict between the prohibitionist, broad harm reduction philosophy, requiring elimination of illicit drug use, and the harm reductionist philosophy, which does not require such elimination. The Minister here endorses the prohibitionist stance of the criminal law and reasserts the superiority of this law over 'harm reductionist' aims, particularly in the unique, highly controlled environment of the prison, in which systematic breaches of the criminal law cannot easily be condoned. Furthermore, he explicitly invokes the wider philosophy of harm reduction by means of elimination of drug use and implies that an active prohibitionist approach will eventually solve the problem and reduce harm by successfully ending intravenous drug use in prison, thereby undermining the case for the 'micro level' harm reduction approach.

Harm reductionists oppose the Minister's analysis by characterising his view that all intravenous use can be eliminated from the prisons as unrealistic, wishful thinking. The current evidence, they argue, strongly suggests both that past prohibitionist approaches have utterly failed to eliminate drugs from prisons and that it would be impossible to introduce truly effective supply reduction methods in prisons without seriously breaching the human rights of prisoners and taking disproportionately coercive action, which would be the source of new severe harms. In this context, where continued intravenous use is highly likely, harm reductionists argue that it is irresponsible to fail to take steps, such as needle exchange, which have a proven capacity to prevent grave harms, such as the spread of HIV and hepatitis, known to be associated with the sharing of contaminated needles in prison. They argue in effect that it is better to exchange the purist's insistence on consistency in the application of prohibitionist laws, which holds out the alluring but unrealistic prospect of an almost total elimination of drug-related harms in prisons, for the pragmatist's reliance on practical harm reduction, which promises more modest but more certain gains.

The overall strategy objective of the National Drugs Strategy also seems to prioritise the form of harm reduction, which does not require elimination of drug use. However, it lacks clarity and generally fails to address and reconcile conflicts between its own prohibitionist and harm reductionist recommendations. It cannot, therefore, help to resolve the kind of difficult dilemma, to which the Minister draws our attention. Of course, the Minister in forcefully supporting the prohibitionist approach at the expense of harm reductionist approaches was ignoring some important inconsistencies in his own prohibitionist policy for the prisons, since methadone maintenance and other harm reductionist methods are increasingly available within the prison system.

The complex, vexed and often very local nature of conflicts between the harm reductionist and the prohibitionist agendas is further illustrated by the view expressed on the same issue in the report of the Group to Review the Structure and Organisation of Prison Health Care Services.[18] At page 11, they make a recommendation for the provision of disinfectant tablets for the sterilisation of drug using equipment 'without further delay.' However, they did not recommend needle or syringe exchange because 'the risk of attack on staff and prisoners with syringes supplied by the state would appear to be unacceptable' (at page 46). This is a new argument against needle exchange. Although the argument is couched in the language of risk reduction, the Group are in fact balancing one set of potential harms against another. Unlike the Minister, the Group do not align themselves with the purist prohibitionist approach, since they recommend the provision of disinfectants – a harm reductionist measure, which can be seen as condoning continued intravenous use. However, they decide to favour the avoidance of the risk of physical harm to staff or prisoners (and avoidance, subsequent to such harm, of the risk that the state will be found legally liable for damages) over the avoidance of the risk of spread of disease through the sharing of contaminated syringes. This problem is not typical inasmuch as it is tied to the local context of the prison. However, it does typify the way that these disputes have an almost bottomless pit of harms to explore and inevitably raise issues of credibility and evidence.

Summary

Criminal justice policy on drugs is complex and cannot easily be disentangled from broader social and health policy on drugs. The criminal justice legislation on drugs is fundamental but its intentions are not always clear and its variable implementation by the police, the courts and other agents reflects the existence of considerable levels of discretion in the system. Ireland is a signatory to various UN conventions on drugs, which limit Irish autonomy with respect to drugs legislation.[19] Irish policy must also be consistent with EU policy, which is currently seeking to build a more coordinated, 'balanced' approach across all EU Member States.

Recent national and international statements on drug policy have adopted the economic jargon of supply and demand reduction. This has led to a misperception of or under-emphasis on the central role of the criminal law in demand reduction (as a coercive deterrent), and to some confusion over the term, harm reduction. There are three meanings attached to this term which need to be distinguished: 1) as a description of specific harm reduction techniques, such as needle exchange; 2) as the philosophy of harm reduction not requiring elimination of drug use (termed *harm reductionism* in this book); and 3) as the philosophy of harm reduction by means of the elimination of drug use, which is essentially the prohibitionist position underlying and framing current policy. The relatively recent refusal of the then Minister for Justice to allow needle exchange within the prisons is an example of the continuing tension between prohibition and harm reductionism. It also illustrates the potential for confusion around the term harm reduction, since the Minister justifies his decision by invoking the rationale of harm reduction through elimination of drug use.

Notes

1 Some writers have attempted to maintain the important distinction between legalisation (where it is legal to use, produce, market and supply drugs) and decriminalisation or depenalisation (where illicit drugs remain illegal but penalties for personal possession are eliminated, not enforced or reduced for example from a criminal offence to a civil offence, which is not arrestable or imprisonable). Many other writers ignore these distinctions and use the terms legalisation and decriminalisation interchangeably. In this book, except when a more precise definition is explicitly provided, the terms legalisation and decriminalisation will both be used to mean the abandonment of the system of drugs prohibition and suppression through the criminal law.

2 European Monitoring Centre for Drugs and Drug Addiction, *Annual Report 2006*, Lisbon: EMCDDA.

3 Hibell, B., Andersson, B., Bjarnason, T., Ahlstrom, S., Kokkevi, A., and Morgan, M. (2004) *The ESPAD Report 2003: Alcohol and Other Drug Use Among Students in 35 European Countries*, Strasbourg: Council of Europe.

4 ASBOs (Anti-Social Behaviour Orders) were introduced in Ireland on 1 January 2007 for adults and 1 March 2007 for children between the ages of 12 and 18.

5 According to the A.T. Kearney/Foreign Policy Globalization Index 2006, Ireland is the 4th most globalised country after Singapore, Switzerland and the U.S.

6 The Garda Síochána is the single, national police force in Ireland.

7 Department of Tourism, Sport and Recreation (2001) *Irish National Drugs Strategy 2001–2008*, Dublin: Stationery Office.

8 See, for example, Fennell, C. (1993) *Crime and Crisis: Justice by Illusion*, Cork University Press.

9 However, Butler, S. (1991) [in 'Drug problems and drug policies in Ireland: a quarter of a century reviewed', *Administration*, 39, 210] points out that the 1977

Misuse of Drugs Act was the result of a consensual, cross-party approach to the issue and that more partisan political approaches only developed as the drugs problem became more severe.

10 *EU Action Plan 2000–2004* (June 2000), Brussels: The European Council.

11 Cohen, J. and Csete, J. (2006) 'As strong as the weakest pillar: harm reduction, law enforcement and human rights', *International Journal of Drug Policy*, 17, 101–103.

12 *EU Action Plan 2005–2008*, Brussels: The European Council (May 2005).

13 Chatwin, C. (2004) 'The effects of EU enlargement on European drug policy', *Drugs: Education, Prevention & Policy*, 11, 6, 437–448.

14 *National Drugs Strategy 2001–2008*, Dublin: Stationery Office.

15 The policy document, *An Garda Síochána Drug Policy*, is available on the Garda Síochána website http://Garda.ie.

16 Garda Síochána Public Attitudes Survey 1999 (2000), Templemore: Garda Research Unit..

17 *Prisons, Drugs and Society* (2001) [Bern: WHO Health in Prisons Project and The Pompidou Group of the Council Of Europe] states that four countries in Europe (Switzerland, Moldova, Spain and Germany) have syringe exchange programmes in a total of 20 different prisons and that they 'can be useful as an integral part of a general approach to drug and health services in prisons'.

18 Report of the Group to Review the Structure and Organisation of Prison Health Care Services (2001), Dublin: Department of Justice, Equality and Law Reform.

19 UN Single Convention on Narcotic Drugs (1961), Convention on Psychotropic Substances (1971), and Convention Against Illicit Traffic in Narcotic Drugs and Psychotropic Substances (1988), New York: UN.

2

Three major perspectives: drug-free world/ prohibition, drug use as a human right and harm reductionism

Given the discrepancies between the criminal law and actual law enforcement practice and between the criminal law and other official and unofficial expressions of drugs policy, there are obvious difficulties in providing a succinct and accurate description of Irish criminal justice policy on drugs. The approach taken in later chapters of this book is to describe in some detail the development of drugs law and the various practices that are intended or thought to impact on drug use and drug-related crime. This approach acknowledges the fact that criminal justice policy on drugs cannot be reduced solely to statute law or to declared Garda policy, but is a continuously evolving, highly complex process, involving many elements, which are not necessarily cohesive.

The debate on needle exchange in prisons illustrates the central importance of what might be called the clash of grounding philosophies behind policy. Other terms that might be used are perspective, rationale, underlying principles or ideology. However, all of these terms refer to a set of relatively stable, core beliefs and ideas about drugs and how to tackle them. These beliefs and ideas shape political and professional rhetoric, drive policy- and decision-making and influence the transition from policy to practice. The philosophy of harm reduction has already been discussed. It has been argued that the term harm reduction can, in fact, be understood to refer to two quite distinct, indeed in large part contrary, philosophies – harm reduction through elimination and harm reduction not requiring elimination of illicit drug use – as well as to specific techniques and interventions aimed at reducing harm. The language of supply reduction and demand reduction is also confusing because it tends to be used tendentiously to imply an equation of law enforcement with supply reduction and of constructive methods of prevention and treatment with demand reduction. This tends to obscure the key role of law enforcement in demand reduction.

However, I believe it is valid and useful to distinguish three distinct major perspectives, which I will term the drug-free world/prohibitionist, the human rights and the harm reductionist perspectives. It will also be useful to describe some additional, quite widely held sub-varieties of the three major perspectives. The three major perspectives, as described, represent viewpoints, which differ very considerably in logic, in value orientation and in their practical implications. This chapter will provide a brief introduction to and preliminary analysis of the drug-free world/prohibitionist and human rights perspectives but provide substantially more detail on the harm reductionist perspective and its origins. This is useful at this point because the harm reductionist perspective plays a key role in current policy but is particularly complex and frequently misunderstood or misrepresented. Chapters 3 to 5 will provide evidence on the operation and effects of prohibition in Ireland and elsewhere over the last 30 years. Chapters 6 to 10 will return to the drug-free world/prohibitionist and human rights perspectives and provide a detailed critique of their respective merits and demerits based on an analysis of both the empirical evidence and the underlying philosophical and moral issues.

The drug-free world/prohibitionist perspective

U.S. criminal justice policy on drugs epitomises the drug-free world/prohibitionist perspective (henceforth termed simply the prohibitionist perspective). The foundational notion under-girding the American prohibitionist approach is the belief that it is possible through the deployment of law enforcement to attain a drug-free world and thereby abolish all the current harms associated with illicit drugs. The core beliefs are: 1) non-medical drug use is wrong and harmful for the individual and society; 2) it is right, appropriate and useful to deploy the criminal law against the wrong of non-medical drug use, just as it is right to criminalise, prohibit and punish other harmful activities such as theft and violence; and 3) the rigorous application of the law can eradicate or come near to eradicating non-medical drug use, thus greatly reducing harm.

The UN, strongly encouraged by the U.S., also subscribes to these core punitive, prohibitionist notions, despite their seeming naïve optimism. This perspective has, therefore, come to dominate the global discourse on drugs over recent decades. According to Levine,[1] all nations subscribe to some form or other of prohibition but the extent of the global domination of prohibition is consistently underestimated even by experts in the field. Indeed, UN policy has as its express goal the achievement of a drug-free world. The 1998 UN General Assembly adopted the slogan 'A drug free world – we can do it' for its 10-year drug strategy 1998–2008.[2] The UN Conventions of 1961, 1971 and 1988 also strongly support prohibition and explicitly rule out the possibility of national policies designed to introduce regulated forms of distribution of non-medical psychotropic drugs, along the lines of those used to control alcohol and tobacco.

The prohibitionist perspective is logically committed to prohibition and zero tolerance in all arenas involving illegal drugs. Illicit drugs are classed as an unqualified evil, which should never be tolerated. On the contrary, they must be actively repressed. Furthermore, as Zimring and Hawkins argue, in their book *The Search for Rational Drug Control*,[3] current American policy defines the problem as any type of use of any type of illicit substance. By, in this way, equating different drugs and different forms of drug use, which in fact have hugely varying potentials for harm, the prohibitionist approach can quickly shift the focus from the evil and harms of drug use itself to combating drug users' 'defiance of legal authority,' that is to law enforcement for its own sake. Drug use, especially 'non-problematic' or 'recreational' drug use, can easily become a target more because it represents disobedience and a challenge to law enforcement than because it is intrinsically harmful. A vivid example of the way focus can shift from the intrinsic 'moral' and real harm of drugs to disobedience, non-conformity and deviance per se can be found in prisons, where one prisoner on an official maintenance programme may be provided with opiates, while his cellmate, who is not on the programme, is criminalised and open to prosecution or punishment for taking similar opiates.

The prohibitionist perspective promotes a zero tolerance approach to all non-medical drug use, but it has a particularly strong focus on supply reduction, which in theory holds the promise of complete elimination of illicit drug use. Prohibition sets out to abolish illicit drugs from the world by eliminating production, manufacture, trafficking, distribution and even personal possession. On the other hand, the prohibitionist perspective is not exclusively reliant on prohibitionist, law enforcement and interdiction approaches and can also actively embrace, as complementary forms of action, various types of demand reduction, such as education and treatment. However, whenever there is a clash of aims or ways and means, prohibition clearly tends to favour repression over other approaches. As Zimring and Hawkins point out, it appears to be all too easy for prohibitionist law enforcement to become an end in itself and essentially detached from its original harm-reductive purpose.

A major difficulty for the prohibitionist perspective is that in preaching zero tolerance for all illicit drugs it must blur the crucial distinctions between illicit drugs, which actually have very different potentials for harm. For example, one might contrast cannabis and crack cocaine in terms of their potential for harm. At the same time prohibition must strictly maintain the division between all illegal drugs and all legally available mood-altering substances. There are two distinct categories in this latter group. First, there are the socially licensed and regulated mood-altering substances, mainly alcohol and nicotine, which often lead to addiction and have many associated harms. These *drugs* are so widely used that their associated harms easily outweigh those caused by illegal drugs. Then, there are the psychotropic drugs that are developed by pharmacological companies and prescribed by the medical profession, such as tranquillisers, sedatives, sleeping pills, stimulants, pain relievers and mood enhancers like Prozac. There is also much harm associated with the use and misuse of these drugs, which are often used for non-medical purposes or inadequate or inappropriate medical reasons.

While in theory medically licensed drugs are used for the health benefit of patients and are prescribed initially for anxiety, stress, pain, depression or other emotional and physical problems, they invariably lead to a substantial number

of iatrogenic (medically-caused) addictions. These drugs are frequently mispre-
scribed – for example tranquillisers are often prescribed for far longer than the
manufacturer's recommended period and so lose their therapeutic efficacy and
set in train what can become a serious and troubling addiction. A few rogue
doctors, often motivated by profit, knowingly and excessively prescribe certain
drugs to people who will use them non-medically. These doctors, however,
are subject to prohibitionist criminal controls. Also, some people develop a
dependency following self-medication with prescription drugs, which are easily
available because they are so widely and often carelessly used and stored.

Other people deliberately misuse both prescription and over-the-counter
drugs, taking them, for the purpose of intoxication, in excessive amounts or
with alcohol or other drugs. A recent report[4] has suggested that in the U.S.
the annual average number of people using pain relievers non-medically now
exceeds the number of new marijuana users. This national, large-scale study
showed that 11.8 % of young adults, in the 18–25 years old group, had used
pain relievers non-medically in the past year. In Ireland, a recent study has
reported that 22% of people in the 15–64 age group have at some time used
sedatives, tranquillisers or anti-depressants and that one in 20 of these had
self-medicated.[5] Ten percent of the respondents had used these drugs in the
last month and 84% of these had used the drugs on a daily basis in the past
month. This study provided interesting evidence that Irish people are being
prescribed these drugs at younger and younger ages. The age of first use for the
35–64 years old group was 37, but only 22 for the 15–34 years old group.

The Western world, including Ireland, has long made extensive use of
alcohol and is now suffused by mood- and mind-altering prescription drugs
and hugely dependent on them.[6] The broad tolerance and sometimes eager
appetite for socially regulated alcohol and nicotine and for medically prescribed
mood-altering drugs raise difficult questions for those who classify illicit drugs
as inherently evil. The moral basis of the condemnation of cannabis, opiates,
cocaine etc. by those, who rely on valium, Prozac, alcohol or nicotine, is, to put
it mildly, obscure. There is an obvious contradiction in the need to, on the one
hand, equate drugs as different as cannabis and heroin and, on the other, make
an intelligible distinction between intoxication by all the different illicit drugs
on one side and intoxication by alcohol or other legal substances on the other.
This irresolvable contradiction involves prohibition in much equivocation and
duplicitous rationalisation. As this book will demonstrate, this contradiction
cannot be dismissed as irrelevant or as a contrived logic-chopper's quibble
because it is the source of endless difficulties, which undermine prohibition
and ensure its failure.

The pervasiveness and acceptability of both legal alcohol and psychoactive
prescription drugs and the context of increasing recourse to the medical profession to shore up positive mood and banish the pains of normal living not only
make the notion of the inherent evil of illicit drugs indefensible but also run
totally counter to prohibition's key objective of a 'drug free world'.

The full-blown drug-free world/prohibitionist ideology characterises illicit drug use, but not alcohol or prescribed mood-altering drug use, as intrinsically evil. The drug-free world that prohibitionists seek is one free only of illicit drugs, not one free of alcohol or prescribed mood-altering drugs. Clearly, the objection is not to artificially altering mood and consciousness for pleasure, but only to certain ways of doing this. It is certain that future scientific developments and innovations in pharmacology, which will provide better targeted, safer and more reliable psychotropic drugs, will make the notion of a drug-free world appear even more absurd.

Full-blown drug-free world/prohibitionist ideology finds familiar expression in the 'war on drugs' rhetoric and putatively drives much drugs policy in Ireland and elsewhere, but it is not essential that prohibitionists adhere to all the tenets of the position. Some less extreme prohibitionists are persuaded that repression through the criminal law is the appropriate approach even though they do *not* believe that all drug use is harmful and morally wrong, as distinct from officially criminal. Equally, some prohibitionists accept that eliminating drugs entirely is not a realistic, attainable goal. These ideologically less strict prohibitionists tend to base their approach on pragmatism. Their core belief is that prohibition holds out the best hope for reducing the harms linked to drug use. This group might be termed utility-based prohibitionists. They are prohibitionists because they believe prohibition and criminal law repression are the most useful approaches for achieving the maximum reduction in harm.

The human rights perspective

The second widely held view and the polar opposite of prohibitionism is the human rights perspective. The key propositions behind this perspective are: that drug taking is not a wrong, evil or harm in and of itself; and that, moreover, the individual has a fundamental human right to privacy and bodily integrity, which in many circumstances encompasses the right to take mood-altering substances. This book is informed by and advocates a version of the human rights perspective and Chapters 7 and 9 will advance a comprehensive and detailed argument to justify this position.

Unlike the third perspective I will describe, that is harm reductionism, the human rights perspective is unequivocally and diametrically opposed to two of the core ideas of the drug-free world/prohibitionist perspective – that drug use is wrong and harmful and that it should be repressed through the criminal law. The human rights perspective is founded on a substantive, positive principle supporting the individual's freedom of choice to use drugs. The human rights perspective, then, opposes prohibition as a matter of principle and not, as harm reductionism does, only if it can be shown that prohibition causes more harm than it prevents. The human rights perspective is fundamentally opposed to state/criminal justice interference with the individual's choice to use or not use mood-altering drugs, including those currently classified as illicit, at least as long as third parties are not coming to harm.

The philosopher John Stuart Mill provides the classic expression of these principles: 'The only purpose for which power can be rightfully exercised over any member of a civilised community, against his will, is to prevent harm to others. His own good, either physical or moral, is not a sufficient warrant … Over himself, over his own body and mind, the individual is sovereign.' [7] Acceptance of this argument that drug use is a human right implies strong support for the complete legalisation of all drugs and all drug use.

The whole area of human rights and their instantiation and vindication in domestic and international law is, of course, complex and contentious.[8] One key aspect of human rights is the affirmation of the *rule of law,* which effectively protects the citizen from the casual and oppressive use by the state of its overwhelming powers. The rule of law subjects both the citizen and the state and its agents to the same exacting legal code inspired by values and mechanisms such as due process, presumption of innocence and proportionality of punishment. Mill's libertarian principles relate to the restriction of the reach of state authority since they assert the autonomy of the individual over his or her own body and mind and clearly oppose the paternalistic use of state powers to interfere unnecessarily with this autonomy even in situations where the individual chooses to harm him or herself. But human rights also have a constructive focus aimed at the creation of conditions that will optimise the welfare, freedom and dignity of all human beings equally. As David A. Richards has argued: 'Part of respect for human rights is the recognition of the right of persons, as free and rational beings, to determine the meanings of their own lives and projects … The values that some persons place on drug use can be accorded no less respect.'[9]

Despite the force of Mill's libertarian argument, it is obvious that many people do not view the freedom to use drugs as self-evidently a human right. Indeed, as Thomas Szasz points out, society has to choose between two competing value systems: 'We could commit ourselves to the view that the state, the representative of many, is more important than the individual; that it therefore has the right, indeed the duty, to regulate the life of the individual in the best interests of the group. Or we could commit ourselves to the view that individual dignity and liberty are the supreme values of life, and that the foremost duty of the state is to protect and promote these values.'[10] This book favours the latter option as the more desirable, fruitful and morally sound guiding principle for the relationships between the state, the law and the citizen. While accepting that this is fundamentally a value judgment, it is one that is strongly supported by empirical evidence about human behaviour and motivation and by contemporary theories of human nature. Chapter 7 will examine the legal, philosophical and psychological arguments for the recognition of a human right to use drugs and demonstrate how they are mutually supportive of each other.

There are, of course, limits to any human right (and many human rights entail complementary duties) and it is valid for society to interfere with the exercise of a human right, if this is interfering with the human rights of others. However, on principle the human rights perspective accepts with equanimity – as a price that must be paid for freedom – the sometimes inevitable quantum of harm, brought on himself or herself by the individual choosing to use drugs, and the possible spread of drug use in the absence of criminal law deterrents. On the other hand, advocates of the human rights perspective are normally well-intentioned people, who recognise the addiction- and harm-producing potential of drugs and, accordingly, support the general aim of harm reduction. They, therefore, tend to advocate the benefits of moderation and support education, prevention and treatment programmes and the careful regulation of access to drugs, along the lines of the regulatory control systems that are currently in place for tobacco and alcohol. However, despite sharing considerable common ground in this regard with harm reductionists and some ground with drug-free world/prohibitionists, advocates of the human rights perspective stand alone in their principled insistence that prohibitionist policies are wrong because they pre-empt and attempt to foreclose individual choice.

A key insight informing the human rights perspective is that ever since mankind discovered coca leaves or peyote or the arts of fermentation and distillation, the prospect of intoxication (poisoning the brain) has indeed been intoxicating (delightfully and irresistibly exciting) to many people. This insight entails not only a recognition of the historical ubiquity of drug use and the almost certain continuation of mood-altering drug use into the future (however objectionable), but also an endorsement of the beneficial uses of psychotropic substances and their crucial role in making life more palatable or meaningful for many people.

These ideas are rarely expressed in the discourse on drugs and are, indeed, anathema for many drug-free world/prohibitionists and harm reductionists. However, the 2004 *Angel Declaration* has recently been issued in Britain by a group, which includes many professionals working in the drugs area. As summarised by Neil Hunt,[11] the key principles of the Declaration are: 1) drug prohibition is inconsistent with the UK's human rights commitment and that the Misuse of Drugs Act 1971 should be repealed and if necessary international treaty obligations should be renegotiated; 2) drug availability should be controlled through a system of licensing; and 3) beyond the underlying recognition of a right to use drugs, the Declaration articulates a strong, secondary commitment to reducing drug-related harm at the level of the individual, the community and wider society.

Because mainstream professional and governmental argumentation, literature and debate tend to dismiss or simply ignore the human rights perspective, it is very easy to underestimate its influence and importance. However, to marginalise this perspective in this way is to discount and marginalise the critically important views of a great many drug users, who regard their drug use as beneficial to themselves, not harmful to others, and as a matter of private choice, to which they have a natural right. For example, in Western Europe millions, and in Ireland hundreds of thousands, of relatively well-educated, informed and responsible members of society smoke cannabis or use stimulants and many of them, one can infer, believe it is their human right to do so.

The human rights perspective has the very considerable intellectual and practical benefit of permitting acknowledgement of the basic similarities and continuities between the use of currently illegal drugs, such as cannabis and heroin and the use of alcohol, nicotine and medical drugs, such as Prozac. At the same time this perspective, like harm reductionism, has the benefit of encouraging attention to the very significant differences in the potential for addiction and harm between different drugs, types of use and contexts of use, all of which differences prohibitionist discourse is compelled to obscure. The basic facts of the different potentials for harm of illegal drugs and of the similarities between legal and illegal drugs are, of course, known to everyone but, arguably, only proponents of the human rights perspective can address these facts in an objective and consistent manner, by insisting that drug use in itself is not wrong, that it should be decriminalised, and that harm reduction should be entirely supportive and persuasive and, generally, not at all coercive, certainly not by way of criminal law enforcement.

The human rights perspective is self-evidently and unequivocally opposed to the key precepts of the drug-free world/prohibitionist perspective, but it is also opposed to the basic premise of harm reductionism, since it is prepared to countenance a degree of harm and does not prioritise harm reduction above all else. However, despite this significant difference in fundamental values, advocates of the human rights perspective can make a credible case that the kind of total decriminalisation they favour would lead not to an increase in drug-related harms, which on principle they would be forced to tolerate, but, on the contrary, to the substantial reduction of drug-related harms.

There are three main grounds to this claim. First, it is believed that decriminalisation would greatly empower the harm reduction movement and facilitate 'micro-level' harm reduction interventions because it would free them of current prohibitionist constraints and provide them with the human, financial and political resources, which are currently diverted to prohibitionist goals.

Second, it is believed that decriminalisation would greatly enhance the truth, credibility and effectiveness of drugs education. Many people, most importantly many young people, currently feel alienated from prohibitionist authorities, whom they perceive as out of touch, old-fashioned, authoritarian and repressive in outlook. These people tend to be dismissive of or immune to what they perceive to be the exaggerated, unrealistic messages about drug harms emanating from such authorities. This is especially the case when very commonly used drugs, like cannabis and ecstasy, are under consideration. A purely health educational approach, freed of coercive moral and criminal justice import and fully accepting the reality of continued drug use, could focus far more honestly on the pros and cons of drug use and achieve far greater credibility and persuasive power, leading to generally more informed and safer decision-making about drug use.

Third, decriminalisation can be claimed to be the best, if not the only way, to eradicate or greatly diminish the criminal justice-related harms which derive directly from prohibition itself. These harms include the bulk of the drug-related crimes of theft and, most particularly, the crimes of violence, intimidation and tax fraud etc. connected to the involvement of gangs in drug production, importation and distribution – gangs who are attracted by the immense profits created by the 'black market'. It is the unregulated, legally prohibited nature of the drugs trade that allows drug gangs to flourish and generate immense and relatively easily gained profits for themselves. The harms, which can potentially be avoided by decriminalisation, also include the destructive criminalisation and stigmatisation of people merely for using or possessing small amounts of drugs.

It should be noted that decriminalisation is implied by, but is not necessarily tied into, the human rights perspective. In other words, it is possible and indeed quite common for people to support total decriminalisation of all drugs without holding, as a matter of principle, that individuals have a human right to use drugs. These decriminalisers argue on purely utilitarian grounds, believing that total decriminalisation offers by far the best prospect for reducing the net amount of harm associated with drugs. These people might be termed supporters of utility-based decriminalisation. Perhaps surprisingly, economists have been to the fore in arguing the merits of decriminalisation. So, for example, Miron and Zwiebel, on the basis of a hard-headed, economic analysis focusing on outcomes and cost-effectiveness, conclude that 'a free market in drugs is likely to be a far superior policy to current policies of drug prohibition ... on net, the existing evidence suggests the social costs of drug prohibition are vastly greater than its benefits.'[12] This is not a fringe opinion amongst economists, since Thornton, who has surveyed a relatively large random sample of American professional economists, reported that 'in 1995 a majority of economists, though not a strong consensus, favoured changes in public policy in the direction of decriminalisation'.[13]

Indeed, in 2001, the influential magazine *The Economist* made a forceful case for a gradual move towards total decriminalisation. In a leader article they wrote:[14]

> To legalise will not be easy. Drug-taking entails risks, and societies are increasingly risk-averse. But the role of government should be to prevent the most chaotic drug-users from harming others – by robbing or by driving while drugged, for instance – and to regulate drug markets to ensure minimum quality and safe distribution. The first task is hard if law enforcers are preoccupied with stopping all drug use; the second, impossible as long as drugs are illegal. A legal market is the best guarantee that drug-taking will be no more dangerous than drinking

alcohol or smoking tobacco. And, just as countries rightly tolerate those two
vices, so they should tolerate those who sell and take drugs.

Perhaps the most famous economist to advocate on behalf of decriminalisation is Milton Friedman, a Nobel Laureate in economics and a well-known,
conservative libertarian, who supports the right of individuals to choose to
use drugs. In an open letter to Bill Bennett, the drug tsar of President George
Bush Senior, he stated:[15]

> You are not mistaken in believing that drugs are a scourge that is devastating our
> society ... Your mistake is failing to recognise that the very measures you favour
> are a major source of the evils you deplore. Of course the problem is demand,
> but it is not only demand, it is demand that must operate through repressed
> and illegal channels. Illegality creates obscene profits that finance the murderous
> tactics of the drug lords; illegality leads to the corruption of law enforcement
> officials; illegality monopolises the efforts of honest law forces so that they are
> starved for resources to fight the simpler crimes, of robbery, theft and assault.
> Drugs are a tragedy for addicts. But criminalising their use converts that tragedy
> into a disaster for society, for users and non-users alike.

Harm reductionism

The third, widely held perspective is what I have termed *harm reductionism*
to distinguish it from the broader concept of harm reduction, the avowed,
ultimate aim of almost all drugs policies and harm reduction by means of the
elimination of illicit drug use, the avowed aim of prohibition. The defining
propositions of harm reductionism are: 1) the reality of continued drug use
must be acknowledged; 2) the elimination of all illegal drug use through
prohibition and law enforcement is, in many respects, an unrealistic, purely
aspirational aim, which should not be allowed to overrule a practical approach
to current harms using interventions of proven value; 3) the primary, overriding objective and focus of policy and practice should be the reduction and
ideally the minimisation of the many diverse harms associated with illegal
drug use, even if this process involves accepting or condoning continued use.
According to White and Gorman, harm reductionists believe that 'the fundamental objective of drug control policy should be to limit the harm caused by
drugs and that reducing prevalence, although one means of pursuing this end,
should have no special status or overarching role'.[16]

Harm reductionism favours non-coercive prevention, education and treatment over repression, but does not necessarily see these positive methods as
always incompatible with prohibition and rigorous law enforcement. However,
a critically important aspect of harm reductionism is that it envisages the
possibility that the central component of the prohibitionist perspective, that is
the prohibition and interdiction of drugs through the criminal justice system,
can itself be not only the definitive creator of criminal harms, but also a major
cause of drug-related health and social harms. Prohibition creates new crimes

and new opportunities for crime, but it also promotes situations which lead drug users to put themselves and others at unnecessary, avoidable risk.

Harm reductionism will frequently attempt to curtail the application or abbreviate the reach of prohibitionist law enforcement in order to make a harm reductionist intervention possible or more effective. It follows that some degree of challenge, but by no means total opposition, to the prohibitionist perspective is intrinsic to harm reductionism. As Levine states, 'harm reduction is not inherently an enemy of drug prohibition. However, in the course of pursuing the reduction of harm, harm reduction necessarily seeks to reduce the criminalized and punitive character of U.S.-style drug prohibition.'[17] Harm reductionism does not take a definitive position on the issue of the appropriate role of the criminal law nor, despite its insistence on tolerance of continued drug use in certain circumstances, does it necessarily have a view one way or the other on the inherent evil of drug use. Levine makes this point succinctly: 'harm reduction seeks to reduce the harmful effects of drug use without requiring users to be drug-free. Harm reduction also seeks to reduce the harmful effects of drug prohibition without requiring governments to be prohibition free.'

The intricate and subtle relationship between harm reductionism and prohibition is significant. Contemporary harm reductionism, as a philosophy and a practical movement, developed historically within the context of and as a critical response to the dominance of the prohibitionist perspective. It remains a reactive, countermovement within global and local prohibitionist systems, or at any rate a movement essentially defined and driven by the existence of drug prohibition. It would be an exaggeration but only a slight exaggeration to state that harm reductionism, in contrast to harm reduction requiring the elimination of drug use, is focused more on the harms created by prohibitionist approaches than on the harms of drug use per se.

The harm reductionist approach is often viewed as primarily concerned with the elimination or reduction of the obvious health-related harms associated with drug use, such as physical and psychological dependence, physical injury and psychological or emotional disturbance, death by overdose or suicide, hepatitis and HIV. But it is also sometimes equally or even more concerned with the reduction of associated social and behavioural harms such as violence, child and spousal abuse, loss of motivation and productivity, intoxicated driving, the disturbance and degradation of the quality of life in neighbourhoods, intimidation and crime.

Harm reductionism has a special status relative to the other major paradigms, since it is primarily focused on practical outcomes rather than on moral principles. MacCoun and Reuter suggest: 'treatment and prevention programmes are frequently required to show that they are cost effective, a standard never imposed on drug enforcement'.[18] If scientific evaluations indicate that a specific harm reduction strategy is not reducing the harms it is designed to target or is creating new harms that outweigh in seriousness the harms it does reduce, then it is likely to be abandoned. For harm reductionism, practical effective-ness, measured according to transparent criteria such as reduction in the spread of HIV amongst injecting drug users, is the final arbiter. On the other hand, the failure of specific harm reductionist interventions does not under-mine the overall harm reductionist project. Indeed, it is an intrinsic strength of harm reductionism that it is responsive to the evidence of scientific evalua-tion. Despite this ostensible reliance on evidence, harm reductionism, just like the other two perspectives, is not in a position to conclusively substantiate its claims and projections and, in the absence of convincing proofs, is often forced to invoke a moral rationale, that is the self-evident rightness of pragmatically reducing harm and enhancing public health and well-being.

Harm reductionism has a long history and has taken a variety of distinct forms, which will now be described. I will distinguish five different approaches, which are driven by quite distinct motives and values and involve different structures and practical responses. In turn I will examine: 1) 'strict medical rationale' harm reductionism; 2) the related, but more socially oriented metha-done maintenance project; 3) public health inspired harm reductionism; 4) theory-based, anti-prohibitionist harm reductionism; and 5) social justice-driven approaches. Contemporary harm reductionism is an eclectic, often cacophonous blend of these disparate tunes.

'Strict medical rationale' harm reductionism

Harm reductionism is mainly a movement of professional workers, whose tasks involve, in various ways, coming to the assistance of individual drug users. The medical profession has a pre-eminent, if not entirely dominant, position in the movement because of its expertise with drugs, long-standing thera-peutic interest in addictions of all kinds and regulatory role in the prescrip-tion of drugs. The early roots of contemporary harm reductionism can be seen in the partial British adoption of harm reductionist principles and practices throughout most of the twentieth century. This was initially inspired by the medical profession, which categorised serious addiction to drugs, but not the casual use of them, as a legitimate medical problem. Under the British system, following the Rolleston Report of 1926,[19] heroin was made available to heroin addicts under prescription by general medical practitioners. This harm reduc-tionist approach with an evident medical rationale was to be the chief response to opiate use in Britain for many decades.

This early type of harm reductionism might be termed *strict medical rationale* harm reductionism. As recently as 1965, the second report of the Brain Committee summarised the British stance as follows: 'the addict should be regarded as a sick person; he should be treated as such and not as a crim-inal, provided he does not resort to criminal acts'.[20] This clearly implies, albeit exclusively in the case of diagnosed *addicts*, that the possession and use of illicit drugs should be tolerated and not prosecuted by the criminal justice system. The substitution of medical for legal authority in this specific domain was a key policy mechanism, which permitted the supply of otherwise illegal drugs to addicts. These drugs, of course, remained illegal and continued to be prohibited for all non-addict users. The subtle but all-important differentiation between the sick and the criminal user was simultaneously created and legitimated by the legal process of medicalising use and possession by addicts.

Crucially, the power to define, what constituted *addiction,* lay with the medical profession. Once the diagnosis of addiction was made in any individual case, the prohibition laws became irrelevant. However, at a time when heroin use was rare, this carefully targeted medicalisation process did not present any serious challenge to the general operation of drug prohibition and interdiction. The medical claim to a superior, virtually monopolistic, interest in the addict also reminds us that this form of harm reductionism is grounded in the ethical convictions and principles of the medical profession and intrinsically linked to the profession's sense of moral responsibility for healing and caring for the sick.

The medicalisation of the supply of drugs, as in the British system of heroin prescription, is a classic form of harm reductionism that challenges prohibition and not only countenances but relies on continued use of illicit drugs. But it represents a uniquely creative legal solution, which differs very significantly from most other harm reductionist interventions. Most obviously, it is different because it challenges prohibition not by opposing and restraining the enforcement of prohibitionist laws for specific, stated harm-reductive purposes, but by actually removing the prohibition and in effect legalising the use of heroin under medical supervision. By means of a deft legal manoeuvre, this policy created a new space in which the addict could use and be supplied with heroin without fear of the law. Heroin prescription and the more recent system of methadone maintenance, unlike most other harm reduction interventions, do not involve ongoing tension and negotiated compromise between the generally prohibitionist system and concession-seeking harm reductionists. In this particular instance, the sponsors of prohibition, that is the government, the legislature and indeed the state itself, have in fact cleverly redefined the legal landscape so as to create a decriminalised zone for certain categories of drug user. In effect, the normally prohibitionist state has itself, within certain carefully demarcated boundaries, metamorphosed into a full-fledged harm reductionist.

It is an interesting, if little regarded fact that this parallel, medically regulated universe, which contrasts starkly with the highly intolerant, prohibitionist universe, differs only marginally from the kind of arrangements that would exist under a regime of legalisation of drugs with alcohol-type regulation of supply. The notable differences are that, in the medical decriminalised system, heroin supply is under strict medical control and doctors are the sole gatekeepers, controlling access to drugs through their power to diagnose addiction. In other words, the medical system, unlike most proposed systems of full legalisation, does not allow users to decide how much they will use nor does it allow non-users to make a personal decision to initiate use. Otherwise, and this fact is insufficiently acknowledged, the medical system is to all intents and purposes tantamount to the legalisation of heroin use.

The expanded, socially oriented harm reductionism of methadone maintenance programmes

While heroin prescription still exists in certain jurisdictions, this special form of medico-legal harm reductionism now thrives mainly in the shape of methadone maintenance programmes. Methadone maintenance has quite a long history as a treatment modality[21] and became especially popular in the U.S. in the 1970s.[22] It was estimated that there were 78,000 heroin users on methadone maintenance programmes in the U.S. in 1980.[23] In Ireland since 1995, when fewer than 500 were on such programmes, methadone mainte-nance has expanded to such an extent that in 2007 it now involves over 8,000 clients, probably more than half of all opiate users in the country.[24] The current Irish methadone maintenance programme is more restrictive than the former British system of heroin prescription, inasmuch as methadone is rarely the client's preferred drug, and the programme does not permit intravenous use, strictly limits the supply of methadone and tests for the use of other psychoac-tive substances. Nevertheless, it is in all essentials an identical medico-legal approach, which in effect legalises and publicly funds opiate use by those who are medically diagnosed as opiate-dependent.

There is, however, an important distinction between Rolleston-style heroin prescription and more recent methadone maintenance programmes. This relates to the underlying rationale. According to Rolleston, heroin mainte-nance was entirely justified as a valid medical treatment undertaken in the best medical interests of the addict patient. This is a strict medical rationale, which asserts medical authority, focuses on the 'sick' individual and stresses the sanctity of the doctor–patient relationship. Methadone maintenance, on the other hand, very quickly came to be explicitly justified in terms of its effec-tiveness at reducing a whole plethora of harms, criminal and social as well as medical; some afflicting the addict and some afflicting members of the wider community or society itself.

The medical rationale has not been abandoned; indeed the legal recog-nition of the authority of the doctor is still at the heart of the methadone maintenance approach. But the focus has shifted from the duty of care owed to the individual patient to the wider obligation to promote general public health by way of helping and controlling the individual. Methadone main-tenance is expressly justified because it can help stabilise the chaotic lives of addicts, making them more amenable to abstinence-directed treatments, more resistant to criminal involvement and more responsible in respect of conduct, which is dangerous to themselves and others. Ironically, Rolleston-style heroin prescription was seen as effective and endured for so long, not only because of the persuasiveness of its original medical rationale, but also to a large degree because it had a positive harm-reductive impact, similar to that of methadone maintenance. In particular, it was valued because it successfully contained the criminal black market in heroin.

From early in the twentieth century the more sympathetic construal of the addict as a needy patient, a victim of an overpowering physiological and/or psychological addiction process, provided an alternative to the prohibitionist's characterisation of the same individual as the criminal perpetrator of wrongs. However, it is worthy of note that the methadone maintenance approach also differs from the original Rolleston-style heroin prescription in its differentiation of types of drug user. The Rolleston system distinguished between sick, addicted patients and all others who took drugs when they had no medically recognised need for them. This latter group were seen as legitimate targets for prohibitionist law enforcement.

By contrast, contemporary harm reductionists, including the sponsors of methadone maintenance, tend to draw a distinction between problematic drug users and non-problematic or recreational drug users. Problematic drug users are people who put themselves and others at risk through their drug use, whether they are addicted or not. Harm reductionist interventions, including methadone maintenance, are mainly targeted on this group of problematic drug users. Moderate, safe, controlled, non-criminally involved and responsible drug users are, in fact, exemplars of the kind of behaviour that harm reductionists are trying to promote. They tend, therefore, not to be a target for active treatment.

It is not an essential tenet of the harm reductionist perspective that this non-problematic drug user group should not be targeted by prohibitionist law enforcement, but, probably, a majority of harm reductionists take a benign and tolerant view of non-problematic drug users and generally favour a relaxed approach to law enforcement in their case. Accordingly, both harm reductionist intervention with problem users and the dominance amongst harm reductionists of tolerant attitudes toward non-problem users promote a process of normalisation of drug use. Prohibitionists, of course, tend to take issue with this normalisation process, arguing that it fosters ever-wider drug use and directly challenges zero tolerance approaches.

Public health inspired harm reductionism

It is often said that the major factor shaping the current harm reductionist agenda was the relatively sudden realisation in the mid-1980s that untrammelled prohibitionist approaches promote behaviours linked to the spread of the newly discovered, highly dangerous AIDS virus as well as other blood-borne viruses. So, for example, prohibitionist law enforcement is seen to promote the sharing of contaminated syringes and needles and consequently make the spread of blood-borne viruses far more likely. Through various pathways, such as accidental piercing by discarded needles and unprotected sex, the public health risks extend well beyond the drug using population.

The serious threat, posed by HIV, lead to the rapid introduction of new forms of harm reduction with more circumscribed, health-related objectives. These included needle exchange and safe injecting rooms. However, as we have seen this was not the beginning of harm reductionism but rather the grafting on of new types of intervention propelled largely by a new and urgent, public health rationale. In fact, the arrival of AIDS caused a drastic change in the putative cost/benefit analysis of prohibition and created a new political reality, in which it would have been politically untenable to fail to introduce measures that might reasonably be expected to reduce the spread of blood-borne viruses by drug users. As a result, the case for both new 'micro-level' harm reduction interventions and the internationally already well-established, harm reductionist techniques, such as methadone maintenance, was greatly strengthened. From the mid 1980s, in Ireland as elsewhere, these approaches were more readily supported, under the banner of public health and general health promotion, even though in the case of the new harm reductionist techniques this almost always required the relaxation of prohibitionist law enforcement.

There is an obvious intersection between harm reductionism and public health and health promotion models and, since the AIDS epidemic, the latter have been an immense influence on harm reductionism. However, harm reductionism and public health are by no means synonymous. The public health model relates to a much broader arena than drug use and is focused on the health of the whole community, customarily advocating coercive action, such as the quarantining of carriers of infectious diseases, the banning of smoking in workplaces, fluoridisation of water supplies and compulsory immunisation. These approaches prioritise the health of the social group over the rights and freedoms of the individual. Harm reductionists disagree amongst themselves on whether similar coercive action can be validly deployed against drug users on public health grounds.

Moreover, many public health advocates, citing solely health grounds, insist on total abstinence as the ultimate aim for harm reductionist treatment, just as they might insist on total abstinence from cigarettes. These public health advocates are likely to offer only qualified support for methadone maintenance, insisting that it should always be accompanied by active, abstinence-directed treatment. They are also likely to place considerable priority on lowering the prevalence of illicit drug use and, consequently, to a degree favour supply reduction and prohibitionist approaches. Indeed, it is difficult for public health practitioners, who are acutely aware of the health damage routinely caused by drug use, to oppose prohibition. It is clear that public health harm reductionists represent a specific brand of harm reductionism which is based on the public health value system and methodology and which is distinct from the Rolleston style, 'strict medical rationale' harm reductionism and the broader, more socially attuned version of the 'strict medical rationale' that emerged with the methadone maintenance movement.

Theory- and evidence-based anti-prohibitionist harm reductionism

So far, then, I have identified three separate brands of harm reductionism or, at least, three different strands of influence on the development of harm reductionism: 'strict medical rationale' harm reductionism; the broader, socially and medically oriented version of this that underpins methadone maintenance; and public health inspired harm reductionism.

Another important source of influence on harm reductionist thought can be identified. This is the articulation, begun long before the arrival of AIDS, of a generally anti-prohibitionist theory of harm reductionism, which did not stem from a medical model. This more radical and intrinsically tolerant, harm reductionist movement was propelled by a growing dissatisfaction with prohibitionist approaches and a growing realisation that on all the available evidence prohibition was both unworkable and counterproductive. The key insight driving this new harm reductionist theory was that prohibition was not preventing and probably could not prevent as much drug-related harm as it engendered. Importantly, the theory also utilised a more sophisticated, holistic conception of drug use and the addiction process – a conception which placed as great an emphasis on the economic and socio-cultural context of use as on the potency of drugs and as on individual physical and psychological vulnerability factors. This theory also emphasised that controlled and minimally harmful use of psychotropic substances was possible and indeed commonplace and should be tolerated and even actively encouraged as a more realistic alternative than abstinence for excessive and addicted users.

An important statement of this more theoretically nuanced, radical harm reductionism was made by the Drug Abuse Council of New York, a major government-funded think tank, which reported in 1980 and concluded that society's primary goal 'should be to minimise the harm and dysfunction that can accompany the misuse of any psychoactive substance whether that drug is currently classified as licit or illicit. To accept this goal entails accepting factors which up until now have not enjoyed wide acceptance, e.g. the continued use of illicit drugs by many Americans. It also entails accepting that not all illicit drug use is necessarily harmful. Further, it indicates that seeking to minimise harm from drug misuse is not synonymous with seeking to eliminate drug use.'[25]

This statement enunciates all the key tenets of harm reductionism: the acknowledgement of continued use of illicit drugs; the abandonment of any a priori commitment to the prohibitionist principle of harm reduction through elimination; and the prioritisation of practical harm reduction. However, it goes further than this in rejecting the prohibitionist stance on the differentiation of legal from illegal psychoactive substances and by asserting that not all drug use is harmful. This latter assertion directly counters the prohibitionist policy of zero tolerance for all illicit drug use and, indeed, implies the need for tolerance of non-harmful forms of use. In fact, the Drug Abuse Council of New York went on to espouse total decriminalisation of all drugs, including opiates.

This rational, evidence-based rejection of prohibitionism and adoption of harm reductionism was associated with and supported by a new research emphasis on controlled use of potentially harmful substances and by an emerging academic analysis of drug use, which focused on the interaction of drug, set and setting – a conceptualisation, which was adapted from the concept of the epidemiological triangle of agent, host and environment and which is now most commonly associated with Norman Zinberg.[26]

Writing in 1979, Zinberg and Harding[27] explained that the new emphasis was a rejection of the 'reigning stereotypic and moralistic view that all illicit drug use is bad and inevitably harmful, addictive, and that abstention is the only alternative.' They argued that two long held mythologies were giving way under the weight of accumulating evidence – that illicit drugs are altogether harmful and that licit substances, such as tobacco, alcohol, caffeine, sugar and various food additives, are altogether benign. The central issues were perceived to be who uses drugs, how they use them and with what effects. These outcomes were seen to be determined by *drug* variables, i.e. the pharmacological proper-ties of the drug or drugs being used, *set* variables, i.e. the attitudes, personality and predispositions of the user, and *setting* variables, i.e. the social, cultural, economic and physical environment, in which use occurs.

Although this new conceptualisation does not deny the importance of physiological mechanisms and psychological dependence processes, it encom-passes them within a wider canvas, which depicts a multi-factorial causation of drug use. The main point is that an addiction is not fully explained by the biochemical facts or the psychological facts of dependence and habit, but also has to be understood as propelled by the addict's reaction to his or her place in the social and cultural world. In other words, the study of the *setting* of drug use and of the personal functions drug use serves for individuals, which depends on both *set* and *setting*, is vital for its key insights into both motiva-tional processes and outcomes.

In particular, by providing a focus on *setting* and the interaction of *setting* with *set*, that is of the person and their context, the new conceptualisation was able to do justice to the abundant evidence that the more serious, reckless and destructive forms of drug use tend to be highly concentrated in marginalised and deprived communities, which suffer a plethora of social, economic, health and educational disadvantages and experience a pervasive climate of rejection, stigmatisation, lack of opportunity and hopelessness. These communities also suffer from high rates of alcoholism, psychiatric and social problems, general ill-health, chronic unemployment, vandalism, crime and violence. Erich Fromm captures the shift in the understanding of the motive force behind addiction, from an emphasis on the power of the drug and the susceptibility of the individual personality to an emphasis on social and cultural factors, in his conclusion that 'criminality and drug addiction are largely forms of protest against boredom and coercion'.[28]

The personal functions, which drug use serves, differ from person to person and, particularly as an addiction develops, from time to time for each person. But the motives that drive drug use include the desire for immediate pleasure and excitement, the need for relief from the distress of the withdrawal syndrome, the desire for psychological escape from current personal burdens, and, especially for those with an already established habit, the search for oblivion from painful memories, guilt and shame. Motives for drug use, amongst the socially marginalised and those with little hope, can also include the search for a sense of meaning and engagement in life and for the sense of social belonging, interdependence and personal worth, which can all to some extent be provided by the drug-user community and by involvement in drugs-related activities. The theoretical focus on this intricate web of social psychological causation of drug use inevitably leads to an analysis of the way social and economic conditions, especially relative deprivation and marginalisation, can create a special susceptibility to drugs through the personal experience of adversity of various kinds and associated feelings of powerlessness, frustration and hopelessness.

Social justice inspired harm reduction

The new pessimistic analysis of the utility of prohibition and the new conceptualisation of addiction and controlled use of drugs emerging in the 1970s together served to underpin harm reductionism with a rational basis, which, on the one hand, implied the rejection of prohibition and, on the other, articulated a clear-cut, non-medical rationale for harm reductionism. The new perspective on drug use, particularly the focus on *setting*, also turned the spotlight on the social and psychological motivation for drug use and on the local contexts and conditions that give rise to high concentrations of the kind of feelings and experiences, which make people especially prone to the use of more dangerous drugs and more dangerous forms of consumption. This in turn introduced a whole new socio-political dimension to the discourse on drugs and to the harm reduction movement.

Why destructive drug use is concentrated in marginalised communities

Much of the stress of poverty and social exclusion results from the direct experience of relatively harsh material conditions, of more numerous and more severe adversities and of lack of opportunity. At the psychological level this stress frequently translates into a sense of powerlessness, frustration and unfairness and a feeling that one's self-esteem is continually under assault. Michael Marmot has described these psychological reactions to one's social situation as the major components of the 'status syndrome',[29] which he has linked to the disproportionate burden of early mortality and ill-health suffered

by the relatively less well-off.[30] Poverty and the associated psychological processes of the 'status syndrome' are important *setting* and *set* factors, which help
explain the susceptibility of marginalised communities to drug problems as
well as to ill-health.

The epidemiological evidence, notably Marmot's studies of Whitehall civil
servants, demonstrates a social gradient in illness and mortality, with people
experiencing distinctly poorer health outcomes even than those immediately
above them in the social and workplace hierarchy. This strongly implies that
the root of the problem is not absolute poverty itself. Poverty, of course, has
an important role through increased exposure to the hazards of malnutrition,
pollution, unhygienic living conditions, hard physical labour etc. However,
it appears that even more important are the psychological and behavioural
reactions of the relatively disadvantaged to their unfavourable position in the
social hierarchy. The more severe the inequalities and the more disadvantaged
the individual, the more likely it is that a health-damaging sense of subjec-
tion, exclusion and inferior status will result. Richard Wilkinson[31] believes that
'even if we managed to remove all the health problems associated with poverty,
the greater part of health inequalities would remain untouched'.

According to Wilkinson, the key psychosocial stress factors linked to
vulnerability to poor physical and mental health are a sense of social inferiority, perceived low evaluation in the eyes of others, reduced ability to control
one's circumstances and work, lack of friends or community involvement
and an early childhood that does not provide a positive, nurturant basis for
later adult competence and self-confidence. A key insight is that 'inequality
and low social status are assaults on our sense of dignity and self-worth'.[32]
Such assaults can have highly deleterious effects on health and well-being by
producing depressed or over-anxious affect, weakening the immune system
response to infection, undermining optimism and the sense of self-efficacy,
and encouraging unhealthy coping mechanisms, such as reliance on alcohol,
overeating and smoking. Social comparison inevitably focuses on the pervasive inequalities across society and provides a constant source of challenge to
an individual's sense of self worth. In particular, those in the lowest echelons
of society cannot escape the implications of their low status and their lack of
wealth, power, status, consumer choice and opportunity.

The same, essentially psychological experiences of being undervalued and
lacking control, which have such a drastic effect on people's physical and
mental health, provide many people from marginalized communities with
strong reasons to seek solace, oblivion, distraction, excitement and possibly
even a sense of self-fulfillment in drug use. The use of mood-altering substances
is frequently an emotional crutch that helps people cope with the kinds of
hardship and disappointment, which are common in the lives of the relatively
deprived. Psychoactive substances are a popular means of escape from the
severe, although sometimes hidden or disguised, feelings of worthlessness and
hopelessness associated with the 'status syndrome'.

Substance use is especially attractive to people who suffer from the 'status syndrome', not only because it opens up a new universe of powerful gratification, which allows them, at least temporarily, to transcend their inexorable sense of inferiority and failure, but also because, for once, they themselves have the power of control in this new universe. The euphoric and oblivious pleasures of psychoactive substances are valued for themselves, but the satisfaction of personal control over self-gratification is also highly prized.

Another aspect of socio-cultural *setting* which helps account for the concentration of drug problems in marginalised areas is the fact that in poor, socially excluded communities the lure of easy money and the negative glamour of the drug dealer career path are uniquely enticing for many young people, who wish to find success and prove their personal significance but who have failed to benefit from the educational system and lack other legitimate opportunities for advancement. For the young males, who become minor or major drug dealers, drug use usually, though not inevitably, precedes and then co-occurs with drug dealing. It is a matter of profound significance that marginalised communities produce young males who are susceptible equally to the attractions of drug use and to the enticements of criminal drug dealing. In Ireland as elsewhere deprived 'underclass' communities are the traditional breeding ground for the 'criminal classes', and so within the one community there is a ready market for drugs and a ready supply of drug entrepreneurs, who are totally uninhibited about breaking the law. Many disaffected young males respond to their lowly social status and their failure in the increasingly competitive worlds of education and employment by rejecting their rejecters. They have strong motivation to offend, because of their actual material poverty and because they see the wealth that surrounds them and conclude that their own disadvantage is utterly undeserved. Their response to the 'status syndrome' is to seek goods, prestige and the respect of others by developing anti-authority attitudes, adopting a stance of aggressive toughness and simply taking what they want.

The mutually reinforcing interaction of *set* and *setting* factors, of individual vulnerability and enabling socio-economic conditions, is a major part of the explanation why serious drug problems develop in marginalised areas. Adversity and inadequacy at personal, family and community levels and the prevalent values and attitudes in stigmatised communities are powerful determinants, which promote crime, drug use and entry into the drug trade. Just as many individuals in deprived communities are deficient in the protective factors, which would make them more resilient to the drugs culture, so too the communities themselves, unlike most middle-class districts, lack the resources, information, understanding and level of political organisation to effectively resist or cope with the drugs culture. Public services and facilities in such communities, including schools and health centres, tend to be poorly resourced or absent. Educational attainment is generally low and high rates of early school leaving, truancy and unemployment prevail. All these factors feed into what has been termed the 'culture of poverty'. Lee Rainwater has described this fatalistic culture in the following way: 'The lower-class person's experience of himself and his world is highly distinctive for its qualities of pain and suffering, hopelessness, and concentration on the deadly earnest present. It is distinctive for its problem and crisis-dominated character.'[33] Lack of information, suspicion of authority, orientation to the present and lack of appreciation of the benefits of forward-planning and delay of gratification tend to lead to ignorance of the potential dangers of drugs or to a reckless disregard for these dangers.

Deprived communities and their members are, therefore, in double jeopardy, exposed to multiple stressors, which induce individual and collective susceptibility to drugs and crime, and seriously deficient in the resources, information, attitudes and socio-political organisation, which protect against the dangers of drugs. It is this double vulnerability of deprived communities and of many of the people in them, which has often led these communities to rapidly and rather easily succumb to destructive forms of drug use.

With young people especially, peer pressure is an enormously important factor in initiation into drug use. At the very beginning, a drug such as heroin has to be introduced into or pushed at a community, but in vulnerable communities the epidemic process quickly takes hold and, as with any fad or fashion, the spread of drug use soon becomes self-propelling. Peer pressure soon becomes a key element in the exponential growth of drug use. In communities that have passed the tipping point and have a well-entrenched opiate drugs culture, only the more resilient and independent-minded youths can reject peer pressure and resist the negative glamour of what can frequently appear to be a rewarding and exciting drug lifestyle.[34]

It is clear from this analysis of the interplay of *drug, set* and *setting* that the physical aspects of addiction are only the most obvious and undeniable, not necessarily the most important, factors in who uses, how they use and to what effect they use drugs. It is also clear that whole communities, not just particular individuals, can be susceptible to invasion by the opiate drugs culture. When the opiate drugs culture gains a grip within a neighbourhood, this is in large part because of the individual and collective vulnerabilities of the people there. However, after the drugs culture becomes embedded in a community, the likelihood of initiation of young people into drug use is, independent of their individual psychological and physical susceptibility, dramatically increased.

The political implications

The new focus on the social setting or context of drug use, then, provided valuable insights and profoundly changed the discourse on drugs. It added a thoroughly political dimension, which involved directly addressing contentious political and moral issues such as social equity and social justice. Like the strict medical rationale, which construed the addict as a suffering patient, this new perspective permitted a more sympathetic perception of the opiate drug user – now, however, as a relatively powerless victim of social and economic conditions and even of failed political policies. And, just as the arrival of AIDS greatly strengthened harm reductionism based on a public health rationale, this new multi-factorial perspective empowered an innovative form of harm reduction inspired by a social justice agenda. This new approach to harm reduction focused, on the one hand, on assisting generally ill-resourced and disorganised, drugs-ridden communities and, on the other, on primary prevention aimed at abolishing the social and material conditions that make drug use more likely.

In Ireland the role of relative deprivation and disadvantage in opiate drug use had been obvious from the early 1980s and, from the earliest years of the epidemic, had been well documented in epidemiological studies.[35] But it was not until the so-called Rabbite Reports of 1996 and 1997 that the Irish government enunciated an explicit political commitment to social justice inspired harm reduction. In his preface to the first report, Pat Rabbitte, the Chair of the Ministerial Task Force, stated that heroin use is 'concentrated in communities that are characterised by large-scale social and economic deprivation and marginalisation. The physical/environmental conditions in these neighbourhoods are poor, as are the social and recreational infrastructures … The drugs problem is now probably the greatest single problem facing the capital (Dublin). It must be solved.'[36]

The report laid out evidence, based on Health Research Board figures, on the areas of residence of those receiving treatment for drug misuse, overwhelmingly opiate misuse. The concordance between the most impoverished and deprived areas in Dublin and areas with high figures for treatment was remarkable. On this basis, the report concluded, quite reasonably at least in the case of the more destructive forms of opiate use, that drug misuse 'is closely associated with social and economic disadvantage, characterised by unemployment, poor living conditions, low educational attainment, high levels of family breakdown and a lack of recreational facilities and other supports'. Significantly, these factors were named as the 'underlying causes of drug misuse'.

In the second Rabbite Report of the Ministerial Task Force, the Minister, Pat Rabbitte admitted, with uncharacteristic candour for a member of government, that: 'for a decade or more, this State failed to tackle effectively the spread in the illicit trafficking and pushing of opiates, the destruction of the lives of individuals, the havoc wrought in communities. It neglected adequately to address also the underlying forces at work in such communities that fed from within the drug phenomenon – their marginalisation within the formal economy; the geographical marginalisation that reinforced economic marginalisation; misguided approaches to public housing policy. Deficiencies in education and social policies also, for example, compounded the other forces at work. Work itself was made scarce in these communities. The result was a spiral of decline.'[37]

These admissions and the assertion that socio-economic deprivation is self-evidently an underlying cause of drug misuse might suggest that political opinion at that time had been totally swayed by the logic and implications of the *drug, set, setting* analysis. This is doubtful, however, if only because the government's galvanised response to the drug problem in the mid- and late-1990s was mainly a reaction to the public outcry at the murder of Veronica Guerin and to the growing activity and ferocity of the anti-drugs activist movement based largely in inner city Dublin communities.

Despite the intellectual roots of social justice inspired harm reduction in an anti-prohibitionist analysis, the very significant upsurge in supports and interventions aimed at assisting drug-infested areas and at primary prevention, following the Rabbitte Reports, was in reality allied to strongly repressive action aimed at drug-dealers and importers. The community anti-drugs movement, which was led by fearful and angry parents of actual drug users or at risk children, specifically targeted drug dealers and drug dealing. These protesters, who were horrified both by the devastation wrought by drugs on their families and by the degradation of their neighbourhoods, tended to be rigorously prohibitionist and as opposed to cannabis as to opiates. The community movement and government policy now made a critical distinction between drug users, who could be viewed as victims and deserving of assistance, and people who profiteered from drugs, who were to be vigorously targeted by the law, whether or not they were addicts.

This bifurcation in the response to inherent drug crime could be seen as an essential element of the new 'balanced' perspective, which combines tough action aimed at supply reduction with more supportive action aimed at demand reduction. So, draconian laws are aimed at 'drug barons', while quite lenient and relaxed approaches are taken to minor offenders, such as those caught in possession of cannabis for the first time. The concept of bifurcation is associated with Anthony Bottoms,[38] who uses the term to refer to the process whereby governments increase penalties for perceived serious crimes that outrage public opinion (such as violent, sex or drug trafficking crimes) and at one and the same time decrease penalties for less serious and less visible crimes that do not rouse much media or public interest. While the bifurcation process intensified after 1996, seeds of the process were embedded in the 1977 Misuse of Drugs Act and the early shoots of the plant became obvious in the 1984 amendment, which more decisively separated dealers from ordinary users.

Social justice inspired harm reduction, despite its links to theory-based anti-prohibitionist harm reductionism, is, in fact, not specifically harm reductionist. It is not a uniquely harm reductionist approach because it does not directly relate to or require the modification of prohibitionist law. Social justice inspired interventions are entirely compatible with the broader concept of harm reduction, which requires elimination of illicit drug use. It is quite possible for full-fledged prohibitionists to support measures like those designed to improve the environment of deprived areas and the life opportunities of the people who live in them. On the other hand, it has to be acknowledged that social justice inspired harm reduction is often implemented by professional workers, who tend to hold a strongly harm reductionist position, and, at this point in time, social justice approaches have become an integral and very significant part of the harm reductionist discourse.

Contemporary harm reductionism

Harm reductionism is now a widespread and powerful movement. It is not a monolithic movement but rather one that contains a wide diversity of opinion under the banner of the key unifying precept of prioritisation of immediate, practical harm reduction aimed at associated harms rather than the supposed harm of drug use itself. In particular, it is possible for harm reductionists to reject outright or offer various degrees of support to the basic prohibitionist approach of criminalising drug production, distribution and use. Exemplifying the intermediate position are the harm reductionists, who believe that a strong case can be made that the criminalisation of cannabis use creates considerably more harm than it prevents. They support the depenalisation or even the decriminalisation of cannabis use,[39] despite being aware of the carcinogenic and other harmful health effects of cannabis use. In short, there are many varieties of harm reductionist, who differ significantly amongst themselves as well as from drug-free world/prohibitionists and human rights advocates. This diversity of opinion reflects the different professional perspectives of harm reductionists and the different rationales behind various harm reduction methods.

It is clear that harm reductionism is an essentially pragmatic response with a particular focus on interventions such as methadone maintenance, needle exchange, the free distribution of condoms, the testing of the content of drugs at raves and safe injecting rooms, which are aimed at people continuing to use drugs and whose main purpose is the prevention of associated ills, such as the spread of disease, overdosing and crime, rather than the prevention of drug use as such.[40]

The harms associated with drugs are the evil to be abolished. Drug use per se is not necessarily an evil or something that must to be abolished, though some harm reductionists certainly regard it as such. What has become key is that harm reductionist interventions should be evidence-based and that, when they are of proven value in reducing associated harms, they should be implemented and indeed prioritised even at the cost of curtailing or suspending altogether aspects of prohibitionist law enforcement.

Contemporary harm reductionism clearly differentiates between the potential for harm of different drugs, different forms of use and different levels of dependency. So, encouraging users of heroin to smoke heroin as an alternative to intravenous use is a valid and effective harm reductionist intervention. By the same token, harm reductionism today draws important distinctions between problem users and non-problem users and sometimes suggests a tolerant approach to the latter category. Indeed, some harm reductionists advocate various degrees of decriminalisation for the less addictive and destructive substances, like cannabis, and the less dangerous forms of controlled use, like coca leaf tea. Most harm reductionists are content that their public attitudes and actual interventions promote a climate of normalisation for drug use. This encouragement of tolerance and normalisation goes well beyond that which is the inevitable consequence of the limited constraints placed on prohibition for specific harm-reductive purposes. The prohibitionist perspective, however, strongly opposes the normalising tendency of harm reductionist approaches and rejects the distinction between problem and non-problem users, on which this normalizing tendency is based. Prohibitionism is premised on the belief that it is impossible to eliminate the harm of drugs without criminalising drugs and without making a strong, sincere and consistent commitment to rigorous drugs law enforcement against all illicit drugs and all forms of illicit drug use regardless of their differences.

It is worth pointing out that harm reductionism, though a profoundly important, activist perspective on drug use, is not a complete philosophy – it does not offer a comprehensive blueprint for the response to drug use. Unlike the other two major perspectives, which focus primarily on the legal status of drugs, harm reductionism is an incomplete response, precisely because it evades the absolutely pivotal issue of the role of the criminal law in the control of drug use. This is a paradox because, as I have argued, harm reductionism is largely shaped by the existence of the fundamentally prohibitionist, global and national systems and it inevitably involves challenge to prohibition. Harm reductionism in a world without prohibition makes no sense, since without the barrier of prohibition, against which it struggles, harm reductionism would become merely harm reduction – the desired goal of every well-meaning person and institution.

This is a subtle point but an important one, since it reminds us that harm reductionism does not have a monopoly on the noble aim of harm reduction. Prohibitionists and adherents of the human rights perspective also sincerely seek harm reduction, if by different means. This fact is often forgotten by harm reductionists. They frequently perceive the drugs problem as a purely public health issue, as if prohibition and law enforcement were simply incidental, unfortunate nuisances, which sometimes create barriers to good public health practice. Many harm reductionists appear to believe that legal issues have little relevance unless a practical need arises to curtail aspects of prohibition in the interests of a specific harm reductionist intervention. Many harm reduction-ists, especially those who equate harm reductionism with the public health response, appear to believe that the question about whether or not people have a right to take mood-altering drugs is an abstract and remote issue of little real consequence. They fail to recognise that this issue is in fact the unavoidable, momentous crossroads of the whole debate.

However, a world that recognises the right to use drugs and abolishes prohibition is surely something like the Promised Land for harm reductionists, for it is a world in which there are no prohibitionist barriers to harm reduction endeavours or to primary prevention, education and treatment. A world without prohibition is the only world where harm minimisation of drug use can truly be counted as primarily a public health problem. In this world everyone, including former prohibitionists could unite in search of the most effective ways to minimise harm – other than relying on the criminal law and interdiction. So, for example, the current situation whereby many deaths result from the use of drugs of unknown purity and uncertain content could be transformed by the introduction of strict, thorough and ubiquitous quality control of drugs – an approach, which is presently made impossible by prohibition. The irony is that in this world, in which everyone would have an equal interest in harm reduction and untrammelled harm reduction could flourish, *harm reductionism* would lose its raison d'être.

Summary

The drug-free world/prohibitionist perspective is dominant not just in Ireland but globally. It holds that all non-medical drug use is wrong and rightly criminalised because it is harmful for the individual and society. The drug-free world/prohibitionist perspective advocates zero tolerance of illicit drug use regardless of type of drug or type of drug use. This position, however, tends to be undermined by the illogical nature and moral ambiguity of the spurious distinction between illicit drugs and socially regulated drugs, such as alcohol, and the medically prescribed psychoactive drugs, such as tranquillisers. These legal substances often lead to dependence or addiction and worldwide cause more health-related harm than illicit drugs. The prohibitionist position also faces difficulties because it typically fails to do justice to the greatly varying potentials for harm of different drugs and different forms of use. In the area of minimally dangerous recreational drug use, prohibition can be seen as enforcing obedience to the law for its own sake rather than in order to avoid genuine harms.

The human rights perspective is diametrically opposed to prohibitionism since it holds that drug taking is not wrong in itself and that the individual has a fundamental human right to take mood-altering substances. The human rights perspective recognises that the use of mood-altering substances is pervasive in human societies and is likely to remain so. Intoxication to achieve altered consciousness, not necessarily under medical supervision, plays a significant and sometimes beneficial role in human life. The human rights perspective is marginalised in public and political debate but it is the implicit, if largely unarticulated, position of hundreds of thousands of drug using Irish citizens. Most advocates of the human rights perspective, however, are fully committed to the avoidance of addiction and dependence and other drug-related harms through education, persuasion, non-coercive prevention and public health initiatives, which reduce the various risks attached to drug use.

There are weaker utility- rather than moral principle-based versions of both the prohibitionist and the human rights perspectives.

Harm reductionism is the third major perspective on drug use. It is an activist movement rather than a complete philosophy or distinct ideology, partly because it largely ignores or minimises the central role of the criminal law. Harm reductionism envisages the possibility that prohibition of drugs through the criminal justice system can itself be a major cause of drug-related health and social harms and most harm reductionist interventions require the relaxation or suspension of aspects of prohibitionist law enforcement. There are various, sometimes contradictory, strands to harm reductionism and a *strict medical rationale* harm reduction has always been an integral part of prohibition since its inception in the U.S. and Britain. There are several other forms of harm reductionism, which derive from distinct rationales and emphasise different types of intervention. They include public health, methadone maintenance, and social justice driven approaches and a theoretically based, explicitly anti-prohibitionist form of harm reductionism, which was first elaborately articulated in the U.S. in the 1970s. Prohibition as a legal framework is a precondition for most forms of harm reductionism.

Notes

1 Levine, H. (2002) 'The secret of world-wide drug prohibition', *The Independent Review*, 7, 2.

2 UN General Assembly 20th Special Session (10 June 1998) *Political Declaration*, New York: UN.

3 Zimring, F. and Hawkins, G. (1992) *The Search for Rational Drug Control*, New York: Cambridge University Press.

4 Colliver, J., Kroutil, L., Dai, L. and Gfroerer, J. (2006) *Misuse of Prescription Drugs: Data from the 2002, 2003, and 2004 National Surveys on Drug Use and Health* (DHHS Publication No. SMA 06-4192, Analytic Series A-28), Rockville, MD: Substance Abuse and Mental Health Services Administration, Office of Applied Studies.

5 *Drug Use in Ireland and Northern Ireland. 2002/2003 Drug Prevalence Survey: Sedatives, Tranquillisers or Anti-depressants* (2007) Bulletin No. 6, Dublin: National Advisory Committee on Drugs.

6 The widespread prescription and dependence on psychotropics is well-illustrated by the prevailing situation with benzodiazepines. The Report of the Benzodiazepine Committee (2002) [Dublin: Department of Health and Children] states that in 2000 about 1 in 10 of all people in the General Medical Scheme (those receiving free primary health care) had been prescribed benzodiazepines and that 'prescribing tends to be for long periods of time, which would appear to be in conflict with best practice ... with many elderly people physiologically and psychologically dependent.'

7 Mill, J.S. (1982) *On Liberty*, Penguin Books (originally published 1859).

8 See, for example, Pagels, E. (1979) 'The roots and origins of human rights' in (eds McKay, R. and Cleveland, H.) *The Internationalization of Human Rights*, New

York: Aspen Institute for Humanistic Studies.

9   Richards, D. (1982) *Sex, Drugs, Death, and the Law*, New Jersey: Rowman and Littlefield at page 189.

10 Szasz, T. (1994) 'The ethics of addiction' in (ed. Comber, R.) *Drugs and Drug Use in Society*, London: Greenwich University Press.

11 Hunt, N. (2004) 'Public health or human rights; what comes first?', *International Journal of Drug Policy*, 15, at 231–237.

12 Miron, J. and Zwiebel, J. (1995) 'The economic case against drug prohibition', *Journal of Economic Perspectives*, 9, 4 at 175–192.

13 Thornton, M. (1995) ' Economists on illegal drugs', *Atlantic Economic Journal*, 23, 2 at 73.

14 *The Economist* (28 July 2001, 360, 8232).

15 An Open Letter To Bill Bennett from Milton Friedman, *Wall Street Journal* (7 September 1989).

16 White, H. and Gorman, D. (2000) 'Dynamics of the drug–crime relationship' in *The Nature of Crime: Continuity and Change*, U.S. Department of Justice, Office of Justice Programs: Washington DC.

17 Levine, 'The secret of world-wide drug prohibition'.

18 MacCoun, R. and Reuter, P. (1977) 'Interpreting Dutch cannabis policy: reasoning by analogy in the legalization debate'. *Science*, 278, at 47–52.

19 *Report of Departmental Committee on Morphine and Heroin Addiction* (known as the Rolleston Report) (1926) London: Stationery Office.

20 *Interdepartmental Committee: Drug Addiction Second Report* (known as the 2nd Brain Report) (1965) London: Stationery Office.

21 Methadone maintenance was first used in North America, by Halliday in Canada in the late fifties and by Dole and Nyswander in the U.S. in the 1960s: Dole, V. and Nyswander, M. (1965) 'A medical treatment for heroin addiction', *Journal of American Medical Association*, 193, at 646.

22 Newman, R. (1977) *Methadone Treatment in Narcotic Addiction*, New York: Academic Press.

23 The Drug Abuse Council, *The Facts about Drug Abuse* (1980), New York: The Free Press.

24 The *Misuse of Drugs (Supervision of Prescription and Supply of Methadone) Regulations* (1998) [Dublin: Stationery Office] provided the legal and bureaucratic structure for a new protocol governing the involvement of general practitioners and pharmacists in a greatly expanded methadone maintenance scheme. The main points of the new protocol are as follows. All methadone treatment is now free. Only methadone of 1 mg/ml concentration can be prescribed. All patients for whom methadone is started must be registered on the central treatment list. For patients being prescribed methadone in general practice a treatment card, incorporating the patient's details and photograph plus the doctor's details, must be lodged in a specified dispensing pharmacy. Butler, S. (2002) [in 'The making of the methadone maintenance protocol: the Irish system?', *Drugs: Education, Prevention and Policy*, 9, 4, 311–324] has provided an analysis of the social policy developments surrounding this new protocol.

25 Drug Abuse Council, *The Facts about Drug Abuse*.

26 Zinberg, N. (1984) *Drug: Set. Setting: The Basis for Controlled Intoxicant Use*, New Haven: Yale University press

27 Zinberg, N. and Harding, W. (1979) 'Control and intoxicant use: a theoretical and practical overview', *Journal of Drug Issues*, 9, at 121–143.

28 Fromm, E. (1976) *To Have or To Be*, London: Jonathan Cape

29 Marmot, M. (2004) *Status Syndrome: How Your Social Standing Directly Affects Your Health and Life Expectancy*, London: Bloomsbury.

30 For example, the Black Report (1980) [*Inequalities in Health*, London: Department of Health and Social Security] in the UK found that after decades of the National Health Service and of attempts to create a more egalitarian society, the life expectancy of the lowest socio-economic class was 7 years less than that for the highest class. Twice as many in the lowest class died between the ages of 15 and 65 than in the highest class. *Inequalities in Mortality: 1989–1998: A Report on All-Ireland Mortality Data* [Balanda, K. and Wilde, J. (2001), Dublin: Institute of Public Health in Ireland] indicates similar, if not quite as stark, class differentials in mortality in Ireland.

31 Wilkinson, R.G. (2005) *The Impact of Inequality: How to Make Sick Societies Healthier*, Abingdon: Routledge, at page 16.

32 Wilkinson, *The Impact of Inequality*, at page 27.

33 Rainwater, L. (1975) 'The lower class: health, illness and medical institutions' in (ed. T. Millon) *Medical Behavioural Science*, Philadelphia: W.B. Saunders.

34 Gladwell, M. (2000) [in *The Tipping Point*, New York: Little Brown] develops the notion of a tipping point, or sudden threshold, in relation to social epidemics, which, he argues, are characterised by contagiousness and by the fact that they exemplify that little causes have big effects and that change happens not gradually but at one dramatic moment.

35 See Dean, G., Lavelle, P., Butler, M. and Bradshaw, J. (1984) *Characteristics of Heroin and Non-heroin Users in a North-central Dublin Area*, Dublin: The Medico-Social Research Board; Dean G., Bradshaw J. and Lavelle P. (1983) *Drug Misuse in Ireland 1982–83*, Dublin: The Medico-Social Research Board; O'Mahony, P. and Gilmore, T. (1982) *Drug Abusers in the Dublin Committal Prisons: A Survey*, Dublin: Stationery Office.

36 Rabbite Report (1996) *First Report of the Ministerial Task Force on Measures to Reduce the Demand for Drugs*, Dublin: Stationery Office.

37 Rabbite Report (1997) *Second Report of the Ministerial Task Force on Measures to Reduce the Demand for Drugs*, Dublin: Stationery Office.

38 Bottoms, A. (1995) 'The philosophy and politics of punishment and sentencing' in (eds Clarkson, C. and Morgan, R.) *The Politics of Sentencing Reform*, Oxford: Clarendon Press.

39 Depenalisation here refers to the removal or lowering of criminal penalties for the simple possession of drugs, while decriminalisation refers to the legalising of drug use and supply.

40 With respect to testing at raves, see Murphy, T. and O'Shea, M. (1998) 'Dutch drugs policy, ecstasy and the Utrecht CVO Report', *Irish Criminal Law Journal*, 8, at 141–164.

3

Drugs and crime

The basic criminal law framework

The connections between drugs and crime are multiple and complex, but at the heart of prohibition and the 'war on drugs' is the political decision to criminalise certain drugs by way of legislation. With the single exception of opium, the use of drugs is not a criminal offence in Ireland. However, the importation, manufacture, distribution, selling and possession, other than by way of a legitimate prescription, of most psychoactive substances (mind-influencing drugs) are defined by Irish law as criminal offences (Misuse of Drugs Act 1977/84). The term 'inherent' drug-related crime will be used to refer to the specific categories of drug-related crime created by the Misuse of Drugs Act.[1]

It is possible and sometimes useful to separate 'inherent' drug-related crime into two categories: those that are intrinsically associated with personal drug use, such as possession (strictly user offences), and those that are associated with supply to others and might or might not involve an offender who is a user (the dealer offences). A drug user can be charged simply with 'possession' or with 'possession and supply', depending on the amount of drugs in his or her possession. Once the question of supply to others is raised the charge relates to a 'dealer' offence, whether the person in possession is a user or not, and this has certain significant legal implications and consequences.

Chapter 4 will examine how the Irish criminal justice system tackles the 'inherent' drug-related crimes created by prohibitionist legislation. This chapter is concerned with the relationship between drugs and other types of crime. The various types of crime with a putative link to drug use can be termed 'non-inherent' drug-related crimes.

The general picture of the drugs/crime nexus

Because the possession of illicit drugs is by definition a crime and because the association between drugs and other forms of crime is apparently very strong, there is a distinct danger of overstating the drugs/crime nexus and slipping into the trap of automatically equating drug use with crime. In fact, there are a great many drug users who do not commit crime other than the 'inherent' drug-related crimes intrinsic to drug use. Following their comprehensive review of the scientific evidence on the dynamics of the drug-crime relationship, White and Gorman[2] conclude that drug users are very diverse in terms of their levels of criminality and patterns of crime and that, equally, criminal offenders are very diverse in terms of their levels of drug use and patterns of use. White and Gorman, therefore, caution against exaggerating the links between drug use and crime.

Within these parameters, White and Gorman report that their exhaustive examination of the research evidence supports the following key conclusions: 1) that most drug users do not commit any crimes (aside from 'inherent' drug-related crime); 2) that alcohol is the drug most often associated with psychopharmacologically motivated violent crime; 3) that, for most criminally involved drug users, drug use does not cause initial criminal involvement; 4) that although there are common causal factors in both alcohol/drug use and delinquent/criminal behaviour, there exist various subgroups displaying different causal paths into those behaviours; and 5) that a large proportion of drug-related crime, especially violent crime, is a result of drug market forces and that it is not the type of drug per se, but rather the economic conditions of the drug market, which appears to influence the drug–crime connection. These conclusions are obviously critically important to our understanding of the drugs/crime nexus. In what follows in this section, these five conclusions will be examined in the light of the Irish research evidence on the links between drugs and crime in order to determine the extent to which they can be supported in the Irish context.

Most drug users do not commit 'non-inherent' drug-related crimes

While a great deal of acquisitive and violent crime can be attributed to drug users, especially heroin users,[3] when we consider the large numbers of 'recreational' users of cannabis, ecstasy and cocaine, it is clear that the vast majority of drug users in Ireland are not significantly involved in crime – apart from the crime intrinsic to drug use. The problematic heroin-using group, who have a considerable involvement in crime and who loom so large in the concerns of the criminal justice system, are only a small minority of the drug users in Ireland. Community, school and treatment surveys[4] indicate, by European comparison, a relatively high exposure in Ireland to cannabis, ecstasy and other psychoactive substances, including inhalants, cocaine and LSD. Much of this drug use is occasional or experimental, but much of it is 'recreational' and quite regular and cases of dependency and addiction are not infrequent. It is likely that there are hundreds of thousands of people in Ireland who use non-opiate drugs, especially cannabis and stimulants, fairly regularly, while there are probably fewer than 15,000 people who use heroin and other opiates. For example, a recent Oireachtas Joint Committee report has stated that 'there are reliably estimated to be some 300,000 users of cannabis in the state'.[5] Most of the 'soft' drug users are generally law-abiding apart from their 'inherent' drug crimes. There are undoubtedly also considerable numbers of heroin and other 'hard' drug users who maintain their habit without having recourse to acquisitive crime.

It is important to note that there is also an unknown, but probably large number of people in Ireland, who can be described as iatrogenic addicts, because they have become addicted to medically prescribed tranquillisers, and who for the most part continue to be supplied legitimately by medical prescription and are not involved in crime of any sort.

The existence of a very large majority of drug users without a significant involvement in crime is an important fact which is often forgotten in discussions of the drugs/crime connection. Unsurprisingly but unfortunately, these discussions tend to focus in an obviously skewed and stereotyped way on the large proportion of acquisitive crime and serious violence in Ireland and elsewhere which is reliably attributable to drug users or drug traders.

Alcohol is the drug most often associated with violence

Although very little is known about the role that drug intoxication plays in gang-related violence, uncorroborated, anecdotal evidence in Ireland suggests that gang members setting out to commit serious violence often use stimulant drugs such as cocaine. The Arrestee Drug Abuse Monitoring Programme (ADAM)[6] in England and Wales provides interesting data on the drug status of detained arrestees. Bennett[7] describes the results of the ADAM survey of several hundred arrestees over 4 locations in England in 1998/99. Urinalysis indicated that 69% of arrestees had taken a drug other than alcohol in the last few days. Forty-nine percent had used cannabis, 29% opiates and 20% cocaine. These figures indicate the widespread use of drugs by people arrested for relatively serious crimes. The sample was not big enough to make sensible comparisons across offence categories, but there were provocative results for the most common offence, that is assault, for which 41 people were arrested. Perhaps surprisingly, 32% of the 41 were positive for alcohol, but an even larger 34% were positive for cannabis. Of those arrested for assault 24%, 12% and 10% proved positive for opiates, cocaine and amphetamines, respectively. There are no equivalent Irish studies but it would not be surprising to find similar results in a sample of Irish arrestees. The high rates of drug use in arrestees may simply reflect the current widespread use of drugs amongst offending groups and may not point to any role for drug-altered consciousness in the commission of offences. However, this is an area that clearly requires further research.

However, there is considerable evidence to suggest that serious violent crime in Ireland is likely to be linked to alcohol consumption. Keogh[8] who connected most acquisitive crime, occurring in Dublin in the mid-1990s, to 'hard drug users' found that, by contrast, 83% of detected sexual offences and 78% of detected murders (which, unlike undetected murders, were rarely related to drug gangs) and assaults were attributable to non-drug users, many of who were thought to have taken considerable amounts of alcohol immediately before the crime. Millar et al.[9] estimated that 46% of all indictable crime in Ireland was related to excessive use of alcohol, but most of this crime was non-violent. Dooley's studies of homicide in Ireland[10] suggest that alcohol plays a significant role in the majority of solved homicides in Ireland. To this extent, the excessive use of alcohol would appear to be far more prevalent in Irish crimes of serious violence than drug-taking. Conversely, it needs to be borne in mind that gangland killings are rarely solved and there is very little hard evidence on the state of drug or alcohol intoxication of such killers.

Also demonstrating the significant role of alcohol in inducing disinhibited, aggressive and criminal behaviour, a study of public order offences in Ireland[11] found that alcohol had been consumed by the arrested offender in 97% of the 4,239 cases, recorded on the Garda PULSE system in 2001/02, where information on contributory factors was actually noted. However, the researchers also directly observed 177 incidents of public disorder and report that alcohol was only obviously involved in 51% of these cases. Unfortunately, this study did not address the role of drugs in public order offending.

The international research literature on the direct criminogenic effects of drugs concludes that there is little evidence that opiates or cannabis or even stimulant drugs are directly conducive to violent behaviour – that is through pharmacological effects on behaviour. So, Fagan[12] states that, 'there is only limited evidence that consumption ... of cocaine, heroin or other substances is a direct, pharmacologically based cause of crime'. Following an extensive review, Reiss and Roth[13] conclude that: 'There is certainly no basis for a blanket assertion that taking any of them (drugs) causes people to behave violently.' However, the literature does support a drug-violence link in the case of some patterns of use of barbiturates and tranquillisers and does indicate that withdrawal from opiates can increase aggression.[14] While opiates are narcotic drugs, that is sleep-inducing drugs with a depressant effect on the central nervous system, cocaine and amphetamines are stimulant drugs that tend to energise the individual. Certain patterns of stimulant drug use can cause paranoid reactions or an exaggerated sense of potency and invulnerability. As Blum[15] points out, this is a complex area and it would be unwise to understate the significance of the direct pharmacological effects of drug-taking on crime: 'powerful agents can affect behaviour; how they affect it depends on how they are used and by whom, and in what settings and in what amounts'.

Drug use typically does not cause initial criminal involvement

There is also Irish evidence to support the view that most drug users who are involved in acquisitive crime did not originally become involved in crime primarily because of their drug use. In an interview-based study, Keogh[16] spoke to 352 'hard drug' using offenders and 51% of these respondents stated that they had been involved in criminal activity before they had ever begun drug use, while 30% stated that involvement in crime only began following initiation into drug use. This result is consistent with another Irish study of 100 drug treatment centre attenders,[17] which found that drug use is associated more with an escalation in crime than with initiation into crime. The drug-using group, undergoing treatment, had been involved in much non-drug-related, non-violent criminal behaviour prior to drug use, but had greatly increased criminal activity following involvement with drugs. Dillon[18] confirms this pattern in a small prison sample, in which 76% of male offenders serving sentences were found to have been criminally involved before initiation into drug use.

Studies of incarcerated females indicate that women drug-using prisoners may be an exception to the rule that criminal activity tends to begin before drug use. An Australian study[19] of 470 incarcerated women found that only one third of the drug users reported criminal activity before drug use. The researchers conclude that, 'for a substantial portion of female offenders drug use plays a role in shaping onset into a criminal career. Women involved in the sex trade, for example, tended to become sex workers after becoming regular users of amphetamines and heroin.' Dillon's Irish study supports this conclusion, since she found that 7 of 8 female drug-using prisoners, whom she interviewed, claimed that they had no criminal involvement prior to beginning drug use.

Pathways into crime and drug use may overlap but are distinct and complex

There is little fine-grained Irish research on individual pathways into crime and drug use, although much is known about risk factors from retrospective studies of Irish prison and drug user samples. Given the reality of the large number of drug users who do not become involved in crime, and the large proportion of criminals who begin crime before drug use, it would be foolish to propose a direct causal link leading from drug use to crime. Drug use is clearly neither a necessary nor a sufficient cause of crime. However, certain forms of drug use are incontrovertibly major contributory factors in crime, both in the sense that they accelerate the pace of criminal activity (and probably broaden it) and in the sense that they tend to precipitate the initiation of some offenders into acquisitive crime and other types of offending, such as prostitution. Irish studies[20] also confirm that there is very considerable overlap in the personal, demographic, socio-economic and community factors and conditions that create susceptibility, on the one hand, to criminal offending and, on the other, to drug use of the type strongly associated with crime.

Writers such as Seddon,[21] who argues that the empirical evidence does not support the 'belief that addiction to illegal drugs is the motor behind much property crime', and Simpson,[22] who calls the drugs/crime nexus 'a puzzle inside an enigma', critically exploit the inadequacy of simplistic, unidirectional models of causality in the drugs/crime relationship. They point to the fact that involvement in crime can facilitate drug use and lead to initiation of drug use, reversing the normally assumed drugs–crime link, and to the fact that shared third factors can cause both crime and drug use. However, while these points are well made and while it is important to see beyond the drugs/crime nexus to other causal factors that tend to determine involvement in both crime and problematic forms of drug use, these writers fail to do justice to the over-whelming evidence for a connection between crime and certain forms of drug use by certain types of people. A powerful drug like heroin has the particular disadvantage that it is strongly tolerance-inducing. This means that a new user of average means soon finds the already high costs of use rapidly increasing, thus making crime as a source of funds for drugs far more likely. These writers also fail to pay due regard to the equally strong evidence that lowering and stabilising drug use can dramatically diminish involvement in crime.

Bennett in the ADAM study found that arrestees, who were users of heroin and crack/cocaine, spent on average £16,000 per annum on drugs, about three times more than users of other drugs. They claimed to have an illegal income of £13,000, which was again about three times more than that of the users of other drugs and non-drug-using arrestees. The heroin and crack/cocaine users were more than five times more likely than the other arrestees to report being involved in robbery, four times more likely to report being caught shoplifting and three times more likely to report committing burglary. The 9% of arrestees who used heroin or crack/cocaine were responsible for 52% of all the crime reported in the study.

The economic conditions of the drug market dictate the drug–crime connection

White and Gorman's fifth point suggests that most 'non-inherent' drug-related crime is most strongly related to economically driven motives, dictated by the illegal and clandestine nature of the black market in drugs. Irish evidence on this issue, which strongly confirms the influence on crime of the drugs market, will be presented in the next section. However, this is an extremely complex issue in Ireland and elsewhere and in order to address it more comprehen-sively it will be useful to differentiate drug-related crime in terms of its predominant underlying motivations. The next section will utilise Goldstein's influential categorisation of drug crime into three main groups according to motivation – crime provoked by the pharmacological action of drugs, acquisi-tive crime driven by the addict's need to obtain money to pay for drugs and crime committed in the service of maintaining, expanding and defending the criminal market in drugs and its profits.[23]

White and Gorman are particularly concerned to emphasise the key role of the drugs market in contradistinction to the lesser role of the pharmacological effects of drugs. While in general terms, this appears justified, there is a consid-erable amount of 'non-inherent' drug-related crime which is not economically driven or connected to market forces and which tends to be hidden or largely disregarded. Domestic violence, neglect of children and dangerous driving are just some examples. These crimes have a direct relationship to the pharmacological effects of drugs and, in some cases more importantly, to the personality and physiological changes wrought by prolonged dependent use of powerful drugs, such as the opiates or cocaine. These drug-related crimes will also be examined in the next section.

Goldstein's categories of drug-related crime

Goldstein has provided a useful categorisation of the different links between drugs and 'non-inherent' drug-related crime of a violent nature. Goldstein pointed to three ways that drugs can cause violent crime: 1) through pharmacological effects on brain and behaviour; 2) through the 'economic compulsive' need to support continued drug use; and 3) through the 'systemic violence' associated with the control of markets, transactions, debt collection, and supply and distribution networks.

International research[24] and Irish research[25] indicate that the economic need to pay for the next fix and the coercion, intimidation and violence associated with organised drugs gangs account for most recorded 'non-inherent' drug-related crime. When we exclude 'inherent' drug crime, much drug-related crime can, therefore, as White and Gorman suggest in their fifth point, be attributed to the black market in drugs, that is to the illegal nature of the drugs trade, rather than to the psychological and physical effects of drug-taking as such. The hyper-inflated cost of illegal drugs drives much acquisitive crime and the immense potential profits of the black market in drugs drive the financial and violent 'systemic' crime of drug gangs. The black market in drugs is mainly the creation of prohibitionist policies.

In a 1988 research investigation, Goldstein et al.[26] examined all drug- and alcohol-related homicides in New York and allocated them to the three categories of drug-related crime. Goldstein and his colleagues found that 74% of homicides fell into the 'systemic' category, that is killings intended to protect drugs market position or profits, 4% were primarily 'economic compulsive', that is killings occurring during robbery or burglary, and 14% were 'psychopharmacological' in nature, that is they were attributable to emotional and behavioural changes induced by the psychoactive substance. However, echoing Dooley's Irish findings, a majority of a little more than two thirds of the 'psychopharmacological' homicides were related to alcohol. It is clearly possible for crimes of homicide to involve mixed motive forces, reflecting all three categories, 'psychopharmacological', 'economic compulsive' and 'systemic'. Nonetheless, this research by Goldstein et al. is an informative analysis, identifying the primary motivation and pointing to the overwhelming predominance of mainly 'systemic' homicides and the relative rarity of homicides driven mainly by the psychopharmacological effects of drug use itself.

Varieties of 'economic compulsive' crime

Goldstein's categorisation of drug-related violent crime is clearly also a useful tool for thinking more generally about the connections between drugs and non-violent crime or crime involving less serious forms of violence. In Ireland, as elsewhere, the vast bulk of drug-related property crime, including theft, burglary, fraud and robbery, clearly falls into Goldstein's second 'economic compulsive' category. Most of the proceeds of such relatively minor acquisitive crimes are immediately expended on drugs.

However, many of these economically motivated crimes involve the physical confrontation of victims, as in muggings and robberies, and thus involve some level of violence or threat of violence. Drug users attempting to raise money to buy the next fix can be desperate, impulsive and unpredictable. Their actions can create volatile situations with a real potential for serious violence. This kind of violent or potentially violent crime is basically 'economic compulsive' in nature. The direct psychopharmacological effects of drugs may or may not play a significant subsidiary role, but it is likely that the general psychological and physiological effects of prolonged, dependent drug use on the personality and the motivational system are relevant to the motivation for and manner of execution of the crime.

One recent study of a sample of 128 mainly opiate users attending a treatment centre in a Dublin suburb found that 41% admitted to committing a crime against the person, including assault or mugging, and 13% admitted armed robbery – mostly using a syringe.[27] Keogh[28] asked a group of 'hard'-drug-using offenders whether they had ever carried a weapon during the commission of a crime of theft and while 26% did not respond to the question, 46% of the remainder admitted they had done so and 11% admitted carrying a firearm. Clearly, it would be incorrect to classify 'economic compulsive' drug-related crime as non-violent crime, even though it normally involves various kinds of relatively petty theft.

It is generally accepted that the incidence of occupational crime and white collar crime, including fraud, skimming, embezzlement and similar crimes, is under-reported in Ireland as elsewhere.[29] It is probable that there is a considerable amount of such crime driven by the economic need to raise money to pay for an expensive drug habit. A small amount of forging of prescriptions comes to official attention, but this is mainly connected to people who are well known to the police for other crimes. It is possible that quite a large number of otherwise law-abiding people are involved in forging prescriptions in order to secure a supply of a drug on which they are dependent and that these people generally escape detection.

Some drug users turn to prostitution to help finance a drug habit and this may also be categorised as 'economic compulsive' crime. On the other hand, lower level dealing undertaken initially to fund one's own habit may be placed in both the 'economic compulsive' and the 'systemic' categories. In the past, illicitly obtained medical drugs (such as morphine and Palfium) have been widely used as an important alternative source of opiates for heroin users[30] and theft from pharmacies and the forging of prescriptions remains a significant aspect of drug-related crime. These two types of crime may be classified as either 'economic compulsive' or 'systemic', depending on whether the drugs acquired are for personal use or supply to others.

Varieties of 'systemic' crime

Tax evasion and money laundering and similar drug-related financial crimes are non-violent 'non-inherent' drug-related crimes, which are clearly 'systemic' in nature. Some forms of theft may also be drug-related 'systemic' crimes, either because they involve the stealing of drugs, for example from pharmacies, or because they involve the theft of money to finance purchase of a consignment of illegal drugs. Crimes of bribery and corruption connected to the importation or distribution of drugs can also be classified as 'systemic'. Many crimes of serious violence are also clearly 'systemic' in nature, including intimidation, assaults and contracted assassinations. These violent crimes are aimed at debt collection, the silencing of informers, the protection of profits and the enforcement of control of market share and supply lines by drug gangs.

While the immense profits of illegal drug distribution fuel 'systemic' crime and violence, as Collins[31] points out, a typical and highly significant aspect of this phenomenon is that drug distribution system violence tends to occur in socially disorganised areas, where resort to violence in dispute resolution is quite customary. Collins argues that these are areas where 'formal and informal social control is absent or ineffective, which traditionally have high rates of interpersonal violence and which are economically disadvantaged'.

Varieties of 'pharmacological effects' crime

While the short-term, direct 'pharmacological' effects of drugs on behaviour, as opposed to personality and motivational changes due to prolonged dependent drug use, appear to play a relatively minor role in the causation of serious violence and acquisitive crime, there are a number of areas in which these 'mind-altering' effects are of primary importance. These include dangerous driving, spousal or partner abuse and the neglect and abuse of children. So, for example, a recent Irish study which tested 2,000 people suspected of driving under the influence of an intoxicant, found that 50% were over the limit for alcohol but that in addition 36% screened positive for illicit drugs, most commonly cannabis and stimulants.[32] This finding is a reminder that there is a substantial level of drugs-linked offending that rarely comes to notice. Another related issue is drug impairment in the workplace. Drug-intoxicated people in charge of heavy machinery or in particularly hazardous workplaces, such as building sites or fishing vessels, can be criminally negligent or reckless.

Additional categories of drug-related crime

There are some 'non-inherent' drug-related crimes which do not fit neatly into Goldstein's three divisions. In particular, there are the numerous, relatively minor, but cumulatively extremely damaging, nuisance offences of drug users in drug-infested areas. These are offences like minor intimidation, harassment, criminal damage and degradation of the environment. This form of collateral damage is commonplace in areas where IV drug users in particular tend to congregate either to use drugs in so-called 'shooting galleries' or to trade in drugs.

These kinds of offences, which are rarely reported or recorded, are very numerous in certain marginalised communities and can have an immensely negative impact on the quality of life of local people, particularly the elderly and families with young children. Stairwells and play areas scattered with used needles and syringes, which are very possibly contaminated with blood-borne viruses, are just one stark symptom of the physical and social degradation of neighborhoods caused by drug users. People in these areas often feel helpless and hopeless and abandoned to their fate by the state and the forces of law and order. They live in fear for their young children and feel oppressed both by local, drug-using youth gangs and by criminal drugs dealers living in the locality.[33]

The sense of desperation and abandonment felt by people living in drug-infested areas has led, particularly for periods in the mid-1980s and mid-1990s, to forceful collective action by groups of parents and others demanding improvements in their local community and in the state's response to the drugs problem. In the latter period, groups such as COCAD[34] were particularly active and marched on the homes of known drug dealers, sometimes forcing their eviction. They also set up night patrols in certain areas and in this and other ways threatened to usurp the role of the police. Lyder[35] has written about this movement from the point of view of an insider and has claimed that many anti-drugs activists were prepared to use extreme violence. In a notorious case, Josie Dwyer, a drugs user and AIDS sufferer, but not a dealer, was beaten to death when walking home one night in May of 1996. He and a friend were set upon by a gang of about 15 anti-drugs activists, wielding clubs and baseball bats. In an emotive and justifiably angry climate, what starts out as legitimate action can quickly shade into illegal coercion, rough justice and mob rule. Clearly, there is a whole category of drug-related offending, which is committed by over-zealous opponents of drugs. The Sinn Féin party has been particularly supportive of anti-drugs activists in Dublin and fear has been expressed by other politicians of the spread to Dublin of the kind of alternate rough justice, involving beatings and knee-capping and worse, that has been associated with the repression of drugs in IRA-controlled areas of Belfast.

An overview of officially recorded 'non-inherent' drug-related crime in Ireland

'Economic compulsive' crime

There can be no serious dispute about the fact that there is a great deal of 'non-inherent' drug-related crime in Ireland. Some of the most important evidence confirming this picture comes from studies of the incarcerated. A recent survey of the psychiatric status of Irish prisoners estimated that 58.8 % of male sentenced prisoners had a drug dependency problem and 45.1 % an alcohol dependency problem.[36] Only 26.3 % had neither a drug nor an alcohol dependency problem. A national survey of a representative sample of more than 1,000 prisoners found that 52% had used heroin and over 40% had injected heroin.[37] A survey of Mountjoy prisoners indicated that the vast majority of heroin-using prisoners were not convicted for drugs offences but for various crimes of theft.[38] Often these prisoners claimed that they had committed a huge number of acquisitive offences (most of which remained undetected and unpunished) and admitted that they had been motivated mainly by the need to fund their drug habit.

According to recent estimates there are about 13,000–14,500 heroin/opiate users in the Republic of Ireland, mainly in the socially deprived areas of Dublin, but now also, in considerable numbers, in provincial cities and towns such as Limerick, Athlone and Portloaise.[39] This heroin-using group are of special interest not only because they constitute such a large proportion both of known property offenders and of Irish prisoners, but also because they are typically characterised by a notable concentration of the kind of background risk factors, such as poverty, social deprivation, educational failure, family disruption and personal adversity, that predispose to both drug abuse and crime. However, it should be pointed out that these opiate users are frequently poly-drug users and that in recent years they also make considerable use of cocaine, including intravenous use.

A Garda Síochána Research Unit study by Keogh[40] provides the strongest evidence on the extent and seriousness of 'non-inherent' drug-related crime in Ireland or at least in Dublin, where about 60% of Irish crime occurs. This study produced a database of 4,105 'hard drug using' individuals (overwhelmingly opiate users) known to the police in Dublin, of whom 77% had a criminal record. Keogh estimated that 91% of male 'hard drug users' at that time had an involvement in crime, apart that is from their inevitable involvement in 'inherent' drug crime. They were mainly male (84%), under 30 years (80%), unemployed (87%) and single (79%). One might caution that these figures, which indicate that 91% of 'hard drug users' have an involvement in crime and 77% have a criminal record, very probably overestimate the criminal involvement of 'hard drug' users, including heroin users, since they are the 'hard drug' users known to the Garda and it is reasonable to assume that at least some of those not known to the Garda are not known, precisely because they are law-abiding.

After Keogh had established the list of known 'hard drug users', he went on to examine all 19,046 detected indictable crimes, occurring in Dublin in a one-year period spanning 1995 and 1996. Of the 7,757 individuals apprehended for these solved crimes, 3,365 (43%) were identified as known 'hard drug users,' i.e. were on Keogh's list. However, this 'hard drug using' group were particularly prolific offenders and accounted for 66% of the total number of detected, recorded crimes. One drug user alone was responsible for 147 crimes and drug users on average committed three times as many crimes as non-drug users. Burglary, larceny from shops, and larceny from unattended vehicles constituted the majority of detected crimes and 'hard drug users' were responsible for 83%, 50% and 84% of these crimes, respectively. 'Hard drug users' were also responsible for most robbery (82%), armed robbery (78%), mugging (82%), and larceny from the person (84%). These are extraordinary figures, which strongly confirm the drugs/crime nexus in the Irish context, particularly with respect to 'economic compulsive' crime.

In a less methodologically rigorous Garda Research Unit study, relying on the views of individual gardai, Millar et al.[41] estimated the extent to which crime, apart from 'inherent' drugs crime, throughout the country was associated with alcohol or drug use. This study estimated that, nationally, 21% of all offences (other than 'inherent' drug offences) were committed by drug users, but that an even greater proportion of offences (46%) were related to excessive alcohol consumption. Given the relatively small numbers of opiate users outside the capital, the figure for drug user crime, which is still considerable, is unsurprisingly much smaller than Keogh's figure for Dublin.

In a near replication of the Keogh study for the years 2000 and 2001, Furey and Browne[42] found that a far lower proportion of detected 'Headline' (mainly indictable) crimes[43] could be attributed to known opiate users. The percentage declined from 66%, in Keogh's 1995/96 study, to 28%, in Furey and Browne's 2000/01 study. Some of this difference is explained by the fact that Furey and Browne examined figures for the whole country and not just Dublin, which has by far the greatest concentration of opiate users. Even so, by Furey and Browne's estimates, known opiate users were responsible for 37% of all burglaries and 49% of all robberies in Ireland in 2000/01. These two crime categories had the highest rate of opiate user involvement of any crimes.

In fact, between 1995 and 2000 there was a remarkable decline of more than a quarter in the number of recorded indictable crimes in Ireland. The decline was particularly evident in respect of offences, such as burglary and larceny, known to be strongly associated with opiate users. It is a reasonable inference that the greatly extended use of methadone maintenance from 1995 (440 people were on methadone maintenance in 1995 and within 3 years this had risen to 3,630) and other interventions in this period stabilised the chaotic lifestyles of a considerable number of opiate-users and so led to a reduction in the kinds of crime, in which they would otherwise have been involved. If this interpretation is correct, the dramatic reduction in officially recorded acquisitive crime in the late 1990s confirms rather than undermines the drugs/crime link. Given the huge extent of property offending associated with opiate use in the mid-1990s, it is obviously quite feasible that interventions, such as methadone maintenance, which divert large numbers of opiate users from crime or reduce their involvement in crime, could have a significant impact even at the level of national crime figures in certain areas like larceny and burglary.

Other aspects of the Furey and Browne study strongly support this interpretation. In their interviews with offenders, Furey and Browne found that 64% reported that, as a result of receiving treatment in the late 1990s, they were either 'doing no crime' or 'a lot less crime' (58%). Only 13% of their respondents, compared to 59% of Keogh's, reported crime as their main source of income. However, it should be pointed out that further factors were operating at this time, which may have contributed to the five-year period of year-on-year reductions in recorded crime from 1995. It is reasonable to presume that these other factors could also have been effective in reducing crime. Most important were the very rapid economic growth in Ireland during this 'Celtic Tiger' period, a sharply lowered unemployment rate and, perhaps most crucially, an almost 50% increase in the numbers held in prison. In addition there were more energetic and far better funded social inclusion and community and estate development programmes than hitherto. Interestingly, there has been a return to increasing crime rates since 2000, though the picture is complicated by the Garda's adoption of a new computerised system of recording crime, called PULSE. However, the return to higher levels of crime may reflect the temporary nature of, or the effective limits on, the benefits to be derived from suddenly increased levels of incarceration and from a far more extensive programme of methadone maintenance.

'Systemic' crime

The area of overlap between 'systemic' and 'economic compulsive' crime is critically important. Many addicts are recruited into the importation/distribution network at a low level, attracted by the promise of relatively small amounts of money or a continued supply of drugs. Inevitably, occasions arise when the impoverished opiate user faces major temptations. The time comes when their addiction-fuelled desperation and the promise of a supply of drugs eases their path into undertaking street level dealing or other tasks useful to major drug dealers, such as intimidation, smuggling or debt collection. For many opiate users the pattern of 'economic compulsive' crime eventually gives way to a more lucrative pattern of minor 'systemic' crime, which solves both their drug supply and economic problems. The investigation at the Dublin treatment centre, mentioned above,[44] found that just under 60% of those in treatment admitted to selling drugs. Forty percent said they had sold heroin and a further 13% said they had sold methadone.

In Ireland, the extent and seriousness of major 'systematic' drug-related crime is not in doubt. A drugs trade probably worth more than €1 billion is managed by organised crime, involving among other things importation, manufacture, distribution, money laundering and tax evasion. Organised crime has flourished at both sophisticated and more rough and ready levels and there are now a significant number of Irish drugs trade 'entrepreneurs' based abroad, particularly in England, the Netherlands and Spain.[45] The size and frequency of drug seizures, the discovery of manufacturing plants, and the money, goods and property confiscated from drug gang members indicate the necessarily highly organised nature of the drugs trade and the immense scale of both the trade and the profits made from it.

Violent criminal gangs are involved in the distribution of contraband tobacco, so-called 'soft' and 'recreational drugs', such as cannabis and ecstasy, as well as opiates and cocaine and other 'hard' drugs. The seriousness of the problem of 'systemic,' 'non-inherent', drug-related crime is evident from the widespread availability of drugs, the substantial size of drug seizures, the large amounts of money and other assets confiscated by the Criminal Assets Bureau from drug gang leaders and not least from the more than 100 gangland killings which have been committed in Ireland over the last decade or so.

In the case of *Gilligan v Criminal Assets Bureau*,[46] then High Court Judge, Catherine McGuinness, noting evidence that she had heard from senior Garda, concluded that it was established that there was now 'an entirely new type of professional criminal who organises, rather than commits, crime and who thereby renders himself virtually immune to the ordinary procedures of criminal investigation and prosecution. Such persons are able to operate a reign of terror so as effectively to prevent the passing on of information to the Garda. At the same time their obvious wealth and power causes them to be respected by lesser criminals or would be criminals … Nevertheless, in the context of a relatively small community, the operations carried out by major criminals have a serious and worsening effect. This is particularly so in their importation and distribution of illegal drugs which, in its turn leads to a striking increase in lesser crimes carried out by addicts seeking to finance their addiction.'

The involvement of organised criminal gangs in the importation and distribution of drugs has clearly had a major negative effect. These gangs have made huge illegal profits and introduced a climate of violence and intimidation new to the Irish crime scene. In June 1996, one such gang organised the murder of the well-known investigative journalist, Veronica Guerin, who was working to expose their operations. In the year before Guerin's murder, there were 12 gangland assassinations of criminally involved victims. None of these cases led to the conviction of a culprit. Although 2004, with five such murders, had the lowest level of drug gang related killing for some time, the general pattern since 1996 has been extremely negative with a dozen or more, largely unsolved killings per annum. In 2005, there were 19 homicides by firearm, most of which were drug gang related, and, in 2006, there were 27, the highest ever number.

In recent years, a new and ominous development has been the relatively large-scale importation of handguns and even machine-guns and other automatic weapons as part of a drug consignment. On 24 October 2006 a consignment of heroin and cannabis, thought to be worth €15 million, was seized in Clondalkin, West Dublin. Quite typically for large-scale seizures in recent years, the haul also included a Heckler and Koch MP5 submachine gun with a silencer, thousands of rounds of ammunition for various weapons and magazines for block machine pistols. In May 2005, the Garda set up a special operation, named Operation Anvil, targeting illegally held weapons. In the following 18 months, in the course of thousands of intelligence led searches and road checkpoints, 787 illegally held firearms were seized (549 in Dublin and 238 elsewhere) and stolen property valued at €14 million was recovered.

The importation of arms is clearly a symptom of and a major contributor to the spread of a highly dangerous, macho gun culture with an all too casual resort to shooting as a solution to business or personal disputes. These disputes, it sometimes emerges, can be pathetically trivial and banal. Such shootings have frequently set in motion a tragic cycle of tit-for-tat revenge killings.

There were 66 homicides in Ireland in 2006, including 27 using firearms. It is very probable that some of the non-firearm killings were drug-related, but, certainly, most of the firearms killings were drug-related and had some connection to drug gangs. A brief analysis of these killings provides insight into the prevailing gun culture in contemporary Ireland. Two of the victims were women in their twenties. One was shot indiscriminately by a drug gang member, who had been refused entry to a party but returned later and discharged a firearm through the front window of the party house, killing the young woman. The second woman was the victim, for reasons unknown, of a contract killing, probably by people with drug gang connections.

Of the remaining firearm killings, 17 were thought by the Garda to be drug-related. Thirteen of the victims were males in their twenties, 3 in their thirties and 1 in his forties. Fifteen were killed in Dublin, the majority in working class areas of North Dublin, one in Limerick and one in Drogheda. One of the older victims was a known gang leader and was thought to have been killed by members of his own gang, 23 of whom were out on bail at the time. A potential witness to this murder, an innocent, 20-year-old young man who happened to be working in this man's house at the time of the assassination was also cold-bloodedly killed. Several other drug-related killings were thought to be tit-for-tat assassinations connected to gang and personal feuds. Another was a drive-by shooting in which a person who was not the intended victim was killed. Further outraging public opinion, several of the killings took place in busy public places in the early evening in front of numerous witnesses. Two killings, of 21 and 19 year-old men, not included in the 17 clearly drug-related killings, occurred in an estate in Limerick, where gun crime by feuding gangs involved with drugs is relatively commonplace.

The impact of drugs on the nature of crime

It is clear that the arrival in Ireland, in the late 1970s, of serious levels of 'hard' drug use impacted significantly on the quantity of crime. By 1983, recorded indictable crime was at historically high levels and burglary, robbery and larceny from the person in particular had undergone a recent surge, almost certainly linked to opiate drug use.[47] But it is also clear that the Irish heroin epidemic and spreading drug culture have impacted powerfully on the character and nature of crime. Contract killings and callously planned professional hits, of which there were several examples in 2006, were unknown in Ireland, outside of paramilitary activity, before the heroin epidemic. The casual use of guns to settle petty disputes or to extract revenge was also extremely rare before 1980.

While the homicide rate in Ireland has risen dramatically in recent years, partly driven by drug-related lethal violence, and is now about twice the1970s rate, it is still at a moderate level by comparison with neighbouring European countries. In 2001, the homicide rate for Ireland was 14.2 per million, compared with 16.1 per million in England and Wales, 17.3 per million in France, and 28.6 per million in Finland.[48] Even Dublin, with its concentration of drug and gun crime, had a lower rate than London, 18.8 versus 26 homicides per million. However, one unwelcome distinction was that more than a third of Irish homicides were by firearm, a statistic that shows a closer affinity to the U.S. situation, where more than half of all homicides are by firearm, than to that in the U.K., where less than 10% are by firearm. These dramatic, callous and mostly cold-blooded shootings understandably receive immense media attention in Ireland. Ireland is, after all, a small, media-saturated nation with only one large city. Compared to larger countries, these killings have a disproportionate effect, sending shock waves throughout society and raising public fear and alarm about crime. It is also very possible that those involved in this kind of extreme violence relish the publicity and attention they receive in the media and are encouraged by it to live up to and protect their vicious reputations.

The deterioration in the quality of crime is not restricted to the area of lethal violence. Individual addicts who finance their habit through crime commit a very considerable amount of property crime. However, 'economic compulsive' drug-related crime is not simply a problem because of the greatly increased volume of theft, burglary and robbery. There is also the question of significant deterioration in the character of property crime, particularly in regard to the broadening of targets for victimisation and in what is acceptable in the execution of a theft. It appears that property crime now more often involves serious, callous and gratuitous violence and victims from vulnerable groups, such as children, women, the elderly and the disabled.

Addicts in need of an opiate fix can tend to be reckless, desperate and indifferent to victims. A problematic IV addiction to opiates usually involves major change to the person's motivational system and can privilege the craving for drugs over almost all other personal values.[49] In general, it is reasonable to suppose that the social, psychological and characterological, as opposed to the purely pharmacological, changes wrought by a serious addiction will translate into an increase in the ruthlessness and potentially the nastiness of crime. Very crucially, the narrowed perspective and urgent recklessness of the drug addict offender lessen empathy with victims. This process can lead to the breaking of once sacred taboos against victimising the vulnerable, such as the young, the elderly, the disabled and the members of one's own community. These taboos were previously well established and more or less automatically obeyed by the criminal fraternity in Ireland as a matter of personal honour and self-respect.

Old people and women appear to have been targeted in the 1980s to a previously unprecedented degree.[50] An extensive study[51] of newspaper reports of crime over the same three-month periods in 1975, 1985 and 1995 concluded that 'the evidence is undeniable that (in 1995) speedier resort is made to violence by criminals and others; that violence, when used, is more often unnecessary and excessive; and that in some areas, for some people, intimidation and a well-grounded fear for personal safety are constant features of everyday life'. Eamon Barnes, the former Director of Public Prosecutions, who in office gained a unique insight into much of Ireland's serious crime, noted, as early as 1985, that 'crime has become more vicious. It has become more nasty. There is a gratuitous violence now, a gratuitous degradation of people and their property.'[52]

There have been egregious examples such as a number of cases of torture of victims, sometimes involving the meting out of rough justice to drug gang members, but also involving the torture or the torture/murder of old people in the course of a robbery. But more generally, Barnes was referring to his sense that much crime, including relatively minor crimes of theft and everyday assaults, was now accompanied by gratuitous brutality and a lack of restraint. Another new, ghastly phenomenon, which adds to this sense of heightened threat from crime, is robbery using a syringe as a weapon. This involves the obscene threat of infection with AIDS or hepatitis. In 1996 there were 1,104 such robberies mainly in Dublin (see Table 5.1, p. 88) and these were, at that time, not categorised as serious offences against the person but as relatively minor threatened assaults. It is not, of course, possible to attribute the deterioration in the quality of acquisitive crime and the increase in gratuitous violence entirely to the influence of drugs, but it is very likely that drugs have played a significant role in these developments.

Summary

'Inherent' drug crime is that crime created by the Misuse of Drugs Act 1977, such as possession, supply, manufacture and cultivation of illicit drugs, and is distinguished from 'non-inherent' drug crime. 'Non-inherent' drug-related crime takes many forms, including acquisitive crime motivated by the need to pay for drugs; crimes of intimidation and violence committed by drug gangs to protect their profits; a probably small number of crimes of violence driven directly by the psychological and behavioural effects of drug use; tax evasion, money laundering, smuggling and other financial crimes committed by drugs traders; crimes of abuse and neglect of dependents associated with states of indifference and irresponsibility caused by prolonged drug dependence; dangerous driving due to drug intoxication; and public nuisance.

Most illicit drug users are not involved in the more visible forms of 'non-inherent' drug-related crime and it is very probable that a majority of Irish criminally involved drug users became involved in criminal activity before initiation of drug use. In Ireland, IV opiate drug use has been associated with high levels of acquisitive crime. With respect to these offenders, drug use tends not to precede criminality but usually causes a huge escalation in the amount of crime committed. Acquisitive crime committed by addicts, who are in a fragile and volatile mental state, is likely to be more reckless and have greater potential for unplanned violence than normal acquisitive crime.

However, most drug-related violence can be classified as 'systemic' crime, related to the control of the illegal drugs market. The size of drugs seizures and the large amount of assets confiscated from drug gang members indicates the high value of the drugs market. There has, in recent years, been a large number of homicides, other acts of violence, intimidation and gun crime connected to drug gangs. Contract killings and other murders of drug gang members or associated people tend to go unsolved. These murders are probably linked to trading disputes, including turf wars, debt enforcement and the intimidation of rivals or potential informers. However, it is likely that some murders of drug gang members are associated with internecine feuds with roots in personal quarrels and slights. Gangs now smuggle guns into the country along with drug consignments and a culture of gun machismo and mindless, extreme violence is becoming established amongst drug gang members, including many still in their teenage years.

Between 1996/97 and 2000/01 there was a remarkable decline, from a very high level, in the type of acquisitive crime known to be linked to opiate drug users, i.e. burglary, mugging, theft from cars and other forms of theft. This was probably due to a reduced involvement in crime by drug users, which in turn was probably due to a number of factors occurring simultaneously in that period, including the massive expansion of the methadone maintenance scheme, the almost 50% increase in the numbers held in prison, the major improvement in the economy and employment situation and the more mean-ingful and better-resourced social inclusion programmes directed at drug-infested, deprived neighbourhoods.

Notes

1 O'Brien, M., Dillon, L. and Moran, R. (2001) 'Legal framework' in *Overview of Drug Issues in Ireland 2000*, Dublin: Health Research Board.

2 White, H. and Gorman, D. (2000) 'Dynamics of the drug-crime relationship' in *The Nature of Crime: Continuity and Change*, U.S. Department of Justice, Office of Justice Programs: Washington D.C.

3 Keogh, E. (1997) *Illicit Drug Use and Related Criminal Activity in the Dublin Metropolitan Area*, Dublin: Garda Headquarters.

4 See, for example, Hibell, B., Andersson, B., Bjarnason, T., Kokkevi, A., Morgan, M. and Narusk, A. (1997) *The 1995 ESPAD Report: Alcohol and Other Drug Use Among Students in 26 European Countries*, Strasbourg: Council of Europe; (2002) *Annual Report on the State of the Drugs Problem in the European Union and Norway*, Lisbon: European Monitoring Centre for Drugs and Drug Addiction; and Long, J., Lynn, E. and Kelly, F. (2005) *Trends in Treated Drug Abuse in Ireland, 1998-2002*, Occasional Paper No. 17, Dublin: Health Research Board.

5 Joint Committee on Arts, Sport, Tourism, Community, Rural and Gaeltacht Affairs (2006) 'What everyone should know about cannabis', Dublin: Stationery Office. See also *Drug Use in Ireland and Northern Ireland*, Bulletin 3 (2005) [Dublin: National Advisory Committee on Drugs] which estimates, on the basis of a survey, that the lifetime prevalence of cannabis use for 15-34 year-olds in Ireland is 24%, and that the lifetime prevalence rate for all females is 12% and all males is 22%.

6 There is now an international I-ADAM programme involving 8 different countries, including Australia and the U.S.

7 Bennett, T. (2000) *Drugs and Crime: The Results of the Second Developmental Stage of the NEW-ADAM Programme*, Home Office Research Study 205, London: Home Office.

8 Keogh, *Illicit Drug Use*.

9 Millar, D., O'Dwyer, K. and Finnegan, M. (1998) *Alcohol and Drugs as Factors in Offending Behaviour: Garda Survey*, Dublin: Garda Headquarters.

10 Dooley, E. (2001) *Homicide in Ireland 1992–96* and (1995) *Homicide in Ireland 1972–91*, Dublin: Stationery Office.

11 Institute of Criminology, UCD for the National Crime Council (2003) *Public Order Offences in Ireland*, Dublin: Stationery Office.

12 Fagan, J. (1990) 'Intoxication and aggression' in (eds Tonry, M. and Wilson, J.) *Drugs and Crime*, Chicago: Chicago University Press, at page 243.

13 Reiss, A. and Roth, J. (1993) (eds) *Understanding and Preventing Violence*, Washington, D.C.: National Academy Press, at pages 182–183.

14 Connolly, J. (2006) *Drugs and Crime in Ireland*, Dublin: Health Research Board.

15 Blum, R. (1969) 'Drugs and violence' in (eds D. Mulvihill et al.) *Causes of Violence* Vol. 13, Washington D.C.: U.S. Government Printing Office, at page 1513.

16 Keogh, *Illicit Drug Use*.

17 Carr, A.J., Hart, I. and Kelly, M. (1980) 'Irish drug abusers: I; their social background', *Irish Medical Journal*, 73, 12, at 453–457.

18 Dillon, L. (2001) *Drug Use Among Prisoners: An Exploratory Study*, Dublin: Health Research Board.

19 Johnson, H. (2004) *Drugs and Crime: A Study of Incarcerated Female Offenders*, Canberra: Australian Institute of Criminology.

20 O'Mahony, P. (1993) *Crime and Punishment in Ireland*, Dublin: Round Hall Sweet & Maxwell; (1997) *Mountjoy Prisoners: A Sociological and Criminological Profile*, Dublin: Stationery Office.

21 Seddon, T. (2000) 'Explaining the drug-crime link: theoretical, policy and research issues', *Journal of Social Policy*, 29, 1, at 95–107.

22 Simpson, M. (2003) 'The relationship between drug use and crime: a puzzle inside an enigma', *International Journal of Drug Policy*, 14, 4, at 307–319.

23 Goldstein, P. (1985) 'The drugs-violence nexus: a tripartite conceptual framework', *Journal of Drug Issues*, 15, at 493–506.

24 O'Mahony, P. (2004) 'Drugs, crime and punishment: an overview of the Irish evidence', *Administration*, 52, 2, at 3–35.

25 O'Mahony, *Mountjoy Prisoners*.

26 Goldstein, P., Brownstein, H. and Ryan, P. (1992) 'Drug-related homicide in New York, 1984 and 1988', *Crime and Delinquency*, 38, 4, at 459–476.

27 D'Arcy, J. (2000) *Drugs and Community: An Exploration of the Nature and Extent of Drug Use in the Greater Blanchardstown Area,* Dublin: Greater Blanchardstown Response to Drugs.

28 Keogh, *Illicit Drug Use*.

29 McCullagh, C. (1996) *Crime in Ireland*, Cork: Cork University Press.

30 O'Mahony, P. and Gilmore, T. (1982) *Drug Abusers in the Dublin Committal Prisons: A Survey*, Dublin: Stationery Office.

31 Collins, J. (1990) 'Summary thoughts about drugs and violence in Drugs and Violence: Causes, Correlates and Consequences' in (eds De La Rosa, M., Lambert, E. and Gropper, B.) *Research Monograph 103*, Washington: National Institute on Drug Abuse, at pages 265–275.

32 Cusack, D., Harrington, G., Furney, P., Flynn, K. and Leavy, C. (2002) 'Driving under the influence of drugs in Ireland: a growing and significant danger', paper presented at 16th International Conference on Alcohol, Drugs and Traffic Safety: Montreal.

33 Murphy-Lawless, J. (2002) gives an account of the struggle of women against the drugs culture in marginalised housing estates in *Fighting Back*, Dublin: Liffey Press. See also Connolly, J. (2003) *Drugs, Crime and Community in Dublin, Monitoring Quality of Life in the North Inner City*, Dublin: North Inner City Drugs Task Force.

34 Coalition of Communities Against Drugs.

35 Lyder, A. (2005) *Pushers Out: The Inside Story of Dublin's Anti-drugs Movement*, Toronto: Trafford.

36 Kennedy, H., Monks, S., Curtin, K., Wright, B., Linehan, S. and Duffy, D. (2005) *Mental Illness in Irish Prisoners: Psychiatric Morbidity in Sentenced, Remanded and Newly Committed Prisoners*, Dublin: National Forensic Mental Health Service.

37 Hannon, F., Kelleher, C. and Friel, S. (2000) *General Healthcare Study of the Irish Prisoner Population*, Dublin: Stationery Office.

38 O'Mahony, *Mountjoy Prisoners*.

39 Kelly, A., Carvalho, M. and Tejeur, C. (2003) *Prevalence of Opiate Use in Ireland*, Dublin: National Advisory Committee on Drugs.

40 Keogh, *Illicit Drug Use*.

41 Millar et al., *Alcohol and Drugs*.

42 Furey, M. and Browne, C. (2003) *Opiate Use and Related Criminal Activity in*

Ireland 2000 & 2001, Templemore: Garda Research Unit.

43 The Garda Annual Report on Crime abandoned the classification 'indictable crime' in 1999 and replaced it with the term 'headline crime'. The two categories for the most part, but not entirely, map onto each other.

44 D'Arcy, *Drugs and Community*.

45 A number of Irish drug dealers have been murdered in Spain and the Netherlands.

46 [1998] 3 I.R. 185 at 241.

47 O'Mahony, *Crime and Punishment in Ireland*.

48 Barclay, G. and Tavares, C. (2003) *International Comparisons of Criminal Justice Statistics 2001*, Issue 12/03, London: Home Office

49 Orford, J. (1982) *Excessive Appetites: A Social Learning Analysis of the Addictions*, Chichester: Wiley.

50 Brewer, J., Lockhart, W. and Rogers, P. (1997) *Crime in Ireland 1945–1995: Here There Be Dragons*, Oxford: Clarendon Press.

51 O'Mahony, P. (1996) *Criminal Chaos: Seven Crises in Irish Criminal Justice*, Dublin: Round Hall Sweet & Maxwell, at page196.

52 Eamon Barnes in an extended interview with Padraig Yeates, *Irish Times* (29, 30 and 31 July 1985).

4

'Inherent' drug-related crime: the criminal justice system response

The Misuse of Drugs Act (1977) is obviously at the heart of the prohibitionist system and the manner and effectiveness of its enforcement to a significant extent defines the reality of the Irish 'war on drugs'. Prohibition outlaws certain psychoactive substances and thereby creates numerous 'inherent' drug-related offences. The criminal law, as the main instrument by which the 'war on drugs' is executed, is focused on creating a world free of illicit drugs by, on the one hand, disrupting the supply of drugs and punishing those involved in the trade and, on the other, punishing those who use drugs.

Analysis of how the laws against 'inherent' drug crime are actually implemented, and to what effect, can assist the understanding of the Irish drugs problem and system of prohibition in a number of ways: 1) information on seizures and drugs charges can depict the general contours of drug prevalence and identify the various forms drug use takes in Ireland; 2) information on seizures, charges, convictions and sentences can indicate the effectiveness of Irish law enforcement agencies in this area; and 3) the same information can indicate the relative toughness of the criminal justice response to drug offences, providing a revealing picture of the rigour of the Irish 'war on drugs'.

Seizures of drugs and the disruption of cultivation and production

The size of the Irish drugs market

Official annual figures on the number and size of seizures of drugs are potential, if very approximate, indicators of the extent of importation of illicit drugs into Ireland. They can also be taken to indicate the growth or diminution of specific drugs in the Irish market. However, the number of seizures and charges for inherent drug crime also reflect Garda policies and priorities and, as Connolly[1] warns, Garda statistics in this area 'are primarily a reflection of the activities and effectiveness of law enforcement agencies'. Also the Garda figures, as published in the Annual Crime Reports, confuse the picture more than a little by mixing large-scale bulk seizures with small personal amounts seized. Annual figures are prone to being drastically skewed by occasional very large seizures, some of which drug consignments may have been in transit rather than destined for the Irish market.[2]

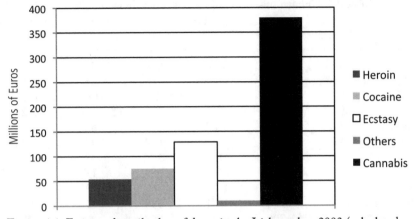

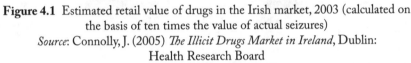

Figure 4.1 Estimated retail value of drugs in the Irish market, 2003 (calculated on the basis of ten times the value of actual seizures)
Source: Connolly, J. (2005) *The Illicit Drugs Market in Ireland*, Dublin: Health Research Board

Connolly estimates, using a multiple of 10 of the annual amount seized as his estimate of the total amount imported in that year, that the illicit drugs market in Ireland was worth about €650 million in 2003. The Garda themselves believe that the drugs market is likely in fact to be worth in excess of €1 billion, but this too is estimated using the 10 times multiplier and based on the fact that in some years since 2000 more than €100 million worth of drugs have been seized by themselves and the Customs and Postal Services.

The estimated total retail market value of cannabis in 2003 was €378 million, of heroin €54 million, cocaine €75 million, amphetamine €10 million and ecstasy €129 million. This indicates that cannabis holds approximately 59% of the market in illegal drugs, ecstasy and amphetamines 20%, cocaine 12% and heroin 9%. These figures, especially the relatively large size of the cannabis market, are a useful reminder that the vast bulk of purchases of illicit drugs are unlikely to be funded by crime, even if most IV opiate use is so funded.

The Irish illicit drugs market appears to be almost entirely dependent on imported drugs, for example, cannabis from Morocco via Spain, heroin from Afghanistan, cocaine from Colombia and ecstasy from the Netherlands. Most drug-producing plants cannot be grown in Ireland's climate, but annually the Garda make charges against 20 or so individuals for growing their own cannabis and occasionally they uncover industrial-scale cultivation of cannabis, including indoors cultivation using heaters and artificial light. Very occasionally the Garda have found manufacturing plants where drugs such as LSD or ecstasy are produced. For example, in 1995, a large-scale factory for the manufacture of ecstasy was discovered in Lucan, West Dublin and destroyed before it could begin production. It is, of course, conceivable that such plants could be active in Ireland but successfully evading detection by the authorities.

Table 4.1 Number of seizures of various drugs: Ireland 1991–2005

	Amphetamine	Cocaine	Cannabis	Heroin	LSD	Ecstasy
1991	4	7	2354	45	34	41
1992	49	11	2643	91	48	65
1993	82	15	2895	81	129	135
1994	391	38	3511	263	116	262
1995	89	42	3205	209	62	571
1996	217	93	3449	664	42	534
1997	475	157	4102	599	48	423
1998	680	151	4513	884	19	509
1999	467	213	4538	767	29	1074
2000	184	206	4641	598	31	1910
2001	162	300	6233	802	6	1485
2002	243	429	3024	714	0	1027
2003	211	566	3705	660	5	1083
2004	145	753	2860	612	7	806
2005	119	968	3417	725	5	653

Source: Garda Annual Reports

Seizures as a guide to the popularity of particular drugs

The annual trends in seizures also provide a tentative guide to the availability and popularity of specific drugs. So, the seizures of ecstasy sharply increased from 1997 (347) to 2000 (1,864) but then declined to 1,083 seizures in 2003. Ecstasy tablets sold for €22 in 1995 but for between €10 and €15 in 2003. This decreased cost suggests that the many seizures in the interim period, some of which were very large, have not succeeded in blocking the supply of ecstasy, which clearly remains widely and now cheaply available. Indeed, the recent decline in price and number of seizures may more than anything reflect the falling out of fashion of ecstasy.

On the other hand, figures for the seizure of cocaine indicate the strong recent growth in the availability and popularity of this drug. Cocaine seizures increased from 42 in 1995 to 986 in 2005, a remarkable increase of more than 2000%. The total amount of cocaine seized increased almost six fold between 2000 and 2003.

Seizures as a guide to the level of Garda supply control activity

In the early 1990s, the number of seizures for all types of drug apart from cannabis – 2,354 seizures in 1991 – was very small. So, in 1991, there were only 41 seizures of ecstasy and 7 of cocaine. This almost certainly indicates a lower level of prevalence of these particular drugs in Ireland at that time. However, the fact that there were also only 45 seizures of heroin in that year, despite the widespread use of heroin in Dublin at that time, seems to point to a generally less active or at least less effective Garda role in drugs interdiction in this period. The abrupt tripling of seizures of heroin in 1996 and the continuing relatively high rate of such seizures since then confirm the more energetic targeting of heroin from that date, as reflected in Operation Dóchas[3] and other supply control initiatives.

In 2002, the Minister for Justice set a target for annual drug seizures (in terms of overall value of drugs seized) to be increased 25% by 2004 and 50% by 2008 – from the baseline of €20 million, the value of drugs seized in 2000. Clearly indicating a degree of prior slackness and the inappropriateness of the targets, the target for 2008 was easily exceeded within one year. A high level of seizures, by comparison with 2000, has continued, ranging in value from around €60 to €100 million.

In short, Garda statistics indicate that the last few years have seen a very significant upturn in the number, the size and the value of drugs seizures by the Irish authorities. These supply control activities often involve Irish law enforcement authorities acting in collaboration with or on information from EU and other international authorities. However, it is clear that this increased activity and/or improved effectiveness in supply control has not stemmed the flow of drugs onto the Irish market nor has it put much pressure on the street price of drugs, which, on the contrary and in line with the experience in Europe, has tended to decrease.

Charges for inherent drug crime

Trends in drugs charges

There has been an increase in 'inherent' drug-related charges (possession, supply, importation etc.) from a very low base of 69, in 1969, to 9,595, in 2005. This amounts to an enormous increase by a factor of 124, which can reliably be taken to reflect the relatively drug-free status of the country in the 1960s and the subsequent surge in drug use. There has even been a huge increase of 470% in drug-related charges since 1983, the year of greatest Garda activity against drugs during the original heroin epidemic. However, there are strong grounds for not taking the growth in number of drug-related charges as an accurate reflection of the growth in the use of illegal drugs.

'Inherent' drug-related offences are police-defined offences – that is they only come to notice when a perpetrator is caught and charged. The figures are, therefore, a reflection of the effectiveness of the Garda in this specific sphere of crime control. The level of effectiveness, in turn, relates to police policy, the resources made available and the competence and commitment of the force in this domain. Garda interest and success in targeting 'inherent' drug crime is, in large part, a result of the organisation's internal prioritisation of goals and of broader policy decisions about deployment of resources.

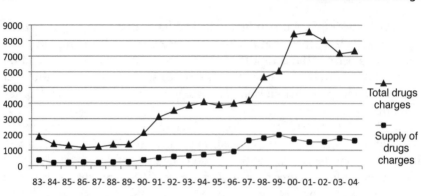

Figure 4.2 Total number of charges for 'inherent' drug offences and
for supply of drugs offences, 1983–2004
Source: Garda Annual Reports

Figures showing changes in the number of charges for different types of drug may to an extent reflect the prevalence within Irish society of various kinds of drugs, but only very approximately. The long-standing predominance, in the figures, of cannabis-related charges and the more recent greater prominence of stimulant- and especially ecstasy- and cocaine-related charges are undoubtedly connected to the popularity and availability of these drugs. However, they also reflect Garda policy and level of commitment as well as differences in the difficulty of detecting and arresting the various types of drug users.

The largest number of charges consistently relate to cannabis. In 2001 there were 5,143 such charges, 61% of the total. There were 2,052 charges relating to ecstasy, amphetamines and other stimulants, 24% of the total, 908 relating to opiates, 11% of the total and 297 relating to cocaine, 4% of the total. In most but not all categories, the number of charges has risen steadily over recent years. Cannabis charges rose from 2,996 in 1993 to 5,143 in 2001, stimulants from 217 to 2,052, opiates from 217 to 908 and cocaine from 15 to 297. Charges relating to LSD, however, declined from 144 in 1993 to 20 in 2001.

The predominance of cannabis-related charges is likely to be linked to the relative ease of detection of this drug due to its comparatively bulky nature, to the less furtive forms of use, including use in groups and in public places, to the comparatively lesser threat involved in challenging cannabis users compared to opiate users, and to the distinctive smell of smoked cannabis. Similarly, the common and relatively overt use of ecstasy in nightclubs and at dance venues makes this drug a comparatively easy target for police action.

While the overall level of drug charges has increased substantially through the years, it is surprising that certain categories of charge have tended to remain low or have declined in number. So, in 2001, the charges for importation were 30 compared to 114 in 1993 and 43 in 1983; for cultivating cannabis were 18 compared to 56 in 1983; and for allowing use of or trade in drugs on premises were nil compared with 24 in 1983.

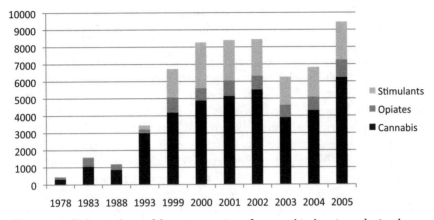

Figure 4.3 Relative share of drug prosecutions for cannabis, heroin and stimulants
Source: Garda Annual Reports

The annual number of drug charges is a 'soft figure' determined by Garda operational policies

It is very obvious that the number of 'inherent' drug-related crime charges per annum, which stood at less than 9,000 in 2001 (or less than 10,000 when one includes the approximately 1,200 'inherent' drug-related crimes involving juveniles and dealt with mainly by police caution) are, in all probability, only a fraction of the number of such crimes committed every single day and only a tiny fraction of such crimes committed in the course of a year.

This means that the annual number of charges for 'inherent' drug crime is a very 'soft' figure, indicative of something, but nothing very clear. This number could be greatly increased by the Garda almost at will, although there are obvious limits to any such increase because of the furtive and easily concealed nature of drug dealing and using. Nonetheless, the trend in the annual number of drugs charges is an important indicator of the changing reality of Garda operations and points to changing Garda priorities in the area of drugs policy.

The annual figures for 'inherent' drug crime, most particularly for possession of amounts for personal use, are clearly the outcome of the exercise of Garda discretion in two senses. First, it is either a deliberate or an incidental result of Garda policy that the number of actual drugs charges remains such a small fraction of the charges that could potentially be made. For whatever reason, the reality of Garda policy is that drug users are not pursued particularly rigorously or consistently. Second, because so few of the many people using drugs are actually targeted by the Garda for the crime of possession, it is inevitable that considerable discretion must be exercised in selecting those against whom the possession laws will in fact be enforced. Very little is known about this latter aspect of Garda operations and, since this is an area that is very open to prejudicial or inequitable use of discretion, there is an urgent need for research on relevant Garda decisions and on the background and other characteristics of people who are charged with possession of drugs in amounts for personal use.

There are certainly major geographical disparities in the number of charges for possession, which might support an allegation of discrimination in law enforcement practice. The risk of arrest and charge for possession of drugs varies hugely between Garda divisions. So, for example, the South Eastern Region (Tipperary, Waterford/Kilkenny, and Wexford/Wicklow) is by far the most active in 'discovering' police-defined 'inherent' drug crime. Compared with the Dublin Metropolitan Region, which has about 6 times the population, this region, in 2001, took 670 proceedings for possession, relating to cannabis resin (Dublin 764); 191, relating to ecstasy (Dublin 217); and 85, relating to amphetamines (Dublin 14). Tellingly, the region took only 14 proceedings for heroin (Dublin 600); a fact that is undoubtedly linked to the general absence of a serious heroin problem in the region. This in turn suggests that regions where there is little heroin may, by comparison with Dublin, be far more proactive in taking action against cannabis and stimulants – effectively net-widening the whole area of 'inherent' drug-related offending in that locality.

Discretion in the prosecution process

There is also considerable scope for discretion in the prosecution process after charges have been laid. Most drug-related offences are triable either way, i.e. they can be defined at the charging stage as either indictable or non-indictable. Defining an offence as indictable creates an option – open to both the prosecution and the defendant – to have a trial before a jury at the Circuit Court. Though certain indictable crimes, for example possession of more than €12,700 worth of illicit drugs, can only be tried at the Circuit Court, many, indeed most of those actually prosecuted, can be tried summarily (without a jury) at District Court level, if both the defendant and the Director of Public Prosecutions agree to this. However, if the charging garda defines a drugs offence as non-indictable, this means that the case will automatically be dealt with at District Court level.

A decision to prosecute or defend a case on indictment at the Circuit Court is critical since, on indictment, the maximum penalty, for possession, is 7 years (3 years for cannabis) and, for supply, a life sentence. On the other hand, the maximum penalty for such an offence, when dealt with summarily, is only one year's imprisonment and a fine and, in the case of the first two convictions for possession of cannabis, a fine only.

According to the Garda Annual Report, 8,721 criminal proceedings were taken against 'inherent' drug crimes in 2001. One fifth of these charges (1,712) fell into the more serious, category of 'Headline', that is mainly indictable, offences. The remaining four fifths (7,009) fell into the less serious

'Non-Headline' offence category. All of the 'Non-Headline' offences, which have been defined as non-indictable by the Garda, were for possession. One can safely assume, given the data on the relative number of charges for the different types of drug, that these latter charges were largely for the possession of cannabis or ecstasy.

All 7,009 'Non-Headline' offences, then, were dealt with summarily at the District Court. However, the vast majority (1,520) of the 1,712 'Headline' offences, which have been defined as indictable, that is as more serious, by the Garda, also involved possession or possession/supply. It is significant that the majority of these supposedly more serious 'Headline' offences were also dealt with summarily, that is as relatively minor offences subject to a maximum of one year's imprisonment and tried by a District Judge sitting without a jury.

In 2001, 1,046 persons were processed for the 1,712 'Headline' drug-related offences and 518 cases were finalised within the year. Only 73 of these finalised cases were dealt with on indictment, which is to say before a jury at Circuit Court level. The remainder (over 80%) was dealt with summarily by the District Court. All but six (8%) of the 73 persons indicted before the Circuit Court were convicted. A further 27 people were awaiting a jury trial at the end of the year.

Amongst the 73 cases commenced before the Circuit Court in 2001 were 20 prosecutions for importation. However, the majority of cases dealt with on indictment before the Circuit Court in 2001 involved possession or supply. Perhaps surprisingly, all cases of importation were not dealt with at the Circuit Court, though all those involving drugs of value €12,700 or more are required to be. Eight evidently less serious prosecutions for importation were dealt with summarily before the District Court. On the other hand, it is interesting that all cases of obstruction (87) and all cases of cultivation or manufacture of drugs (19) were dealt with summarily at the District Court.

The Garda do not provide data which might explain their decision-making in this important area of police discretion. It is not clear whether indictable as opposed to non-indictable charges are made because of a Garda view that the person charged is or is not a dealer, or because of the amount of drugs possessed (when they are worth under €12,700), or because of the type of drug involved, or indeed because of other factors. It is quite possible there may be no systematic basis to the exercise of this discretion. Similarly, there is a lack of data to explain decisions, which involve the Director of Public Prosecutions as well as the Garda, about whether to prosecute indictable charges at the District or at the Circuit Court. This is clearly an area that deserves much greater scrutiny.

Convictions and sentences

Very few of the thousands of people proceeded against annually for drug-related offences are punished by a sentence of imprisonment. This is a very

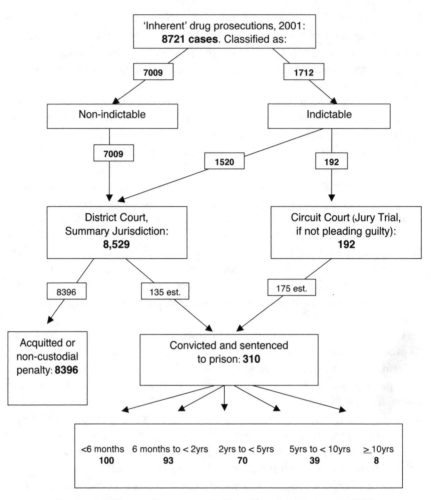

Figure 4.4 Drug offence prosecutions related to outcomes: 2001
Source: Irish Prison Service Report and Garda Report for 2001

different pattern to some other countries. For example, in the U.S. over 40%
of currently detained prisoners have been convicted for 'inherent' drug-related
crime and imprisonment is a common sanction for possession of even relatively small amounts of illicit drugs.

In 1979, when there were 594 drugs crime charges in Ireland, just 9 people
were committed to prison on 'inherent' drug-related convictions. By 1989,
there were 1,344 drugs crime charges and a well-established and very serious
opiate drugs problem, but the figure for prison committals for drugs crime
had increased to only 66. More recent figures for 2001, when there were 8,721
'inherent' drug-related charges, show that 310 people, including 24 females
(8% of the total), were sent to prison under conviction for drugs offences

specifically. Relating these figures to the data on criminal proceedings and convictions for 'inherent' drug crime, it appears reasonable to estimate that considerably less than 5% of all convictions for drug-related offences result in a prison sentence. This annual total of 310 people imprisoned specifically for drug crime is out of a total of 5,160 committals under sentence in Ireland in 2001 for all categories of crime. So, 'inherent' drug-related crime represents just 6% of all crime punished by imprisonment.[4]

Approximately a third (100) of the 310 sentences for 'inherent' drug crime were for less than 6 months and nearly a further third (93) were for periods of at least 6 months, but less than 2 years. In other words, a substantial majority of prison sentences for 'inherent' drug-related crime are for relatively short periods, reflecting the location of many drug-related convictions in the District Court. Only 8 out of 310 sentences (2.5%) were for 10 years or more, 39 for a period of at least 5 but less than 10 years, and 70 for a period of at least 3 but less than 5 years.

The mandatory 10-year minimum sentence

These figures may indicate a degree of unease amongst the judiciary concerning the mandatory 10-year minimum sentence for possession of drugs with a value of €12,700 or more, introduced by the Criminal Justice Act 1999. A number of cases, involving possession of drugs of more than this value, have been reported in the press where judges have exercised or, arguably, over-stretched the limited discretion available to them under the Act and handed down sentences of less and sometimes much less than 10 years.

Actual judicial decisions have tended to undercut the mandatory minimum sentence provision from the start. In 2003 the then Minister for Justice, Michael McDowell expressed his dissatisfaction with the judicial implemen-tation of the provision and warned judges that he would bring in legislation to further restrict their decision-making if they continued to flout the inten-tion of the Act. However, in April 2005 three cases were reported in the press, which indicated that this warning had had little effect.

Judge McCartan reduced the mandatory minimum sentence of 10 years to 2 years for a man who pleaded guilty to possessing €25,000 worth of ecstasy, cocaine and cannabis in Monasterevin, where apparently he had about 25 regular customers. The judge cited 'exceptional and sad circumstances', namely that the convicted dealer had been paralysed from the right knee down as a result of a car accident. The second case, before Judge Joseph Matthews, concerned a chef who was found with €370,000 worth of cocaine hidden under his pillow. The accused pleaded guilty of having it for sale or supply and was given a five and a half years' jail term fully suspended on condition that he undertake urinalysis for 3 years and be of good behaviour for 5 years. In the third case, Judge Yvonne Murphy sentenced a Nigerian, who had been born in Ireland, lived there till he was four and held Irish citizenship, to 10 years, but suspended 2 of these years, taking into consideration that he had no previous convictions and would be serving his sentence in a 'foreign country'. He had been caught with €300,000 worth of cocaine in a hidden compartment of a suitcase and had maintained his ignorance of the drugs, claiming he was duped.

An investigation, undertaken by Patrick McEvoy BL for the Department of Justice,[5] looked at 55 cases tried between 1999 and 2001 and found that only three of these cases resulted in sentences of 10 years or more. McEvoy concluded that 'the Courts have evinced a marked reluctance to impose the mandatory minimum sentence'. In all but one of the cases, the accused pleaded guilty and McEvoy identified this guilty plea and the fact that material assistance had been given to the Garda as the main factors influencing mitigation. However, the cases cited above indicate that judges are also influenced by the personal circumstances of offenders.

Despite this reluctance to impose the mandatory minimum sentence, the number of offenders in the system facing long prison terms for 'inherent' drug-related crime is growing. In the McEvoy cases covered by the mandatory minimum sentence, the median sentence length was 6 years, a relatively long sentence. These convicts are joined by a smaller but also increasing number of drugs gang members who have been convicted for murder and other serious drug-related offences and have received life or very long sentences. On the other hand, some of the long-term prisoners now accumulating in the system are relatively low level couriers or 'mules,' many from foreign countries.

Summary

Most 'inherent' drug-related offences are essentially victimless, police-defined offences – that is there is rarely a complainant to the police and these offences normally only come to notice when a perpetrator is caught and charged. The number of such offences that go unnoticed or ignored is huge in proportion to the number officially recorded. Historically, there have been peaks and troughs in the number and size of seizures. The ease with which the Garda were able to increase the amount of drugs seized after 1996 and again after the then Minister for Justice set specific targets in 2002 suggests that, due to lack of effort or, at any rate, to lack of successful effort, there was considerable untapped potential for further drug seizures in Ireland at these times. In recent years a higher level of international cooperation between law enforcement agencies and better quality intelligence have undoubtedly contributed to the increased level of large-scale seizures. Despite the increased level of seizures, survey and anecdotal information indicates that almost all types of drug are fairly easily available to users, often in their own localities, and that drug prices have not risen significantly but have, in fact, tended to decrease.

It could be argued that the Garda exercise a wide degree of discretion in detecting drug possession charges – the number of offences prosecuted is obviously only a tiny fraction of those that occur. There is also substantial discretion exercised at the prosecution stage. Although certain indictable crimes, most notably possession of more than €12,700 worth of illicit drugs, can only be tried at the Circuit Court, most 'inherent' drug-related offences are triable either way, that is as either indictable or non-indictable. In fact, well over 80% of them are treated as non-indictable offences and, of the remainder, that is the 20% classified as indictable crimes, over 80% are dealt with summarily at the District Court rather than at the Circuit Court. The vast majority of cases are, therefore, treated relatively leniently, since the maximum sentence available to the District Court is 12 months. Less than 100 'inherent' drug-related offences are tried by the Circuit Court each year.

Very few of the approximately 10,000 people proceeded against annually for drug-related offences are punished by a sentence of imprisonment. Instead, they tend to receive a fine, probation, community service or dismissal under the 1907 Probation Act. In fact, considerably less than 5% of all convictions for drug-related offences result in a prison sentence. The 300 or so people sent to prison each year for 'inherent' drug crime constitute about 6% of the total number of people sentenced to prison annually. Only 8 out of the 310 prison sentences for drug crime in 2001 were for 10 years or longer. A third of the 310 sentences to prison were for less than 6 months and almost two thirds for less than 2 years. Since the Criminal Justice Act of 1999, a minimum sentence of 10 years has been in place for offences of possession of drugs to the value of €12,700 or more. However, despite the publicly expressed annoyance of the former Minister for Justice, Michael McDowell, a large majority of such cases have in fact received sentences of less than 10 years and in some cases much less than 10 years. In general, the conviction figures mean that approximately one in every thousand convicted 'inherent' drug offenders receives a sentence of 10 years or more and one in every hundred receives a sentence of 3 years or more.

It is evident from this analysis that the so-called Irish 'war on drugs' is not the relentless and ruthless blitzkrieg implied by the overheated political rhetoric. In fact, the vast majority of the relatively few 'inherent' drug crimes that are prosecuted annually are dealt with quite leniently. Very few of the 'Mr Bigs' of drug importation and distribution are caught and imprisoned and few enough of their important gang members. Indeed, many of the small number of people, who receive lengthy sentences of imprisonment, are, in fact, easily replaceable couriers or other small cogs in the machine, who do not stand to make great profits from their involvement in the drugs trade. The main area of success for law enforcement is in seizures, but it is patently obvious that even supply control is not truly successful. It is limited to causing relatively minor ripples in an estimated billion euro business, which seems to be able to continue its uninterrupted supply, to all areas of the country, of very substantial amounts of illicit drugs at cheaper than ever prices.

Notes

1 Connolly, J. (2005) *The Illicit Drug Market in Ireland*, Dublin: Health Research Board. Also, for a more detailed treatment of the official statistics on drug seizures, see O'Mahony, P. (2004) 'Drugs, crime and punishment: an overview of the Irish evidence', *Administration*, 52, 2, at 3–35.

2 For example, in July 2007, a consignment of more than 1.5 tons of cocaine worth over €100 million was seized in Cork. This consignment, which was worth more than 20 times the total value of cocaine seizures in 2003 and more than the total value of all illicit drugs seized in that year, was discovered by accident following the overturning in rough seas of small craft bringing bales of cocaine ashore from a larger boat.

3 Operation Dóchas was initiated in October 1996 and involved the targeting of street-trading in drugs, mainly opiates. Four hundred uniformed and plainclothes gardai were deployed mainly to patrol known drug-infested areas in Dublin. By September 1998 over 20,000 arrests and over 10,000 charges had been made under the auspices of this operation and more than £7 million worth of drugs seized.

4 Irish Prison Service Annual Reports (2001 and 2005) Dublin: Stationery Office. Figures for 2005, when there were 5,088 committals to prison and 9,595 'inherent' drug crime charges, are very similar. There were 279 committals to prison for 'inherent' drug crime, 150 for a period of 1 year or less, 88 for more than 1 year but less than 5 , 28 for more than 5 but less than ten and 13 for more than 10 years.

5 McEvoy, P. (2001) *Research on the Criteria Applied by the Courts in Sentencing Under s. 15A of the Misuse of Drugs Act 1977 (As Amended)*, Dublin: Department of Justice, Equality and Law Reform.

5

The evolving Irish policy on drugs and drug-related crime

The operational reality pre-1996

The delineation of Irish criminal justice policy on drugs and drug-related crime is, as I have argued, a complex matter open to widely different interpretations. In order to clearly and fully understand the Irish prohibitionist 'war on drugs' it is necessary to juxtapose and somehow collate and make sense of often inconsistent or frankly conflicting components, including legislation, official policy statements, informal political statements, actual Garda operations, judicial decisions, the implementation of sanctions including imprisonment, and numerous disparate initiatives such as the Drug Court, Arrest Referral and health, education, community and welfare actions.

Most Irish official policy and strategy statements are, in fact, amalgams that freely mix ideas from drug-free world/prohibitionist and the harm reductionist perspectives. This is usually done without fully articulating the implications of these ideas, thereby avoiding and failing to address the underlying conflicts and contradictions. We have already seen that recent Irish policy statements are deliberately broad and all-encompassing and tend to be ineffective as instruments for resolving disputes, for example between harm reductionist and prohibitionist approaches. By the same token, such broad policy statements enable a wide variety of philosophies and approaches to operate in varying degrees of isolation from each other or, on rarer occasions, in harmonious synergy with each other. Contemporary drugs policy in Ireland is undeniably characterised by a commitment to the drug-free world/prohibitionist perspective, but, on the other hand, despite the one-sided rhetoric, it maintains a highly nuanced, prohibitionist stance, which fully incorporates substantial concessions to the harm reductionist perspective.

The drugs problem came late to Ireland and, in fact, the original heroin epidemic coincided with the first Reagan presidency, during which the U.S. made a sharp turn away from public-health-dominated drugs policies and from the serious consideration of decriminalisation towards an out-and-out 'war on drugs'. In fact, Reagan chose to ignore the New York Council on Drug Abuse, which was a government-funded think tank, consisting of many of America's foremost scientists from the various disciplines with an interest in drug abuse, which had been given the task of mapping out the best strategy for dealing with the U.S. drugs problem. The Council reported in 1980 in a book entitled *The Facts about Drug Abuse* and recommended a fairly radical decriminalisation approach.[1] Reagan totally repudiated this approach and instead developed a policy which focused increasingly on prohibition, interdiction, eradication of drug crops in producing countries and punishment of drug offences. Even then, however, U.S. policy continued to embrace some significant treatment and harm reduction initiatives.

According to the U.S. National Academy of Sciences,[2] the U.S. by 1980 had successively been through periods in which first a 'cops' approach, then a 'docs' approach and finally a 'cops plus docs' approach predominated. The U.S. has remained in this final phase ever since but, while the U.S. government claims to advocate a multifaceted, balanced approach, its policy is more accurately characterised as fundamentally, robustly prohibitionist with some 'docs' add-ons. At the ideological level, the U.S. is vigorously prohibitionist and promotes a 'drug-free world' perspective at home and abroad. In practice, the U.S. supports many 'docs' approaches in the areas of treatment, education and prevention, which serve to somewhat patchily moderate the harshness of the general system of prohibition. However, law enforcement and repression clearly predominate and have become ever more central since 1980. Strong evidence for this is that U.S. expenditure on law enforcement in the drugs area increased ten fold in the period 1981–99 and that currently the 'war on drugs' costs the U.S. $30 billion per annum; a startling figure, which can be compared to the $7.5 billion cost of the 1991 Gulf War.

Also, confirming the intensifying prohibitionist, law enforcement emphasis of U.S. policy, the number of 'inherent' drug crime offenders in state prisons climbed from 23,900 in 1980 to 289,000 in 1999 – a twelve fold increase. At year-end 2003, the 'inherent' drug offence group constituted 55% of all prisoners held in federal prisons and over 20% of all adult prisoners in state prisons.[3] The U.S. National Academy of Sciences believes that 'it is unconscionable for this country to continue to carry out a public policy of this magnitude and cost without any way of knowing whether and to what extent it is having the desired effect'.

Irish policy in the 1970s and 1980s was undoubtedly influenced by the American thinking of that era and especially by a recognition of the need to combine 'cops' and 'docs' approaches within a general prohibitionist framework. The initial Irish legislation, the 1977 Misuse of Drugs Act, represented a clear attempt to introduce a 'cops plus docs' approach.[4] Although the main purpose of the Act was to criminalise possession and supply, the Act also made careful provision for the preparation of medical and Probation and Welfare Service reports on any drug user brought before the courts and envisaged the provision of drug treatment centres within the penal system. Irish policy in the subsequent 30 years has also tended to mirror the U.S. policy of increasing reliance on law enforcement and of waging an increasingly severe 'war on drugs'. However, in the Irish case, the escalation in drugs law enforcement has been more selectively focused on drugs dealers and, unlike in the U.S., imprisonment has not been widely used as a response to simple possession of illicit substances. In addition, since 1996, the 'docs' elements in Irish criminal justice policy on drugs have, by comparison with the U.S., been far better resourced and more fully integrated into the system.

Interestingly, a more lenient treatment of cannabis users was incorporated in the 1977 law and still applies. As shown in the previous chapter, there is clear evidence that this *de jure* distinction has indeed translated into *de facto* differential treatment of 'soft drug users' by the Garda and the courts. This is the case despite Garda claims that they treat all drugs as equally criminal. Convicted cannabis and ecstasy users are almost invariably treated summarily at the District Court and are very rarely imprisoned. Instead, they tend to be fined or given a community-based sanction for their 'inherent' drug-related offences. This approach undoubtedly reflects the intention of the original legislation and its implicit acknowledgement of key distinctions between 'soft' and 'hard' drugs, or at least between cannabis and all other drugs; but it is also probably linked to the fact that cannabis and stimulant drug users, who do not use opiates, come from right across the social class spectrum and tend not to be involved in crime other than that intrinsic to drug use.

Despite the apparent intentions of the legislation and the actual differential treatment of 'soft' drug users, which is evident from Garda and judicial decision-making, most official statements repudiate any 'soft'/'hard' distinction between illicit drugs. Indeed, it is indicative of the unresolved tensions and contradictions at the heart of Irish policy that the Garda and most politicians continue to adhere to policy statements that explicitly minimise distinctions between drugs and forms of use. For example, the 1993 Garda Annual Report on Crime stated without qualification that 'once again, the major drug of abuse is cannabis resin'. While cannabis may be the most widely used drug and a large majority of Garda charges for drug-related crime involve cannabis, this statement ignored the far more devastating effects of opiate drugs on Irish society, in terms of crime, health and general social well-being.

Current Garda policy remains wedded to this approach, stating that 'the organisation [the Garda Síochána] makes no distinction in terms of criminality with either the physical and or psychological effects of specific drugs of abuse'. This kind of official blurring of distinctions between drugs and types of drug use has also permeated popular attitudes. Surveys show that the public are acutely aware of the connection between drug use and property and violent crime and that, in this context, they tend to see all illicit drugs and their users as inherently dangerous.[5]

The 1977 Misuse of Drugs Act also made significant provision for treatment approaches to all types of drug users and, very significantly, included users who deal in drugs in that dispensation. The Act required the judge to seek medical and welfare officer reports in all cases involving the possibility of serious penalties under the Misuse of Drugs Act. In the language of the Act, at section 28.1 (a), the judge was to '(i) cause to be furnished to the court a medical report in writing on the convicted person together with such recommendations (if any) as to medical treatment which the person making the report considers appropriate to the needs of the convicted person, and (ii) a report in writing as to the vocational and educational circumstances and social background of the convicted person together with such recommendations (if any) as to care which the body or person making the report considers appropriate to the said needs.'

Having considered the reports, the judge, instead of imposing a penalty, could implement, at his or her discretion, a number of treatment options. The judge could, in the words of section 28.2 of the Act:[6]

> (a) permit the person concerned to enter into a recognisance containing such of the following conditions as the court considers appropriate having regard to the circumstances of the case and the welfare of the person, namely—
>   (i) a condition that the person concerned be placed under the supervision of such body (including a health board) or person as may be named in the order and during a period specified in the order,
>   (ii) a condition requiring such person to undergo medical treatment recommended in the report,
>   (iii) a condition requiring such person for such treatment to attend or remain in a hospital, clinic or other place specified in the order for a period so specified,
>   (iv) a condition requiring the person to attend a specified course of education, instruction or training, being a course which, if undergone by such person, would, in the opinion of the court, improve his vocational opportunities or social circumstances, facilitate his social rehabilitation or reduce the likelihood of his committing a further offence under this Act, or
> (b) order that the person be detained in custody in a designated custodial treatment centre for a period not exceeding the maximum period of imprisonment which the court may impose in respect of the offence to which the conviction relates, or one year, whichever is the shorter.

Unfortunately yet indicative of the main thrust of Irish criminal justice policy on drugs, most of these treatment provisions, which promote the view of the drug user as a victim of the addictive process and social conditions and, consequently, in need of medical and other supports, were little used. The Central Mental Hospital (a psychiatric hospital under the control of the Department of Health, but offering inpatient services to the prison system) was the only place designated as a treatment centre for drug-using offenders. The designation occurred in 1980, but the centre was dedesignated a short time later without ever having operated properly as a drug treatment centre. In effect, these were, or at least quickly became, with few exceptions, nominal provisions – mere window-dressing that did not lead to the promised system of treatment-based alternatives to imprisonment for drug-using offenders.

There has, on the other hand, been considerable, if ad hoc, use made by the courts of Probation and Welfare supervision of drug offenders, following a conviction with deferral of sentence. This supervision usually includes the condition of attendance at a drug treatment centre. Fairly wide use has also been made of temporary release from prison of a drug-addicted offender for the purpose of drug treatment. This process occurs under the control and at the discretion of the executive, without reference to the courts. After assessment by both the penal authorities and the receiving agency (for example, the Coolmine Therapeutic Community programme), it is possible for an offender to be released a year or even several years early on condition that he/she attend a treatment course. In most of these cases, the treatment involves a residential programme with the goal of abstinence. Only a small minority of drug-addicted offenders and prisoners, however, have benefited from these provisions.

Despite the potential in the 1977 Act for the creation of a treatment-based diversion system for drug-using offenders, it soon became the norm both for the Garda to not target opiate users for the 'inherent' drug crime of possession and for the criminal justice system to process opiate-using offenders for non-drug crimes without adverting to or in any serious way addressing their status as drug users. It is possible that this was a deliberate policy, which was pursued because it offered an efficient way to avoid the treatment issues, including the pressing issues of lack of facilities and resources, raised by the 1977 legislation.

The 1984 amendment of the Misuse of Drugs Act was intended to strengthen the 1977 Act and close off certain loopholes. In this regard, it increased sentences for drug offences, most importantly raising the maximum sentence for importation and supply from 14 years to life imprisonment. The 1984 (Amendment) Act was the first of several pieces of legislation to take a conspicuously hardline position, targeting what were then commonly termed drug gang 'godfathers' and 'pushers'. In effect, the amendment strengthened the arm of the law in its dealings with drug crime and increased the punitiveness of the criminal justice response. At the same time, the amendment weakened the provisions aimed at a diversionary system of treatment-based alternatives. The amendment made the obtaining of medical and Probation and Welfare reports a discretionary matter. On 19 June 1984, the Minister for Health, explained to the Dail that 'over the years the courts have been hindered in passing sentence on drug pushers as a result of the current mandatory remand provision pending receipt of reports on their medical and social backgrounds. Section 11 of this Bill provides for the substitution of a discretionary remand provision for the mandatory one as it is obviously inappropriate to defer sentences in serious cases such as drug pushing where the problem of addiction does not arise.' This should not be taken to mean that this amendment was made merely to avoid remanding non-drug-using dealers for reports, since on 27 June 1984 the Minister for Justice explained to the Dail that 'the reason

I propose to amend section 28 in this respect is that it is inappropriate to defer sentences on drug pushers who do not have a serious addiction problem while reports are being sought on their medical and social circumstances'. Given the ambiguity of the notion of the seriousness of an addiction, it is not surprising that the amendment was widely interpreted to mean that a dealer should not be remanded for reports even if he were a drug user.

Arguably, this was an important early step on the road to bifurcation, the policy of separating drug-using offenders, who could be regarded as suitable candidates for lenient and constructive approaches, from drug barons and dealers, who were deserving of much harsher treatment, whether or not they were users. Yet, a great many opiate addicts, 'serious' or not, become embroiled, if usually only in a small way, in the drug dealing network. The lack of precision, on the one hand, about the seriousness of the accused's addiction (which would anyway have to be evaluated without the benefit of a medical report) and, on the other, about the seriousness of his or her involvement in dealing, were bound to create practical difficulties and moral dilemmas for the court. Furthermore, these critical issues were not addressed or even mentioned in the 1984 legislation, which restricted itself to carefully unpicking the 1977 Act so as to make assessments of drug-using offenders discretionary. Neither the explanation for this nor the purpose behind it was provided in the law itself. However, since very little progress had in fact been made in establishing treatment-based alternatives, and since many drug users were not even recognised as such, when, as was most common, they appeared before the courts for non-drug crime, this new provision had only marginal effects.

Nonetheless, the change in the law and the negative signals sent out by this change almost certainly facilitated the practice of ignoring the drugs problems of offenders and lowered the chances that treatment services for convicted drug users would be provided on anything like a sufficient scale. Consequently, in the 1980s, the proportion of opiate-using offenders in the prison system, who were almost entirely imprisoned for 'non-inherent' drug crime, rose rapidly until they were the large majority of prisoners in some Dublin prisons and about 40% of all Irish prisoners.[7] Many of these prisoners were not officially known within the prison system as opiate users because they were almost all convicted for property crimes and because they chose not to avail of the detoxification option available on entry to prison. The official lack of focus on the drugs problems of these offenders permitted and promoted for many years the remarkably desultory approach to drug treatment and rehabilitation in a prison system that, with the exception of a few small prisons, was and continues to be totally dominated by a rampant drugs culture.[8]

On the other hand, in theory and at the political level the seriousness and the intrinsically multi-factorial nature of the drugs problem were appreciated as early as 1983, when a Special Government Task Force on Drug Abuse was set up. In 1985, this initiative was followed by the establishment of a National Coordinating Committee on Drug Abuse. Over the following decade, politicians countered accusations of official inaction with repeated promises of a genuinely holistic, properly funded and fully coordinated response to the drugs problem. These statements explicitly acknowledged the extremely detrimental effect of drugs on marginalised communities and the key role of social inclusion policies in any holistic response. However, as was later admitted in the Rabbitte Reports of the mid-1990s,[9] the availability of informed analyses of the problem and the innumerable political promises failed to translate into innovative policy or effective interventions on the ground.

In the mid- to late 1980s, there was a notable political determination to increase state activity in the area of harm reduction, but this was driven mainly by concern over AIDS. At that time, more than half of all known cases of HIV in Ireland were attributed to the sharing of needles by drug users. As part of the new focus on harm reduction, more drugs clinics were established and a number of preventative, educational, needle exchange and outreach programmes put in place. There was also a tacit but significant shift from a disease model of treatment, emphasising detoxification and abstinence, to a harm reduction model, relying substantially on methadone maintenance. This shift would eventually have enormous impact in the criminal justice area.

While these harm reductionist initiatives had some limited positive impact, drug services continued to be severely under-resourced and oversubscribed, certainly until the radical improvements following 1996. Services also lacked coordination and any sense of a coherent, guiding philosophy. In addition, the authorities faced considerable resistance from communities, fearful about disease, crime and nuisance, to locating new clinics in their areas and vociferous complaint about the congregation of drug users around established clinics. That the then current approaches were ineffectual and utterly inadequate and fell far short of the promised holistic response to the drugs problem had become painfully obvious by 1991, when the Government Strategy to Prevent Drug Misuse[10] was published. This failure was obvious not least from the clear evidence that young people, especially in the disadvantaged areas of Dublin, were continuing to become involved with heroin in ever-growing numbers.

The operational reality post-1996: social and health-related initiatives impacting on criminal justice

The year 1996 became a watershed in terms of the official response to the drugs problem in Ireland. In 1996, a number of events converged to stimulate a more proactive and energetic political response. Foremost amongst those events was the murder by a criminal drugs gang of prominent journalist, Veronica Guerin, who was investigating the gang's activities. Guerin's murder made everyone suddenly more profoundly aware of the audacity and ruthlessness of drugs gangs and their apparent sense of impunity. The murder of Guerin coincided with historically high levels of serious crime (102,000 reported indictable crimes in 1995 compared to 62,000 in 1978) and, very significantly, with a

Table 5.1 Trends 1993–2004 for various statistics relating to drugs policy changes in 1996

Year	Syringe robberies & burglaries	Direct drug- related deaths	Drug prosecutions of under-17- year-olds	New HIV cases attributed to IV drug	People on methadone maintenance programmes	Average daily number detained in prison
1993	154	20	3	52	380	2171
1994	295	19	4	20	400	2141
1995	453	36	185	19	440	2156
1996	1104	44	163	20	1960	2179
1997	893	78	134	21	2820	2300
1998	442	82	248	26	3630	2370
1999	384	122	232	69	4250	2763
2000	361	113	323	83	4900	2919
2001	371	93	440	38	5760	3126
2002	221	90	479	50	6200	3166
2003	287	96	459	49	6880	3176
2004	171	112	444	71	7000	3199

Source: Garda Crime and Irish Prison Service Annual Reports and *drugnet*: Ireland

highly emotive people's protest movement against drugs and drug dealers and against perceived government, health service and Garda Síochána indifference and inaction. This protest movement, of parents and families in drugs-damaged communities, involved mass meetings, street marches leading to the forcible eviction of alleged drugs dealers, community self-policing and other vigilante-type activities.[11] By 1996 this movement threatened to usurp Garda Síochána authority in certain manifestly deprived, drugs-ridden localities and was attracting substantial media attention not just in Ireland but also from abroad.

The most important expression of the new level of commitment at Government and statutory agency level was the Ministerial Task Force on Measures to Reduce Demand for Drugs, which issued two reports, in October 1996 and May 1997.[12] Among other things, this initiative led to a realistically funded organisational structure for dealing with and coordinating the response to the drugs problem across all its dimensions, including a Cabinet committee on drugs, a National Drugs Strategy Team, a National Advisory Committee on Drugs, 14 Local Drugs Task Forces and, more recently, 3 Regional Drugs Task Forces.

Following 1996, the newly galvanised government response to the drugs problem placed considerable focus on strengthening law enforcement. This aspect will be dealt with in the following section. However, there was also a quantum leap in the commitment to and investment in harm reductionist and broad harm reduction measures, including some with a social justice and long-term, preventative perspective. There was a clear acknowledgement of the urgent need to greatly improve treatment for addicts and a new, more sincere determination to provide the necessary resources. There was also a reinvigorated will to tackle the root causes of drug abuse and invest in broadly based as well as narrowly targeted preventative actions. In part, this more serious recognition of and response to the role of social exclusion in the Irish drugs problem resulted from the pressures exerted by the anti-drugs activists and their supporters.

In practical terms, this new emphasis has been most clearly demonstrated by the work of the 14 Local Drugs Task Forces in specific drug-afflicted and socio-economically marginalised areas, which had previously considered themselves abandoned by the statutory agencies. Thirteen of the Task Forces are in the Greater Dublin area and one in North Cork City. The Task Forces have received substantial government funding and have developed and continue to deliver locally based treatment, rehabilitation and preventative/educational programmes to reduce the demand for illicit drugs. The Local Drugs Task Forces explicitly follow a social partnership model, involving collaboration between the statutory, community and voluntary sectors, who all have representatives on the Task Forces. They also work within an explicit harm reduction framework though a considerable number of community members of Task Forces take a strong, prohibitionist, zero tolerance line and are not fully supportive of all harm reduction approaches.

The recognition of the vital role of social exclusion has prompted the development of many programmes expected to impact positively on drug misuse and drug-related crime. For example, there has been considerable investment in the building of youth and community centres and in various projects designed to raise standards in social housing and improve the security, ambience and community solidarity of local neighbourhoods. A few formerly marginalised and very derelict areas have been transformed by substantial investment in youth and community facilities and by the upgrading of social housing and its immediate environment. There have also been many individual-focused programmes, which set out to empower disadvantaged people by way of education, training and increased employment opportunities. Much of this work has been facilitated by social partnership arrangements and interagency cooperation and this has included improved links between the Garda and local communities through Joint Policing Committees, Community Policing Fora, the Juvenile Liaison Scheme (a diversionary programme, usually involving a caution for young offenders, who admit their offence) and the Garda Projects (community-based, preventative programmes run by the Garda in collaboration with community workers and aimed at 'at risk youth' in marginalised communities).[13]

In treatment terms the most dramatic change following 1996 was the massive expansion of the methadone maintenance programme. This programme became the government's preferred and principal harm reduction response to the opiate drugs problem. In 1995, there were about 440 heroin users registered for methadone maintenance, with 300 more on an 'active' waiting list and a further 700 on a so-called 'inactive' waiting list. The media were, in 1996, drawing attention to the plight of desperate mothers who were approaching general practitioner after general practitioner in an attempt to find maintenance treatment for their addict children, who were languishing on impossibly long waiting lists. By 1998, the numbers actually registered for and receiving methadone maintenance had increased to 3,630 and by 2005 to over 7,000 – an eighteen fold increase in 10 years. This increase has largely occurred in drug treatment centres, but there has also been a considerable expansion in the numbers of addicts receiving maintenance from general practitioners.

While there was some increase in the number of counselling, rehabilitative and abstinence-focused programmes available to opiate-users and other drug users, these are still very insufficient and methadone maintenance has remained the first choice and predominant treatment modality in the years since 1996. There are still only 20 residential drug addiction treatment beds in the state and a very poor ratio of counsellors to addicts at maintenance centres. Recently, the Director of the Merchant's Quay Project, the state's largest voluntary drug treatment centre, has argued that while stabilising chaotic addicts by the provision of expanded maintenance programmes was very necessary in 1996, it is now essential to move beyond this by providing more readily available rehabilitation, support and counselling services aimed at helping addicts achieve abstinence.[14]

There have also been some developments in the drugs treatment area within the prison system, which mainly reflect the changes in the community. In 2000, a report was published by a Steering Group on Prison Based Drug Treatment Services.[15] This report emphasised the importance of 'equivalence of care' between the prison and the wider community and of through-care and aftercare services. In 1996, a designated drug-free prison was established in the Training Unit adjacent to Mountjoy Prison and a 7-week drug detoxification and rehabilitation programme was introduced in Mountjoy Prison. Recently, however, there has been an expansion of methadone maintenance approaches in the prison system to include not only HIV positive prisoners but also all new committals who have been on approved maintenance programmes in the community. At the time of writing in early 2007, there are upwards of 400 Irish prisoners (from a total of about 3,300) who are receiving daily methadone maintenance.[16]

However, a recent study by Lines concludes that high-risk behaviours for the sexual and intravenous transmission of HIV and hepatitis C are still widespread in Irish prisons. Lines concludes that the Irish Prison Service falls far short of its own objectives in terms of both the provision of HIV and hepatitis C prevention measures and the provision of adequate and consistent access to care for prisoners living with HIV/AIDS and/or hepatitis C.[17] Nonetheless, in 2004 the then Minister for Justice, Michael McDowell, reverting to a no-nonsense zero tolerance approach, proclaimed his intention to rid the prison system entirely of drugs. As part of this policy there has been a decision to impose mandatory random drug testing at the planned rate of 68,000 tests per annum. Ironically, this is occurring just after the Scottish Prison Service has announced the abandonment of its 10-year mandatory drug-testing scheme. The Scottish Prison Service has recently declared the scheme a failure which actually encouraged the use of heroin and which wasted resources that would be better spent on the improvement of treatment services for prisoners.[18] A British Home Office study concluded that mandatory testing had reduced the use of cannabis in prison but had not impacted significantly on heroin use. It seemed that prisoners were influenced by the fact that cannabis was detectable in urine tests for a far longer period than heroin.[19]

In general, there has been insufficient research on the effects of this large-scale reliance on methadone maintenance as the main response to the opiates problem since 1996. However, it seems clear that the programme has had some significant success in diminishing the level of property crime associated with opiate drug use. There may also have been significant harm reduction gains in the area of health, including reduced spread of disease and lowered rates of overdose and corresponding gains in the social well-being of users and their families. It is not obvious, however, that the programme has succeeded in stemming the recruitment of young people to opiate use or in challenging in any way the burgeoning non-opiate drugs culture. The greatly increased emphasis on methadone maintenance has not been able to halt the geographic spread of opiate use outside Dublin, since Portloaise, Athlone, Limerick and other urban centres have developed a relatively serious heroin problem in recent years. Indeed, it is possible to argue that methadone maintenance on this scale normalises drug use of all kinds and creates a climate of greater tolerance.

As the U.S. National Academy of Sciences states: 'Critics of harm reduction strategies often contend that such approaches send the wrong message – potentially undermining attempts to discourage drug use.'[20] It is, indeed, arguable that a large-scale methadone maintenance programme, which is not embedded within a broader plan to urgently help all opiate users attain abstinence and which makes few specific efforts to promote abstinence, will inevitably send the wrong message and encourage the spread of the drugs culture. However, there is also anecdotal evidence that prisoners from outside Dublin, who themselves first began IV opiate drug use in a Dublin prison, may have played a very significant role in bringing heroin use to provincial towns on their return to their home communities after release from prison.

As well as a dearth of descriptive and evaluative research, there has been a lack of analysis of the policy implications of the methadone maintenance approach. Methadone maintenance is undeniably a harm reductionist, public health type approach and in the Irish context represents a major intensification of the medicalisation of the drugs problem. It is very similar to the approach to opiate addiction that dominated and proved highly effective in Britain for many decades following the Rolleston Report of 1926, that is the continuing prescription of heroin to addicts by licensed doctors. It can, therefore, be interpreted as a form of decriminalisation by stealth. The state pays for the opiate drugs, manages and regulates the distribution through the medical profession and oversees the whole process of continuing addiction in a benevolent way that neatly avoids the question of law enforcement. It is, in effect, an experiment with the kind of regulation and infrastructural supports and normalisation of drug use that are envisaged as essential components of the 'human rights' approach to drug use.

These implications are rarely articulated. Equally little attention is paid to the inevitable tensions created by a methadone maintenance system of this scale for the drug-free world/prohibitionist model, to which the Garda Síochána still strictly adhere. The current approach highlights the victimhood and illness of the opiate user rather than his criminality and, when users are compliant and avoid 'illegal' drugs and crime, there are obvious and substantial personal gains for the addict and social benefits for society at large. The Garda have to reconcile the 'legality' of this kind of state-sponsored opiate use with their deeply ingrained mindset that cannabis, ecstasy, cocaine and heroin are all equally criminal and with the fact that they have a duty to constantly enforce the laws against possession of these drugs. Arguably, the Garda have managed their dilemma in two ways, by drawing an ever-sharper distinction between 'victim' drug users and 'criminal' drug dealers and by a division of labour, in which different and very differently oriented gardai undertake, on the one hand, the community policing/social partnership role, and, on the other, the repression of drug use role.

The operational reality post-1996: law enforcement and criminal justice initiatives

'Tough' legislation

If harm reduction, treatment and preventative approaches were very significantly boosted following 1996, there was, in the same period, at least an equal emphasis on tougher and more repressive law enforcement approaches. A number of legislative initiatives, prompted by the events of 1996, introduced new forms of social regulation of drug-related activity and set out to generally strengthen law enforcement in the drugs area.[21]

The galvanised political response manifested itself chiefly in the rapid progression and often intensification of actions, which were already being planned or actively developed. Government responded to the demand for effective action and took advantage of the heightened levels of public concern by pouring resources into the area and pushing through legislation, which up until that time had been resisted by opponents anxious about the erosion of civil liberties. Politicians were very much concerned with the 'optics' of the situation and eager that their response would be perceived as tough and unyielding. They correctly assumed that doubts about the impact of legal changes on civil liberties were a minority concern and that the broader public wanted a hardline response, irrespective of the implications for due process and the presumption of innocence.

Relevant Acts introduced following 1996 include: Criminal Justice (Drug Trafficking) Act 1996; Criminal Assets Bureau Act 1996; Proceeds of Crime Act 1996; Housing Act 1997 Licensing (Combating Drug Abuse) Act 1997; the Criminal Justice Act 1999; Non-fatal Offences against the Person Act 1997; and Criminal Justice Act 2006.

The Criminal Justice (Drug Trafficking) Act 1996 laid down quite draconian rules for the detention, search and interrogation of suspected drugs dealers, including the possibility of detention for up to 7 days for the purposes of interrogation. This legislation also restricted the 'right to silence' since it allows inferences to be drawn by a court from the failure of an accused person to mention particular facts during questioning. Most of these provisions were borrowings from the emergency powers made available by the Offences against the State Act 1939 and previously only used in tackling paramilitary, subversive activity by groups such as the Provisional IRA.

The Criminal Assets Bureau Act and the Proceeds of Crime Act set up the Criminal Assets Bureau and the necessary statutory legal framework to support it. These Acts provided the Bureau with specific powers to focus on the illegally-acquired assets of criminals involved in serious crime by identifying criminally acquired assets and freezing or confiscating them. These also provided for the collection of unpaid taxes on illegally-acquired income.

The Housing Act 1997 created powers which enabled local authorities to evict individual tenants for antisocial behaviour, particularly if it was drug-related. The Licensing (Combating Drug Abuse) Act 1997 created powers to suspend intoxicating liquor licences and to permanently disqualify holders convicted for drug offences. Possible offences leading to loss of a licence were to include knowingly allowing consumption or sale of drugs on their premises.

The Non-fatal Offences against the Person Act 1997 was specifically designed to combat crime involving possibly infected syringes. It created crimes involving the possession of a syringe or container of blood with intent to threaten or injure, injuring a person with a syringe or threatening to do so and abandoning a syringe in any place in a manner which injures or is likely to injure any person. The penalties for these crimes range from 5 years to life imprisonment. This Act was a response to the perceived inadequacy of current law for dealing with syringe attacks. The number of crimes of robbery and burglary using a syringe in 1997 was 893. This number has steadily and quite dramatically declined since then and was 165 in 2005 (see Table 5.1). This is plausible prima facie evidence that this new legislation has been effective in lowering the prevalence of crime involving syringes.

The Criminal Justice Act 1999 introduced mandatory minimum sentences of ten years for certain drug dealing crimes involving relatively large amounts of drugs (with a street value of €12,700 or more). The judge is permitted to mitigate the sentence under certain circumstances, for example if there is a timely admission of guilt or if the convicted person has materially assisted the Garda. Interestingly, the mandatory 10-year sentence could also be reduced, by way of a mid-sentence review, in the case of addicts, if the addiction was a substantial factor in the commission of the offence. This provision indicates a concern to distinguish between addict and non-addict dealers to the extent that the addict who takes advantage of the opportunity to become abstinent from drugs presented by the prison sentence could have this fact taken into consideration at mid-term review and could have the remainder of his or her sentence suspended. There is, however, no available data on the extent to which this provision is used. This provision is similar to the distinction contained in the 1984 Misuse of Drugs Act, which made obtaining medical and Probation and Welfare reports discretionary. The implicit intention behind the 1984 amendment, however, appears to have been to draw a distinction between victimised users and victimising dealers, whether they are users or not.

The Criminal Justice Act 2006 had a number of provisions aimed at drugs crime and introduced mandatory minimum sentences for possession of firearms in suspicious circumstances. The Act created the offences of participation in a criminal organisation and supplying drugs to a prisoner and extended the power of gardai to issue search warrants. It also strengthened the legislation covering mandatory minimum 10-year sentences for those caught with €12,700 worth of drugs or more, limiting the discretion of the courts in this area by requiring the judge to take into consideration the convicted person's previous convictions for drug trafficking offences. The Act also made provision for a Drug Offenders Register, analogous to the Sex Offender Register. This required drug offenders, on release from prison, to subject themselves to monitoring by the Garda. On 13 February 2007 the Cabinet approved a new package of anti-crime measures, many of which were aimed at 'rebalancing' criminal justice procedure and toughening sentencing. The proposals included new restrictions on the right to bail and, perhaps most alarmingly, the extension of the curtailment of the right to silence and 7-day detention of suspects to criminal suspects more generally. Repeat offending in the area of organised crime, it was proposed, would be subject to particularly harsh sentences of imprisonment.

Bifurcation

The putative creation in the 1984 amendment to the Misuse of Drugs Act of two categories of user (dealing and non-dealing) may be interpreted as an attempt to maintain a 'cops plus docs' approach towards the non-dealing user, who was a 'victim' of pushers, whilst permitting a harsher, more punitive, mainly 'cops' approach towards dealers and pushers, whether they were users or not. The amendment, which made the medical assessment of drug-using offenders a discretionary matter, was an important step in a bifurcation process, which has continued and, indeed, intensified, since 1996, despite the specific provision in the Criminal Justice Act 1999 for a more sympathetic approach to dealers and smugglers with an addiction problem. Bifurcation, in the drugs context, promotes the coexistence within the criminal justice system of relatively lenient approaches to the mass of less serious drug offenders and draconian approaches to those labelled as especially heinous offenders – the profiteering traffickers, pushers and gang leaders.

In fact, because of a lack of professional assessment services and genuine treatment options for offenders, it is reasonable to conclude that the 1984 provision had little in the way of practical consequences. If the rehabilitative potential of the 1977 Act had been fully realised, then the implementation of this amendment might have had negative consequences for many drug-using offenders suspected of dealing, who but for the amendment would have received the benefit of automatic medical assessment and treatment. In reality, relatively few drug-using offenders were properly assessed and very few received treatment, whether or not they were dealing.

Even if the services had been available, it would have been inherently difficult to implement the 1984 amendment in a fair and humane manner, ensuring continued access to assessment and treatment for those who needed them. This is because so many ordinary drug users, particularly opiate users, get caught up in small-time dealing. The whole point of the amendment was to facilitate the rapid conviction and imprisonment of those involved in possession and supply of drugs by circumventing the nuisance of compulsory medical assessment and by avoiding the issues of treatment which such an assessment might raise. Yet many small-time suppliers become part of the dealing network because of their addiction – not in order to exploit others but primarily to assure their own continued access to drugs. With respect to the offence of possession for the purpose of supply, it is possible to imagine a continuum of wrongfulness from relatively 'innocent' user/dealers, who deal only in a small way in order to obtain a supply of the drug for themselves, to the most 'guilty' dealers, who are users or have become users, but who have deliberately and callously set out to exploit others for their own profit. However, the legislation did not invite judges to make distinctions of this kind between classes of dealers and preempted the medical assessment necessary to a sound judgment on the question of the accused's level of drug dependence. The legislation, in effect, encouraged a harsh response to anyone who was tainted by dealing, regardless of the scale of dealing or of the fact that it might be mainly driven by addiction. Given the paucity of assessment and treatment services at the time and the fact that most convicted drug users were in prison for non-drug crime and their addiction status was frequently ignored by the criminal justice system, this provision was largely redundant and ineffectual. However, it was important as a policy statement which made a clear commitment to the bifurcation approach. Its main purpose seems to have been rhetorical – to signal the government's distaste for and intent to suppress drug dealers. The questionable morality and justice of promoting the withholding of treatment for addiction from those who need it because of their involvement in dealing, at whatever level of the network, was not addressed. In fact, the provision of assessment and treatment for offenders with drug problems is a moral onus on the state. This duty of care, like all medical care is, surely, owed to every convict who has a drug problem regardless of his or her crimes.

The apparently more sympathetic provision in the Criminal Justice Act 1999, which allows for a more lenient sentencing approach to addict as opposed to non-addict dealers and smugglers, takes an entirely different, indeed diametrically opposed approach. Contrary to the 1984 legislation, which appears to have been designed to lessen the likelihood that addiction will be considered a mitigating factor in the offence of dealing, the 1999 legislation appears to establish addiction as a significant mitigating factor in dealing and smuggling. The addict convicted of possession of €12,700 or more worth of drugs and facing a 10-year mandatory minimum sentence, who stays drug-free in prison, can in effect, at the discretion of the judge, halve his or her sentence. This provision, surely, introduces serious unfairness and profound moral ambiguity into the sentencing and penal process. Non-addict 'mules' are frequently exploited by large-scale dealers and are sometimes caught with large amounts of drugs, which they are smuggling on behalf of others for a relatively trifling personal profit. Why should these people be treated more punitively than large-scale 'professional' dealers and smugglers, who have been caught with similar amounts of drugs but who happen to be addicts?

However, it would be a mistake to interpret the 1999 provision as a deliberate reversal of the bifurcation approach. The historical context of increasingly harsh approaches to the specifically targeted group of drug traffickers, pushers and gang leaders makes this extremely unlikely, And after all, this provision for the favourable treatment of addict smugglers and dealers that remain drug-free in prison was part of tough new legislation that introduced 10-year mandatory minimum sentences. Mandatory minimum sentences are generally opposed by the Irish judiciary and regarded as an attack on judicial discretion and independence. In fact, it is most probable that this 1999 provision was chiefly designed as a sop to the judiciary and as a demonstration that judicial discretion was far from completely undermined in these cases. The provision for differential treatment of addicts eased the passage of innovative legislation, which for the first time outside of murder cases introduced severe mandatory minimum sentences. This 'sympathetic' provision may also have been regarded as politically expedient because it helped prevent public sympathy for addicts and support for medical and treatment approaches from interfering with the

ratcheting up of the criminal justice response to dealers and also, inciden-
tally, because it incentivised people to stay drug-free in prison. Whatever the
motives behind the legislation, the differential penal treatment of addicts who
deal and smuggle and dealers and smugglers who are not addicts raises difficult
jurisprudential and moral questions, which were not addressed in the political
debate leading to the Criminal Justice Act 1999.

On this account, then, the 1999 legislative provision, which appears to mitigate culpability on the grounds of addiction, is, in spite of appearances, mainly
a mechanism for sharpening the bifurcation within the system. It permits
the targeting of certain people involved in drugs with new, relatively extreme
measures, while, at the same time, seeming to support the general principle
of more tolerant, harm reductionist measures for the kind of amenable, drug-
using offenders who can be regarded as victims insofar as they have been
led into crime by their addiction more than by greed or other objectionable
motives.

In 1984 and 1999, there was broad political and public support for a bifurcation approach. This support extended to the drug-ravaged communities themselves. For example, in the mid-1990s massed anti-drugs protesters evicted
'known' drug dealers from their homes without any pretence at due process.
The Housing Act 1997, which allows for such evictions with a rather limited
form of due process, can be seen as an appropriation and legalisation by the
state of this vigilante intervention. Indeed, since so many of the demonised
local dealers were themselves users, the bifurcation distinction between 'ordinary' users and pushers or dealers who were also users was vital to the protest
movement. Mothers and fathers, concerned to get help for their user children,
were quick to identify and condemn dealers and gang members, who, unlike
their own children, deserved to face the full weight of the law. Interestingly,
people from drug-infested communities also tended to be in full accord with
the Garda in their indiscriminate, zero-tolerant condemnation of all drugs,
including cannabis.[22]

Curtailment of the right to bail and other civil liberties

The obvious material success of the drugs gangs, their impunity, their apparent
increasing involvement in armed robbery and the continuing, appalling spec-
tacle of numerous brutal assassinations within the underworld of organised
crime clearly convince the public at large of the need for relatively extreme
action. An important aspect of this is the perception, which may or may not
be well founded, that loyalist and republican paramilitaries and ex-paramili-
taries have a significant role in the drugs trade. These kinds of consideration
have meant that the public are quite prepared to see the extension of emergency powers, intended only for use when the security of the state is in immi-
nent danger, to the treatment of suspected drug dealers. Indeed, much of the
political rhetoric in response to the drugs problem from 1996 onwards has

emphasised that drugs gangs are a threat to the security of the state on a par with the threat once posed by terrorists and politically motivated subversive organisations.

The new dispensation on civil liberties and the public apathy about previously cherished, hard-won rights were demonstrated most clearly by the introduction of 7-day detention for suspect drug dealers and the curtailment of their privilege against self-incrimination. They were also demonstrated by the passing in 1996, by a majority of about 80% to 20%, of an amendment to the Constitution, which would legalise preventative detention by way of refusal of bail, in a case where it was reasonably suspected that the person charged would continue to commit crime if released on bail. Up until that point, preventative detention had not been permitted in Ireland because of several pivotal Supreme Court judgments to the effect that refusal of bail – on the grounds that the accused was likely to commit new offences while on bail –was unconstitutional.[23] Consequently, many drug abusers, who were prolific offenders and highly likely to continue offending in order to finance their drug habit, would, in the pre-trial period, be at liberty on bail. Much of the political discourse promoting this new way of restricting access to bail focused on the fact that the pre-trial period could be very long (over 12 months) and drug abuse and drug-related crime were likely to continue unabated during this time. Little thought was given to the fact that, by the same token, refusing bail would mean that, in some cases, an innocent person or one against whom the state could not make a satisfactory case would languish in jail for an unconscionably long period.

The Criminal Assets Bureau

The establishment in 1996 of the Criminal Assets Bureau was perhaps the most innovative and probably the most effective initiative of this period. The Criminal Assets Bureau is a multi-agency unit with officers drawn from the Revenue Commissioners and the Department of Social, Family and Community Affairs as well as the Garda Síochána. It was set up by the Criminal Assets Bureau Act 1996 and supported by the fairly radical Proceeds of Crime Act 1996, which allowed for the seizure of assets, even if no conviction had been recorded, unlike the previous Criminal Law Act of 1994, which provided only for the forfeiture of criminal assets following a conviction. The Proceeds of Crime Act 1996 was amended in 2005 to allow the Garda to seize cash in any location in the state once they believed it was the proceeds of, or linked to, criminal activity. This has enabled gardai to seize large sums of money found in course of searches for drugs. While the Criminal Assets Bureau has been credited with breaking up a number of organised drugs gangs, it is also arguable that the initial success of the policy of targeting the wealth of drug dealers has led directly to a situation where successful, large-scale drug dealers have based themselves abroad and the local drugs trade has become a chaotic arena, riven by rivalry and internecine feuding between less well-organised and controlled and even more ruthlessly violent gangs.

The Criminal Assets Bureau is a major departure because it targets large-scale, organised crime via the civil law, financial route, thus benefiting from the lower standard of proof applicable in the civil courts. That is it works to the more relaxed criterion of 'balance of probabilities' as opposed to 'beyond reasonable doubt'. This approach also benefits from the reversed burden of proof in matters of taxation. Those indicted are not presumed innocent but are, rather, required to explain how they came into possession of their wealth and how they have fulfilled their tax obligations. The Bureau focuses on tax evasion and the freezing and confiscation of assets of suspect and unexplained origin. The proceeds of drugs trafficking were the initial target and, in the words of the Garda Annual Report, remain 'of particular interest to the Bureau, but a substantial part of its activities involves the targeting of … living off immoral earnings, corruption and money laundering'.[24] This statement describes a situation which exemplifies how relatively extreme actions, initially justified by a specific rationale relating to the threat posed by violent drugs gangs, can easily be extended to other areas of criminal activity. This example of legislative and operational creep points to the very real potential for adverse knock-on effects on the fundamental rights of ordinary citizens from the ever-broadening application of restrictions on civil liberties, originally introduced to combat serious drugs offenders.

The Criminal Assets Bureau is considered successful because it has disbanded a number of major drugs gangs, whose members have lost very considerable assets and been faced with crippling tax bills. By the end of 2003, the Bureau had been operational for a little over 7 years and had frozen a total of €50 million of suspect assets. It had been instrumental in the collection of about €43 million of tax from persons suspected of being involved in criminal activity. The Bureau has introduced not only a financial means for attacking drugs gangs, but also a financial means for measuring effectiveness. On the other hand, many members of organised drugs crime gangs are thought to have exiled themselves abroad because of the threat posed by the Bureau. Some of these have there become successful dealers on an even larger scale than when they were based in Ireland.[25]

Partly inspired by the way the effectiveness of the Criminal Assets Bureau can be measured in clear-cut monetary terms, current criminal justice policy has adopted a new 'business model' managerial approach, which focuses on quantifiable performance indicators. For example, in 2002, the then Minister for Justice, Michael McDowell, using the 2000 seizures figures as a baseline, set specific targets for seizures by the Garda. He expected them to increase drug seizures 25% in monetary value terms by 2004 and 50% by 2008. The figure for 2000 was €20 million and, already by 2003, seizures were valued at €100 million, far surpassing the target for 2008. The figures for 2003 were unusually high because of the seizure of one particularly enormous consignment. In 2006, the total value of seizures was just under €74 million, still more than twice the targeted figure for 2008.[26]

Evaluating the new tougher policies

This quantitative evaluation and target-setting process is clearly problematic not only because of the variable street value of drugs and the fact that the Garda have the power to determine this value,[27] but also because increased seizures may merely be an indication of the increased supply and availability of drugs in the market rather than proof that their availability is being restricted. Given the reality of ample and widespread availability of drugs throughout Ireland, the increase in the value of seizures, from what was a very low base by comparison with neighbouring countries, may in fact mean little and may be creating a seriously misleading mirage of effective supply control action. The reality is that across Europe drugs are both more available and cheaper than ever before. In its Annual report for 2006,[28] the European Monitoring Centre for Drugs and Drug Addiction found that the price of drugs had fallen over the past 5 years with the price of some drugs, including ecstasy and (brown) heroin, almost halving.

It would be a mistake to conclude that all the tougher law enforcement responses since 1996 have focused exclusively on serious criminals and the leading, profiteering members of drugs gangs. It has been mentioned above that many 'mules' caught in possession of more than €12,700 worth of illicit drugs are imprisoned for long periods but are not serious criminals. In addition, several law enforcement initiatives, following 1996, were aimed at low-level street dealing in heroin and at curbing 'shooting galleries' in specific drug-infested areas. The first and largest of these was Operation Dóchas, which involved the deployment of over 400 gardai in Dublin's inner city. Other street level initiatives followed, including Operations Nightcap and Clean Street, which involved undercover gardai monitoring the sale of small amounts of illicit drugs in licensed premises and other public places and 'if feasible purchasing drugs from the dealers to effect prosecutions.'[29] The Garda National Drugs Unit was set up in 1996 to better coordinate drugs-related intelligence, but also to support local divisional drug units 'with their primary focus being local drug dealers and users'.[30] Also, the new bail laws and the opening of the new remand prison of 400 places (in 1999) led to the imprisonment of large numbers of drug users who were often involved in relatively petty crime and not seriously involved in dealing.

On the other hand, the increased level from 1996 of law enforcement on the streets can be interpreted as mainly an attempt to support local drug-ravaged communities and to convince them that the Garda could be trusted to deal with the problem and that there would be no future need for the vigilante-type activities so prevalent in the mid-1990s. In reality, this largely temporary increase in Garda activities against street-level drug users did not represent a major change in policy, whereby opiate and other 'hard' drug users would be targeted and routinely prosecuted for 'inherent' drug-related crimes like possession. Similarly, the refusal of bail to drug-using offenders did not mark a new focus on 'inherent' drug crime, since those refused bail tended to be facing other charges and the large majority of imprisoned users continued to be prosecuted and convicted for property crime.

Treatment approaches within the criminal justice system

Since 1996, there have also been a few small-scale projects within the criminal justice system that promote the 'docs' element of the 'cops plus docs' approach. The two most significant initiatives have been the establishment of a pilot Drug Court in Dublin in 2001 and the arrest referral scheme.[31] Both of these initiatives are essentially treatment-based diversion programmes that offer an alternative to custody for drug-using offenders at, respectively, the trial and arrest stage. However, these initiatives have, so far, been experimental and small-scale and thus little more than symbolic gestures, which create hardly a ripple in the mainstream criminal justice system response to drug-using offenders.

The Drug Court approach allows judges the option of diverting non-violent, drug-using minor offenders from the prison system to court-supervised treatment for their drug problems. The pilot Drug Court was set up with its sphere of activity restricted to the North Inner City area of Dublin, where dedicated treatment and rehabilitation services were available to it. An evaluation of the first year of operation of the Drug Court has been published.[32] Of 61 offenders referred to the court, 37 were accepted as eligible and suitable. They were mainly males in their late twenties, unemployed and of low educational attainment. They were all primarily heroin users but were almost always poly-drug users, who were on average using 5 different drugs. Thirty-five of the offenders had amassed a total of 872 prior convictions. Their current charges overwhelmingly involved larceny and only a handful were for drug-related offences per se. The percentage of 'negative for opiates' urine tests increased significantly as the programme progressed, from 42% in the first 3 months to 82% in the last three months.

The authors of the evaluation report state that it is 'far too early to comment conclusively on the overall effectiveness of the programme' but they do believe that preliminary results show a marked decline in offending behaviours (the rate at which participants were arrested, charged or had their bail revoked) and an increase in compliance as the programme progressed. A positive, but modest 30% of the offenders were clean of all illicit drugs by the end of the evaluation period. In their view, this means that the 'Drug Court will have the desired impact if it can succeed in retaining participants over the early months'. They recommended the continuance and extension of the Drug Court provided that timely access to treatment services can be guaranteed.[33] An evaluation of the arrest referral scheme is underway.

Summary

While the Misuse of Drugs Act 1977 was fundamentally prohibitionist, it strove to include a 'docs' approach alongside the 'cops' approach. It explicitly placed cannabis in a less severe category and it made provision for the medical and social/educational assessment of offenders and for alternative treatment-oriented forms of sanction. It made provision for sentences of imprisonment that would be served in specialist custodial drug treatment centres. However, the potential of these 'docs' provisions was never fully realised.

While almost all convicted, non-opiate drug users convicted for possession escape a sentence of imprisonment, it is the norm for the system to imprison opiate-using offenders for their acquisitive crimes rather than for their 'inherent' drug crime. Medical and other services within the prison system have been generally very poor and, until recently, the addiction status of prisoners has generally been ignored, apart from the provision of a rather abrupt methadone detoxification on arrival in prison. Many prisoners have chosen not to mention their drug use to prison officials and many have continued using opiates in prison. By the mid-1980s the Irish prisons, especially in Dublin, were infested with drugs and dominated by a rabid drugs culture.

The 1984 amendment to the Misuse of Drugs Act was the first of many pieces of legislation designed to strengthen the powers of law enforcement against drugs offenders and increase punishments for 'inherent' drugs offences. A maximum life sentence was introduced for importation and supply of illegal drugs. This amendment also made the court's obtaining of medical and social/educational assessments of addicted offenders discretionary, ostensibly in order to separate the treatment of dealers and non-dealing addict offenders. This can be regarded as the beginning of a process of bifurcation, in which an ever harsher approach would be taken against dealers, whilst maintaining a relatively lenient approach to the drug users, who are seen as their victims.

In the mid-1980s the threat of HIV and AIDS bolstered state support for harm reduction and public health inspired measures, such as needle exchange and methadone maintenance; nonetheless for many years drug services of all kinds remained under-resourced and utterly insufficient to meet the obvious needs and demands of drug users and their families.

The investigating journalist Veronica Guerin was murdered in 1996 by a drugs gang, which felt threatened by her inquiries. This event, which outraged public opinion, coincided with a period when there was already widespread public concern over historically high levels of crime, especially drug-related acquisitive crime. Simultaneously, families of drug users and other members of deprived communities devastated by a rampant and largely unchecked drugs culture were involved in an increasingly vociferous and proactive protest movement, which highlighted the failures and inaction of law enforcement, health services and government. Vigilante actions against drug dealers and mass protests, including evictions of 'known' drug dealers, were beginning to attract intense media interest. All these factors finally convinced government that dramatic action had to be taken to tackle the drug problem and drug-related crime problems. The Rabbitte Reports in 1996 and 1997 spelled out the multi-factorial nature of the drug problem and crucially recognised the vital contribution of deprivation and social exclusion to the problem, especially in respect to opiate drugs. The reports presented a blueprint for a coordinated, social partnership, community-based response to the problem and for an extensive bureaucratic, operational and advisory structure to support such a response.

Since 1996, following the galvanised response of the government, there has been a major expansion of drug services, harm reductionist interventions, and primary preventative programmes aimed at improving training and educational opportunities, recreational facilities for youth and the built environment of deprived areas. Initially the flow of funding was relatively generous but an adequate level of funding has not always been maintained. Some showcase areas, such as Ballymun and Fatima Mansions, have been dramatically improved, but many, usually more peripherally situated, housing estates remain relatively neglected and insufficiently supported. In terms of drug treatment, the main emphasis has been on methadone maintenance and the numbers on such programmes have increased about twenty fold since 1995. While community-based services often emphasise counselling and employment training, these areas and abstinence-based treatment approaches have generally taken a secondary role to methadone maintenance.

Services for drug-addicted prisoners were also expanded. Drug-free regimes and a longer more supportive system of detoxification were introduced in the prisons. Methadone maintenance was also introduced for those who had been on such programmes before their committal as well as for HIV positive prisoners. However, drug use has remained widespread within the system and the majority of imprisoned addicts remain largely without treatment or support. More recently, the then Minister for Justice, Michael McDowell, has announced a shift in policy towards a more hardline approach aimed at ridding the prisons of drug use and relying on greater surveillance, interdiction of drugs, mandatory testing and sanctions for those found using drugs.

Many legislative changes relating to the criminal justice system followed 1996. These new laws were mainly intended to toughen the response to drug crime and increase the powers of the police and other relevant agencies. A plethora of 'hardline' legislation was introduced between 1996 and 2006, which, among other things: limited civil liberties and due process safeguards for suspect drugs dealers; introduced mandatory minimum sentences of 10 years for people found in possession of drugs to the value of €12,700 or more; permitted local authorities to evict drug-using tenants on account of antisocial behaviour; and allowed for the permanent disqualification of holders of liquor licences if they knowingly allowed consumption or sale of drugs on their premises. These new measures, which were tough on drug crime, and, politically, clearly intended to be seen as tough, were introduced alongside the much enhanced harm reduction and social inclusion programmes. The conflict between these two paradigms was obscured by the reinforced bifurcation approach and by the binary approach of official policy, emphasising both demand reduction and supply reduction. The more constructive and supportive treatment and preventative approaches were subsumed under the heading of demand reduction and the more punitive, deterrent and condemnatory approaches under the heading of supply reduction.

Between 1996 and 2000, there was a remarkable increase of almost 50% in the numbers held in prison and many of this increased number of prisoners were drug users, refused bail under the 1997 Bail Act. On the other hand, new schemes for treatment-based diversion of drug-addicted offenders at either the arrest or court stage have been established. So far, these schemes have been experimental and very small scale, but they are a clear attempt to reinvigorate a 'cops plus docs' approach within the criminal justice system. However, perhaps the most significant, single, law enforcement initiative following 1996 was the introduction of the Criminal Assets Bureau. This inter-agency Bureau tackles organised crime by freezing and confiscating assets which cannot be properly explained and by collecting unpaid taxes. This approach benefits from the lower level of proof required in civil cases and the reversed burden of proof in taxation matters. This approach has had considerable success in breaking up drug gangs, who seemed invulnerable to the law. But there are signs that the Bureau are now finding it increasingly difficult to trace and identify the assets of drug dealers, who have become wiser to the methods of the Bureau and the implications of the law in this area.

Notes

1 Drug Abuse Council (1980) *The Facts about Drug Abuse*, New York: The Free Press.
2 U.S. National Academy of Sciences (2001) *Informing America's Policy on Illegal Drugs: What We Don't Know Keeps Hurting Us*, Washington, D.C.: National Academy of Sciences.
3 Harrison, P.M. and Allen, J.B. (2006) *US Department of Justice, Bureau of Justice Statistics, Prisoners in 2005*, Washington, D.C: U.S. Department of Justice.
4 Butler, S. (1991) ('Drug problems and drug policies in Ireland: a quarter of a century reviewed', *Administration*, 39, at 210) suggests that the Misuse of Drugs Act 1977 was influenced by the Report of the Working Party on Drug Abuse (1971) [Dublin: Stationery Office], which he describes as a balanced, caring document that states, inter alia, 'persons who have become dependent on drugs … should be regarded as sick people in need of medical care to be treated with sympathy and understanding'.
5 For example, see Bryan, A., Moran, R., Farrell, E. and O'Brien, M. (2000) *Drug-related Knowledge, Attitudes and Beliefs in Ireland: Report of a Nation-wide Survey*, Dublin: Health Research Board. These researchers found that 94% of a representa-

tive sample of 1,000 adults considered drugs crime a major problem in Ireland and 91% considered the drug problem out of control. Negative and often punitive attitudes towards addicts were widespread. Fifty-three percent believed that almost all drug addicts are dangerous; 43% saw drug addicts more as criminals than victims; 57% thought that those with a drugs problem had only themselves to blame; 70% agreed that Irish society is too tolerant toward drug users; and 51% believed that tougher sentences for drug misusers is the answer.

6 Misuse of Drugs Act 1977.
7 O'Mahony, P. (1993) *Crime and Punishment in Ireland,* Dublin: Round Hall Sweet & Maxwell; (1997) *Mountjoy Prisoners: A Sociological and Criminological Profile,* Dublin: Stationery Office.
8 Hannon, F., Kelleher, C. and Friel, S. (2000) *General Healthcare Study of the Irish Prisoner Population,* Dublin: Stationery Office; O'Mahony, *Mountjoy Prisoners;* Allwright, S., Barry, J., Bradley, F., Long, J. and Thornton, L. (1999) *Hepatitis B, Hepatitis C and HIV in Irish Prisoners: Prevalence and Risk,* Dublin: Stationery Office.
9 Rabbite Reports (1996) *First Report of the Ministerial Task Force on Measures to Reduce the Demand for Drugs* and (1997) *Second Report of the Ministerial Task Force on Measures to Reduce the Demand for Drugs.*
10 Department of Health (1991) *Government Strategy to Prevent Drug Misuse,* Dublin: Department of Health.
11 A recent book (Lyder, A. (2005) *Pushers Out: The Inside Story of Dublin's Anti-Drug Movement,* Toronto: Trafford) provides a history of the movement from an activist's point of view.
12 Rabbite Reports.
13 Connolly, J. (2003) *Community Policing and Drugs in Dublin,* Dublin: North Inner City Drugs Task Force; Bowden, M. and Higgins, L. (2000) *The Impact and Effectiveness of the Garda Special Projects,* Dublin: Department of Justice.
14 Tony Geoghegan cited in *The Irish Times,* 'Shake-up sought in drug addiction policy' by Holland, K. (25 April 2003).
15 Report of Steering Group on Prison Based Drug Treatment Services (2000), Dublin: Irish Prison Service.
16 Personal Communication from Governor of Mountjoy Prison (February 2007).
17 Lines, R. (2002) *A Call for Action: HIV/AIDS and Hepatitis C in Irish Prisons,* Dublin: Merchants Quay Ireland and Irish Penal Reform Trust.
18 Dean, J. (2005) 'The future of mandatory drug testing in Scottish prisons: a review of policy', *International Journal of Prisoner Health,* 1, 2–4, at 163–170.
19 Singleton, N. et al. (2005) 'The impact of mandatory drug testing in prisons', London: Home Office Online Report 03/05.
20 U.S. National Academy of Sciences, *Informing America's Policy on Illegal Drugs,* at page 63.
21 O'Brien, M., Dillon, L. and Moran, R. (2001) 'Legal framework' in *Overview of Drug Issues in Ireland 2000,* Dublin: Health Research Board.
22 Lyder, *Pushers Out.*
23 See *The People v O'Callaghan* (1966) I.R. 501 and *The Director of Public Prosecutions v Ryan* (1989) I.R. 399.
24 Annual Report on Crime (2001) Dublin: Garda Headquarters.
25 *Prime Time Investigates* (12 June 2006) described the multi-million euro operation

of one Irishman living in the Netherlands for the last few years. Other Irish large-scale dealers are known to be based in Spain.

26 Figures released by the Garda National Drugs Unit, January 2007.

27 The questionable nature of Garda estimates of the street value of drugs is also a vitally important matter in the prosecution of people found in possession of €12,700 or more worth of drugs and facing a mandatory minimum 10-year sentence.

28 *Annual Report 2006*, Lisbon: European Monitoring Centre for Drugs and Drug Addiction.

29 *Annual Report on Crime 2001*, Dublin: Garda Headquarters.

30 *Annual Report on Crime 1997*, Dublin: Garda Headquarters.

31 Working Group on a Courts Commission (1998) *Fifth Report: Drug Courts*, Dublin: Stationery Office.

32 Farrell, M. and Farrell Grant Sparks Consulting (2002) *Final Evaluation of the Pilot Drug Court*, Dublin: Irish Courts Service.

33 On 1 February 2006 the Irish Courts Service announced that the Drugs Treatment Court was to be put on a permanent footing and extended on a phased basis to all court districts in the Dublin Metropolitan Area.

6

A balanced policy? Effective compromise or confused muddle?

The post-1996 response to the drugs problem represents a major escalation in effort and investment and a notable diversification in the type of anti-drugs activities that are undertaken. There can be little doubt that the reshaped prohibition incorporating stronger harm reductionist and social justice driven projects is a more balanced approach than the previous stricter form of prohibition. The most obvious markers of the more vigorous and constructive response since 1996 are the greatly expanded methadone maintenance programme,[1] the community-based preventative programmes, including social and inter-sectoral partnerships, youth facilities, improved housing and enhanced environments, and the more active Garda response through the Criminal Assets Bureau, supply control measures and community policing. However, this gearing up of the level of response to the drugs problem does not translate into a significant transformation of criminal justice policy on drugs as such or an abandonment of the fundamental commitment to prohibition.

Despite the massively increased investment in the drugs area and the introduction or consolidation of harm reductionist initiatives and social justice inspired harm reduction, the Irish criminal justice system itself has over the last 10 years steadfastly adhered to its traditional 'cops plus docs' approach. This approach is characterised by an underlying, doctrinaire prioritisation of the drug-free world/prohibitionist perspective and by a token, minimalist approach to treatment and treatment-based diversion within the criminal justice system. In other words, Irish criminal justice policy on drugs, which has always in theory taken a 'cops plus docs' approach, continues to do so, but equally continues to be hot on 'cops' and at best lukewarm on 'docs'.

There have been some attitudinal and minor policy changes within the criminal justice area, but these have largely been required in order to accommodate to the changing broader realities following 1996. These attitudinal and policy changes have been a pragmatic response to the many new non-criminal justice interventions with drug users, including those who are criminally involved. They have been driven by the need to adjust to the enormous expansion of harm reductionist measures, such as methadone maintenance, and to the new emphasis on social inclusion and community-based approaches. They have not been driven by any direct critical analysis of policy or challenge to the received prohibitionist wisdom.

In recent years, health, social welfare, educational and criminal justice policies and interventions on drugs issues have converged more than ever and there are now many inter-sectoral initiatives, such as community policing fora and community-based programmes for at-risk youth. The criminal justice area has had to make various adjustments to fit in with the new inter-sectoral 'balanced policy' agenda, but the orientation of legislation, law enforcement and political thinking in criminal justice policy on drugs remains essentially unchanged.

In 2004, the then Minister for Justice, Michael McDowell, announced an unequivocally drug-free world/prohibitionist policy for the prison system. This plan – to totally eliminate drugs from the prisons – is widely regarded within the system as unworkable and utterly unrealistic. It is also considered inconsistent with many of the harm reductionist approaches now adopted within the system. As we have seen in Chapter 1, this hardline prohibitionist approach also has a very real potential to obstruct further development within the prisons of harm reductionist approaches, such as needle exchange. The Minister's plan relies on a tightening up of supply control measures, such as increased surveillance of visits, glass barriers between prisoners and their visitors and sniffer dog patrols. It also involves a system of mandatory drug testing of a kind that has recently been abandoned after many years' experience by the Scottish system because, in their view, it was wasteful and counterproductive.[2] In the Irish system the plan is to randomly select up to 10% of prisoners per month and test for the presence of illicit drugs through urinalysis. Special incentives, such as enhanced meals, are to be offered to people who volunteer for testing. The prisoners who test positive will face sanctions such as loss of visits or of remission time, while those caught in possession of drugs will face a Garda investigation and possible prosecution. The Scottish experience of such a regime indicates that it fails to impact on the prevalence of drug use and may encourage prisoners to use potentially more dangerous 'hard' drugs such as heroin since they are easier to conceal than cannabis and remain detectable to testing for a shorter period of time.

The differentiation of drugs

Also indicating the continuing ascendancy of the drug-free world/prohibitionist perspective, the blurring of critical differences between types of drug, types of use and contexts of use still typifies official thinking, as does the strict adherence to a theoretically, practically and morally questionable differentiation between the misuse of illegal drugs and the misuse of legally condoned and medically prescribed drugs. The World Health Organisation[3] has calculated that, globally, all illicit drugs together account for 0.6% of 'disability-adjusted life years' compared to 6.1% attributable to tobacco and alcohol. This suggests that the latter cause 10 times more health-related harm, yet this sobering fact has impinged hardly at all on the drugs discourse in Ireland. At the UN level, however, the inconsistencies in the response to licit and illicit mood-altering substances have received some recognition. In 1994, the then executive director of the UN Drug Control Programme[4] stated 'it is increasingly difficult to justify the continued distinction among substances solely according to their legal status and social acceptability … pursuing disparate strategies to minimise their impact is ultimately artificial, irrational and uneconomical'.

Recently, Judge Elizabeth Dunne made an interesting and relevant comment on sentencing in a case for possession of cannabis, which qualified for the mandatory minimum sentence of 10 years (*DPP v V.*). She said 'it seems to me, in considering this matter it does not matter in practical terms in dealing with the sentence whether the quantity concerned is €10,000 or €13,000 worth of cannabis or €1 million worth of heroin, I am not entitled to take into account those differences'. This thinking seems to accord with the stated Garda policy that they treat all illicit drugs similarly. However, the case was appealed and the Court of Criminal Appeal noted the differential treatment of cannabis in the 1977 Act and stated that 'offences relating to cannabis might be treated less severely'. Crucially, on the other hand, they went on to state that 'It is, however, an argument of very little value.' This somewhat equivocal support for the more lenient treatment of cannabis cases did, however, translate into the suspension of two years of the sentence handed down by Judge Dunne.

This case points to the persistent tensions, difficulties and disparities arising from the system's failure to distinguish clearly between types of drug. The 1977 Act singles out cannabis for more lenient treatment, but other than this there is no attempt in Irish law to categorise drugs according to their inherent dangerousness. In reality cannabis and several other substances, such as ecstasy, tend to be treated more leniently, but there is no legal basis for the extension of lenient treatment from cannabis to other substances, and official policy, especially Garda policy, adamantly proclaims the equal illegality and seriousness of all illicit substances, including cannabis.

Two other recent events illustrate similar tensions in Irish criminal justice policy. On 31 January 2006, in response to the self-killing of an apparently hallucinating man who had purchased and ingested 'magic mushrooms', the Minister for Health, Mary Harney banned the sale and possession of such unprocessed, hallucinogenic mushrooms. Prior to this there had been a 'loophole' in the drugs control law, which had banned all processed psychoactive mushrooms, but not those in their natural state. What is surprising in this is not the government's predictable recourse to strict prohibition, which was inevitable given the current legal framework, but the fact that more than 20 shops in the commercial areas of Irish towns had for several years been openly, casually and confidently trading in these mood-altering mushrooms and other psychoactive substances, such as BZP and Salvia, which are technically legal because they have so far escaped the attention of the law. They had been serving a small but significant counterculture of self-proclaimed 'heads' and other people wishing to experiment with the hallucinogenic mushrooms and other drugs – evidently without arousing much public outrage. This phenomenon indicates the new complexity of the drugs scene in Ireland and, arguably, highlights the beneficial, 'civilising' or socialising effects of a tolerant approach. Certainly the traders have responded by suggesting that the distribution of 'magic mushrooms' will now fall into the hands of criminal gangs and quality control will be relaxed, leading to a far greater presence of toxic mushrooms in the market. The largely unproblematic presence of these shops, within a system that claims strict adherence to prohibition, demonstrates emphatically the immediate feasibility of forms of partial legalisation, in which 'less dangerous' drugs are split off from the criminal drugs market.

The second event was the announced introduction in February 2006 of a new adult cautioning scheme in which a police caution would replace prosecution for certain categories of minor offender, including those found, for the first time, in possession of small amounts of cannabis for personal use. This move clearly signalled the minor nature of this offence and could be seen as another step in the bifurcation process, which relaxes the approach to minor drug offenders, whilst strengthening the punitive response to dealers and traffickers. However, illustrating the enduring problems of the Irish system with the differentiation of drugs, the then Minister for Justice, Michael McDowell, made a public statement on these changes affirming that in fact there was no change in the law and the Garda remained as committed as ever to the war on drugs. He stated 'there is no question of the guards depriving themselves, or the Director of Public Prosecutions depriving himself, of a discretion to prosecute for these offences. But in many cases it may make sense, instead of queuing up for court time in three or six months time to confront an offender who accepts his or her responsibility with the facts now, to bring them before a senior officer of An Garda Síochána, to administer a caution and to draw their attention that they are committing a very serious offence.' In other words, reinforcing the equivocation of the Irish system, the authorities would now be able to treat this kind of possession of cannabis as a relatively trivial offence, but they must continue to label it 'a very serious offence' and pretend that they are treating it as such. In fact, presumably due to pressures exerted on the Minister, the adult cautioning scheme was finally introduced without listing possession of cannabis as a scheduled offence amenable to the adult caution.

Of course, tension between the fact of more lenient treatment of cannabis and other less dangerous drugs and equal condemnation of all illicit drug use is implicit in the zero tolerant, prohibitionist position. However, the Irish system is particularly confused because the 1977 legislation singled out cannabis and only cannabis (and not, for example, 'magic mushrooms') for more lenient treatment and because it has never attempted to address the vexed issue of categorising drugs in terms of their dangerousness and devising a graduated scheme of punishments scaled to dangerousness.

The original singling out of cannabis in 1977 was no doubt a common sense reaction by legislators to the perceived lesser threat of cannabis, but the way in which the drugs scene has evolved over recent decades has created new powerful motivation for the continuing reluctance to address differences between severe, socially and personally destructive addictions and largely non-problematic recreational use of drugs. Some of the most important factors are that: 1) the use of cannabis and stimulants is widely perceived to act as a gateway to heroin and poly-drug use and therefore to seriously self-destructive addictions; 2) poly-drug use has become common (most criminally involved drug users are poly-drug users and heroin and other opiates are increasingly being 'marketed' as part of a package including cocaine and other recreational drugs); and 3) perhaps most importantly, organised criminal gangs with a proclivity for serious intimidation and violence are as prominent in the importation and distribution of recreational drugs (and even tobacco) as of heroin.

However, none of these arguments justify the failure to respond to the very real differences between different drugs and methods of use in their potential for harm. Despite the fact that many hard drug users will have first used cannabis (and before that tobacco), the gateway theory has little credibility. This is because, in reality, only a tiny proportion of cannabis users go on to use opiates. For example, it is estimated that about 50 million Americans use cannabis but only about 1 million of them use opiates. When we look at severely addicted, hard drug users it can seem that they have inexorably slid down a slippery slope of increasing dependency on ever more dangerous substances. However, in reality the vast majority of the far greater number of 'recreational' users has clearly been able to halt their slide before dependency becomes a serious problem. Cannabis use is probably a common, but certainly not an essential, behavioural stepping stone to hard drug use. The Keogh[5] and Furey and Browne[6] studies offer useful insight on this topic, because large proportions of the hard drug users they interviewed reported using heroin before cannabis – 32% and 27% of the total, respectively. But who would suggest that heroin is a gateway drug for cannabis?

The other two arguments, which hinge on the interconnections between 'soft' and 'hard' drug use and the criminal involvement in 'soft' drug distribution, can as easily be regarded as arguments for legalisation or selective legalisation along the lines of the Dutch experiment with cannabis. The Dutch have in effect legalised the cultivation, distribution, possession and use of cannabis within the Netherlands but claim that they still conform to their prohibitionist obligations under international law. The Dutch, by decriminalising cannabis, have had considerable success in separating the cannabis market from the criminal market, lowering the probability that a cannabis user will turn to hard drugs, maintaining a considerably lower level of cannabis use than prevails in the U.S. and the U.K. and depriving criminal gangs of substantial drug-related profits.[7] The, until recently, 'legal' largely unproblematic sale of magic mushrooms in Ireland clearly illustrated the advantages of maintaining the trade in psychoactive substances within the legitimate sphere.

The 'criminal' drug user

While drugs differ in their potential to create addiction and drugs and methods of use differ in their potential for disruption of personality and lifestyle and for collateral damage, it is important to remember that even dangerous drugs like heroin can be used in a controlled, relatively non-problematic way. As a report from the British Department of Health has recently stated: 'drugs are not, of themselves, dangerous, with the risk residing in the interaction between the substance, the individual, the method of consumption and the context of use'.[8]

On the other hand, the very much greater involvement of heroin users, compared to the much larger group of 'recreational' drug users, in 'economic compulsive' crime is of profound importance. It highlights the fact that relative social deprivation combined with severe personal adversity, that is an interaction between *set* (personality and personal capacities) and *setting* (the socio-economic and cultural context), tend to underlie the predisposition to both crime and the more socially and personally destructive forms of drug use. The relatively powerless, undereducated, personally and politically disorganised person with little stake in the socio-economic system is far likelier to turn to crime and to fall prey to chaotic, uninhibited and excessive forms of drug use. In this regard, it is a critically significant fact that the evidence shows that many criminally involved heroin users would have become involved in crime even if they had avoided drug use.

Official policy and especially Garda and penal policy is still vitiated by a lack of clarity about and inattention to the significant behavioural differences between different types of drug user, both with regard to how this impacts on mode of drug use and on involvement in crime. The official policy of condemning all drugs and modes of use equally prevents the system from appreciating and reacting appropriately to the powerful effects, on who uses drugs and how they use them, of socio-cultural setting and other background factors.

The Garda, possibly in order to facilitate a much invigorated focus on supply reduction, continue, in their policy statements, to totally downplay their role as law enforcers in demand reduction. This is apparent not only from their failure to articulate their role in policing 'inherent' drug crime at the street level, but also from the selective and relatively sparing manner in which they do actually enforce the law on 'inherent' drug crime involving small personal amounts of illicit drugs. Of course, targeting users of all kinds and all social backgrounds through the prohibitionist laws and filling the prisons with 'inherent' drug criminals from the middle classes would not only be a severe drain on time and resources, but also risk alienating popular support. In addition, it would tarnish the 'morally purer' and more noble aim, which the government and the Garda are happy to embrace, of crushing violent, organised criminals and ruthless dealers/traffickers/pushers.

With respect to the whole gamut of drug-using and drug-dealing offenders, a tripartite categorisation has now been established and dictates the tenor of the criminal justice response. This is not the result of a deliberate policy of *trifurcation*, but an inevitable consequence of the failure of bifurcation policies to always neatly distinguish minor from major drugs offenders and 'victims' of pushers from the pusher/victimisers. The original 1977 legislation focused on the medical and social needs of the drug-dependent person and the 1984 legislation began the bifurcation process of separating the treatment of drugs dealers from that of drugs users. While, the distinction between ordinary user and dealer remains of paramount importance, the new tripartite division is concerned mainly with the issue of compliance. First, there are the compliant, 'ex-offender', mainly opiate users who are 'given a chance' and encouraged to 'go straight' and to generally stabilise their lives by making use of methadone maintenance and other supports. They now benefit from much improved facilities and opportunities and much more tolerant and sympathetic attitudes.

At the opposite extreme are the dealers/traffickers/pushers, who have become 'Public Enemy No. 1' and are demonised as violent, evil profiteers, who create and benefit from other people's misery. They are specifically targeted with tough law enforcement and with highly punitive measures. In order to combat these 'drug barons', state agencies have been provided with special powers – some of which are borrowed from the antiterrorist domain and are highly questionable from a civil liberties point of view.

Between these two categories lies the third category – the intransigent, opiate-drug-using offenders, who are likely to be involved in small-scale dealing and generally petty property crime in order to fund their habit. These are people who tend to avoid state drug services altogether and continue to commit drug-related, acquisitive crime. Or they are people who take advantage of methadone maintenance and other available services but, nonetheless, continue using heroin and other drugs and continue their involvement in crime. This still numerous third category continue to be treated by the criminal justice system as they always have been, that is to say they are often imprisoned for their non-inherent drug-related crime and within the prison system their drug addiction status is largely ignored. Arguably, they are, if anything, treated somewhat less sympathetically, because they have spurned the various offers of 'social rehabilitation' now open to them.

'Constructive ambiguity'

In 1995, the head of the National Drugs Squad, Superintendent John McGroarty,[9] stated that 'we are committed to tough, unrelenting law enforcement, although it is very clear to us that something more effective is required'. This can be read in two ways: as a plea for a multifaceted approach to support law enforcement or as an admission of the failure of prohibition. The current situation is clearly far removed from the one he faced and preventative and harm reductionist measures now have a strong and stable presence in Ireland. However, the drugs problem continues to fester and indeed strengthen its grip on Irish society and it is clear that 'something more effective' is still required.

Criminal justice policy in the drugs area is now thoroughly infused by what has been famously called in another context 'constructive ambiguity'.[10] There has been a major, if decidedly partial, dismantling or curtailing of prohibition in order to accommodate methadone maintenance and other harm reductionist interventions. The fundamental commitment to prohibition, however, remains unaltered. Harm reductionist techniques, most particularly methadone maintenance, have become key weapons not only in the public health domain but also in the war against crime – without ever being fully recognised as such. Certainly, the fact that methadone maintenance is in essence a form of legalisation goes completely unremarked.

An intensification of bifurcation since 1996 enables the strange conjunction of extremely hostile, condemnatory approaches toward dealers and more tolerant and supportive approaches towards more compliant, 'ordinary' drug users. As Cohen and Csete[11] state: 'the "balanced approach" is often expressed as meting out harsh punishment to drug traffickers and organised criminals, while treating drug users as "patients" in need of support and treatment'. However, bifurcation is more of a success at the theoretical and political level than at the practical, because so many drug users and drug traders fall between the two extreme stools of 'victim' and victimiser and tend to end up being processed by the criminal justice system along a third route.

The Garda and the courts, by exercising their wide powers of discretion, add to the ambiguity and ambivalence of the system. In practice they recognise significant differences between drugs and types of drug use and drug user, but they simultaneously maintain an official posture of zero tolerance, which ignores such distinctions. Similarly, tolerant, normalising treatment approaches are now commonly available outside the prison system and increasingly, in the shape of methadone maintenance, within the prison system, while, by contrast, the official policy for prisons declares a hardline, prohibitionist, zero tolerance approach. Moreover, despite the expansion of methadone maintenance within the prisons, drugs and psychiatric treatment is still grossly under-resourced within the penal system and there is a clear failure to institute the promised 'equivalence of care' with the outside community.

The new forms of harm reductionist accommodation to drugs since 1996, which have been introduced alongside enhanced, but still less than energetic enforcement of the possession laws at the street level, strongly revitalised supply reduction efforts and ever more repressive approaches to dealers, are signs of the profound fuzziness and ambiguity imbuing official Irish prohibitionist policy. However, it can be argued that this ambiguity is constructive, insofar as it allows harm reduction and prohibition to coexist, indeed in some respects to flourish, alongside each other.

It is often said that pragmatism is the hallmark of the harm reductionist movement. This is undeniable, but what has developed in Ireland and many other jurisdictions, over recent years, is actually an entirely pragmatic form of prohibition, which through compromise manages to assure the continuing, secure presence of a significant level of harm reductionist approaches without breaking the system's fundamental adherence to prohibition. This results in a form of prohibition which is riddled with inconsistencies and ambiguities, not to say hypocrisies. But, the overall policy is probably more correctly labelled ambivalent than ambiguous. It is a so-called 'balanced policy', which in effect promotes the parallel implementation of harm reduction and prohibition.

Harm reductionism and prohibition, though intrinsically opposed, are both endorsed and served in the current system – not entirely, but to a significant degree. Although the balancing process relies on a degree of fudging and conceptual ambiguity the support for both prohibition and harm reductionism is unambiguous. Inevitably, prohibition places constraints on harm reductionism and vice versa, but there exists a workable and functional compromise between the two, which is ambiguous only to the extent that it is not overly concerned with its own logical inconsistencies.

On the other hand, as I have argued, the basic framework of Irish policy remains prohibitionist and, accordingly, harm reductionism and prohibition are not served equally. The default position and the design bias of legislation, policy and of the criminal justice system still clearly privilege prohibitionist solutions. Because of this, the ambivalence, which is achieved by compromise and has proved so functional for the system, still works to ensure that prohibition will trump harm reductionism, whenever this is truly necessary. Harm reductionism and prevention have gained new ground, but they are not the sole possessors of their own territory. They securely occupy this new ground, but always only as rent payers – the freehold ownership remains firmly in the grasp of prohibition. So, for example, the continuing dominion of prohibition ensures that the notion of a human right to drug use is ruled out as, by definition, utterly misguided. Consequently, the human rights perspective on drugs is almost entirely absent from policy and public debate.[12]

Reinarman[13] assuming a position of solidarity with the harm reductionist movement, has recently argued the benefits of a degree of ambiguity for harm reductionism, specifically ambiguity about the human right to use psychoactive substances. He states that 'most movement members have long supported the basic human right to use drugs and some form of decriminalisation. But for over a century prohibitionists have so demonised drugs and poisoned policy discourse that avoidance of the question of legalisation is often the only politically sensible strategy for accomplishing anything in the way of harm reduction.' While this appears to be a plea for prudent recognition of the realpolitik, it is also consistent with my argument that the harm reductionist approach only makes sense as a challenge made within a prohibitionist framework. This is the case not least because many harm reductionists are not anti-prohibition. The harm reductionist movement remains as cohesive and effective as it is only because it focuses on practical issues in the here and now. When push comes to shove, harm reductionists always avoid the question whether or not the criminal law should be used against drugs because so many of their number, particularly the public health harm reductionists, are not actually opposed to prohibition. In fact, in order to make his point, Reinarman has greatly exaggerated the consensus amongst harm reductionists about the right to use drugs. He has also not paid due attention to the fact that even for the harm reductionists, who believe there should be such a right, the first priority is actually reducing harm in the here and now and this practical approach will always take precedence over arguing against prohibition.

Butler and Mayock[14] have recently provided an analysis of Irish drugs policy which leans on Reinarman's positive view of ambiguity but stretches the concept of ambiguity far beyond what the latter intended. They suggest that Irish policy-makers have failed either to commit themselves to 'the fundamental truths of the war on drugs and to the sole implementation of abstinence-based healthcare strategies' or to 'provide a detailed ideological justification' for the actual harm reductionist interventions which they have introduced. Instead, they argue, policy-makers 'shroud the policy process in ambiguity by introducing harm reduction practices without debate, announcement or a clearly presented rationale'. They take the view that this is in keeping with a political culture, in which 'citizens have been accustomed to high-level ambiguity and within which abstract statements of political ideals are not regarded as literal truths demanding action'. They go on to suggest that ambiguity, in the sense of lack of certainty about underlying principles, may be essential to the harm reductionist movement in Ireland because 'strident public debate on moral issues is as likely to lead to polarisation and policy paralysis as it is to agreed and effective solutions'. They point to the history of Irish debate and development of policy on abortion as an example of this.

This argument is rather contrived, conjuring up a quasi-problem out of the facts 1) that Ireland does not provide *ideological* reasons for harm reductionist approaches, and 2) that Ireland does not conform to a narrow, fundamentalist form of prohibitionism of a type which does not occur outside certain Islamic states (in their treatment of alcohol). Against the first point, it can be argued that harm reductionism nowhere attracts or requires elaborate ideological rationalisation. After all harm reductionist approaches are by definition justified by their practical effects. Against the second point, it can be argued that Butler and Mayock, in order to set up a straw man, are utilising an exaggerated stereotype of purist prohibitionism, which does not represent the forms of prohibition found in Western democracies, including the U.S., the fount of modern drugs prohibitionism. This stereotype ignores the compassion for the addict, which has always been part of Western prohibition and has from the beginning allowed for non-abstinence-based treatments. More broadly, Butler and Mayock's argument greatly exaggerates the uniqueness of both the Irish compromise on drugs policy, the Irish failure to wage an uncompromising, blitzkrieg war on drugs and the Irish predilection for political fudging on controversial issues. In fact, the kind of compromise on the war on drugs and the kind of political fudging found in Ireland are virtually universal phenomena within Western democracies. The Irish may have a deserved reputation for whimsy, but the tendency for politicians to promote fairytales is rife in all countries. Political ideals are never 'literal truths'.

Their argument might be of only passing interest, but for the fact that Butler and Mayock go on to make the bizarre, scaremongering claim that the Drug Policy Action Group,[15] an Irish lobby group seeking improvements in drug policy, by campaigning publicly for drug law reform, might 'mobilise opponents of harm reduction and ultimately lead to the dismantling of existing harm reduction systems'. Butler and Mayock state that 'to break the silence on harm reduction through the creation of a national debate on the moral issues inherent in drug policy might in fact prove to be counterproductive for those committed to harm reduction'. Their position clearly implies that books such as this one should not be written for fear that the government would respond to public debate on prohibition by curtailing harm reductionist approaches and returning to a more strict form of prohibition.

The main message of Butler and Mayock's exploration of Irish drugs policy appears to be that drug policy issues in Ireland should effectively be left unexplored. However, it is clear that they greatly overstate both the ambiguity surrounding harm reductionism and the capacity of the Drug Policy Action Group or of any critics of prohibition to stir up 'paralysing and polarising' moral controversy. Needle exchange, methadone maintenance and perhaps even prohibition itself – it seems clear from the general lack of public interest in them over the recent years of change – simply do not have the same potential in Ireland as issues like abortion to stir hearts and minds or provoke general political protest. Moreover, Butler and Mayock greatly underestimate the strength, rationality and inevitability of the state's commitment to harm reductionism. Government may well be reluctant to spell out this commitment, but, as I have argued, a prohibitionist policy without strong harm reductionist elements is now politically unviable.

In reality, harm reductionism does not rely on obscurantism for its continued existence. The ambivalence and deliberate uncertainty that typify some aspects of drugs policy are not an essential camouflage for the operation of harm reductionism, but an incidental side-effect of the successful introduction of harm reductionist approaches. A strong case can be made not only that harm reductionist measures are now, due to their obvious usefulness, politically secure, but also that prohibition could not possibly survive politically without the concessions it has already made to harm reductionism.

'Constructive ambiguity' is not the decisive issue. One cannot demand or expect complete logical consistency from multifaceted policies, which address highly complex, human and social problems. Many areas, such as health and education, involve inconsistencies and anomalies in policy and sometimes even attempt the parallel implementation of quite contradictory approaches. But it is plainly wrong and self-defeating to encourage, as Butler and Mayock do, a culture of *omerta* and denial. Avoidance of inquiry and debate cannot possibly help a system that already suffers from the signal failure to examine and test its own policy assumptions and to objectively measure the effectiveness of its responses. It is obviously legitimate, useful and, indeed, necessary to question the current Irish compromise system and the logically incoherent framework of prohibitionism which ultimately shapes it.

Unfortunately, the suppression of any form of dissent, that is any form of advocacy of the abolition of prohibition or of the human right to use drugs, characterises the whole drug-free world/prohibitionist perspective. This is especially true at the highest level of the UN, which is concerned to present a show of what Jelsma[16] calls 'an apparent unanimity in its endorsement of prohibitive drug control'. But Jelsma argues that this actually screens 'a long-standing conflict within the UN system between nations wanting to maintain the prohibition regime and those hoping for a more pragmatic approach'. Jelsma documents how dissenting countries, which question the existing drug control framework, such as Mexico (on the North–South, consumer–producer divide) and countries like the Netherlands and Australia (that are at the fore-front of harm reduction experimentation, including forms of decriminalisation) are marginalised and deprived of a voice. Recently the then Irish Minister for Justice, Michael McDowell,[17] also declared his distaste for dissenting views on drugs policy, stating: 'Anybody who in public argues that it is somehow acceptable to consume prohibited drugs, and to be in possession of them in small quantities, is suffering not simply from moral confusion but a complete absence of a critical faculty of any kind.'

The drug-free world/prohibitionist perspective is waging a 'war on drugs' and is zero tolerant not just of all illicit drugs but also of all views that oppose prohibition. It is in the interests of prohibition to send out the message that prohibition is the only way and that deviations from it cannot be toler-ated, because they are defeatist, enfeebling and give succour to the 'enemy'. However, the reality of the Irish response to drugs, detailed in Chapters 4 and 5, belies the implicit claims of the official, zero tolerant drugs war rhetoric that rigorously pursued prohibition against all illicit drugs is the only real, political option. Even the most powerful sponsor of international prohibition, the U.S., has more than a dozen states, including Oregon, Ohio, California and New York, which have seen fit to experiment with the decriminalisation of cannabis. In fact, as the *World Drug Report*[18] concludes, the reality is that: 'Laws – and even the international Conventions – are not written in stone; they can be changed when the democratic will of nations so wishes it.' And, of course, the democratic will should be informed by open, honest and thorough inquiry into all aspects of the drugs issue, including the possible abandonment of prohibition.

Summary

There has been a sea change in the response to drugs in Ireland, but, arguably, criminal justice policy on drugs itself has changed hardly at all or at best only superficially. The response to drugs is now far more diverse, sophisticated and complex, but the vast bulk of law enforcement activity against drug-related crime focuses, as it always has, on possession offences, mostly of cannabis, small-scale trading transactions and relatively petty property crime committed by opiate users. Policy is now imbued with ambivalence since fundamentally conflicting approaches are simultaneously endorsed. The supply versus demand reduction dichotomy and the bifurcation approach are mutually supportive ideological positions, which help maintain and justify the underlying prohibitionist structures. Present policy is a confused muddle, but it is also to a degree functional, underpinning a new form of pragmatic prohibition, which in large measure supports harm reductionism and broader preventative harm reduction through social justice driven projects. However, prohibition's ingrained intolerance of the arguments for the human right to drug use and for decriminalisation continues and is misguidedly supported by some harm reductionists, who underestimate the political necessity and long-term security of harm reductionism.

Notes

1 It needs to be remembered that by no means all opiate users who seek a place are guaranteed a timely place on a methadone maintenance programme. In May 2005, Judge Gerard Haughton commented in the Athlone District Court that addicts can face a wait of 14 months for methadone treatment. He was dealing with the case of an individual who had at one time needed €200 a day to pay for heroin. The judge pointed out that this means that in the 14 months awaiting treatment this offender would need to raise about €80,000, which could mean stealing goods worth €400,000, since a thief can only expect to redeem about 20% of the value from stolen goods. The judge said 'the treatment would cost a fraction of that, and why we continue to have waiting lists of that length for different types of treatment is beyond me'.

2 Howie, M., 'Prison drug tests "failing to have impact"', *Scotsman*, 30 May 2005.

3 Epidemiology and Burden of Disease Team (2001) *The Global Burden of Disease*, Focus 5, Brief 2, Geneva: World Health Organisation.

4 UNDCP (1994) *Statement by the Executive Director of the United Nations Drug Control Programme at the Thirty-seventh Session of the Commission on Narcotic Drugs*, Vienna, 13 April.

5 Keogh, E. (1997) *Illicit Drug Use and Related Criminal Activity in the Dublin Metropolitan Area*, Dublin: Garda Headquarters.

6 Furey, M. and Browne, C. (2003) *Opiate Use and Related Criminal Activity in Ireland 2000 & 2001*, Templemore: Garda Research Unit.

7 See Leuw, E. (ed.) (1991) ' Drugs and drugs policy in the Netherlands' in *Crime and Justice: Annual Review of Research*, 12, Chicago: University of Chicago Press;

Drugs Policy in the Netherlands: Continuity and Change (1995) The Hague: Ministries for Foreign Affairs, Health, Justice and the Interior; MacCoun, R. and Reuter, P. (1997) 'Interpreting Dutch cannabis policy: reasoning by analogy in the legalization debate', *Science*, 278, at 47–52; Uitermark, J. (2004) 'The origins and future of the Dutch approach towards drugs', *Journal of Drug Issues*, 22, at 511–532.

8 Best, D., Gross, S., Vingoe, L., Witton, J. and Strang, J. (2003) *Dangerousness of Drugs: a Guide to the Risks and Harms Associated with Substance Use*, London: Department of Health.

9 Addressing the Irish Farmers' Association Conference on Rural Crime.

10 President of Sinn Féin Gerry Adams has recommended the usefulness of 'constructive ambiguity' about the relationship between the IRA and Sinn Féin within the context of talks with the British and Irish governments.

11 Cohen, J. and Csete, J. (2006) 'As strong as the weakest pillar: harm reduction, law enforcement and human rights', *International Journal of Drug Policy*, 17, at 101–103.

12 A notable exception is Tim Murphy who has made a number of powerful and eloquent contributions to the debate from an anti-prohibitionist perspective; see Murphy, T. (1996) *Rethinking the War on Drugs*, Cork: Cork University Press; Murphy, T. (1996) 'Drugs, drug prohibition and crime: a response to Peter Charleton', *Irish Criminal Law Journal*, 6, at 1–18; Murphy, T. (2002) 'Drugs, crime, and prohibitionist ideology' in (ed. O'Mahony, P.) *Criminal Justice in Ireland*, Dublin: IPA.

13 Reinarman, C. (2004) 'Public health and human rights: the virtues of ambiguity', *International Journal of Drug Policy*, 15, at 243–249.

14 Butler, S. and Mayock, P. (2005) '"An Irish solution to an Irish problem": harm reduction and ambiguity in the drug policy of the Republic of Ireland', *International Journal of Drug Policy*, 16, at 415–422.

15 Website at http://drugpolicy.ie.

16 Jelsma, M. (2003) 'Drugs in the UN system: the unwritten history of the 1998 United Nations General Assembly Special Session on Drugs', *International Journal of Drug Policy*, 14, at 181–195.

17 O'Regan, M., 'McDowell urges judges to reflect on drug terms', *Irish Times*, 25 May 2006.

18 United Nations Drug Control Programme (1997) *World Drug Report*, UNDCP/Oxford University Press.

7

The general failure of prohibition to prevent drug use: underlying reasons and key implications

Taking the critiques of prohibition seriously

In Ireland it is necessary to confront the fact that the drugs problem is continuing to grow despite decades of increasingly fierce, prohibitionist rhetoric and increasingly severe criminal justice responses. In this context, it would be foolish not to seek answers to the following key questions: 1) Has prohibition as a legal framework succeeded? 2) Is the current, recently enhanced 'cops plus docs' compromise between prohibition and harm reductionism working? Depending on the answers to these first two questions, a final crucial question can be addressed: 3) Is there a case for a radical change in drugs policy along the lines of total abolition of drugs prohibition?

Many powerful critiques of prohibition have now been published. The Transform, Drug Policy Foundation,[1] as one example, articulates its position as follows:

> Prohibition is a globalised legal system that mandates criminal sanctions in an attempt to eliminate the production, supply and use of certain drugs from society. This policy has failed in its own terms, with drug use and misuse rising dramatically, and drugs cheaper and more available than ever. The collision of prohibition with rapidly rising demand for drugs has created serious problems associated with illegal drug markets, maximising drug related harms to users and the wider community. Policy related harms include: the creation of crime at all levels; a crisis in the criminal justice and prisons system; harm maximisation for drug users; political, economic and social instability in drug producer and transit countries; and mass criminalization and the undermining of human rights. Enforcement is either ineffective or actively counterproductive and policy related harms are now far greater than harms caused by drug use. Harm reduction initiatives are largely mitigating against harms created or exacerbated by prohibition, whilst new resources for drug treatment are primarily an attempt to reduce prohibition-related crime. Neither addresses the intractable problems associated with illegal drug production and supply.

This is a devastating critique of prohibition, which spans a wide spectrum of reasonably well proven and, in some cases, undeniable propositions about the harm prohibition causes, from increased risk to innocent individuals to geopolitical instability. In Ireland the legal academic Tim Murphy[2] has eloquently made the case against prohibition in the following terms: 'I regard prohibition as ineffectual, irresponsible and illegitimate. It is ineffectual because it is falling far short of its objectives, it is irresponsible because it is contributing directly and indirectly to the creation of greater social problems and it is illegitimate because it employs incarceration and other criminal sanctions in an improper and excessive manner.'

It is perhaps surprising that prohibition has not collapsed under the overwhelming weight of such forceful critiques. I have already argued that the survival of prohibition is in large part due to the fact that it is a faith and emotion-based belief system, which discounts or ignores counterevidence and successfully shields itself from criticism with various cunning rhetorical devices and logical manoeuvres. However, before attempting to deal with the even stiffer barriers presented by substantive prohibitionist ideology, it is necessary to confront two influential, apparently reasonable, first line defences of prohibition. These are 1) that the growth in the drugs counterculture is a cultural product, which cannot be blamed on any failure of prohibition; and 2) that prohibition has not worked because it has not been sufficiently strictly implemented. I will address these defences in this section and, after presenting the evidence for the failure of Irish prohibition in Chapter 8, I will address the faith-based nature of prohibition and prohibition's other inbuilt strategic and rhetorical advantages in Chapter 9. In the remaining sections of this chapter, I will present a theory explaining the inevitability of the failure of drugs prohibition and will expand on the implications of this theoretical analysis.

Cultural change and drug use

It is clear that many of the issues raised in the typical critique of prohibition are complex and contentious. In particular, opponents of prohibition need to be, but rarely are, careful to distinguish the harm caused by prohibition from the inevitable harm of drug use itself. In any event, this distinction is by no means always clear-cut. It is, therefore, easy to overstate the strength and particularly the practical implications of the standard anti-prohibition argument.

Even the undeniable, key truth that prohibition has failed to halt the growth of drug use lends itself to credible interpretations, which do not attribute any significant degree of blame for this failure to prohibition. I will investigate in the next chapter the distinct question whether or not prohibition has actively and independently contributed to the growth of the drugs counterculture, but, at this point, I will focus on the not unreasonable, broader suggestion that the growth in the drugs counterculture owes much to social, economic and cultural factors, which have no fundamental or necessary connections to prohibition.

These factors include globalisation and improved transport and communication links. Such political and technological changes have increased international trade, travel, cultural homogeneity and, crucially, marketing opportunities for drug producers and dealers. Other factors relevant to increased drug use, particularly in the developed West, include greater affluence, consumerism, individualism, hedonism, stress, alienation and ennui, all of which may in their different ways contribute to an increased appetite for drugs. These factors, which are themselves intimately linked to economic, technological, political and socio-cultural change, are likely to have been a major influence on drug use even in the absence of prohibition. The continuing existence of political instability in drug-producing regions, especially the existence of so-called 'rogue nations', such as Afghanistan, and, in Latin America, of large rebel areas within national territories, has facilitated the supply to the West of immense amounts of heroin and cocaine. Opponents of prohibition, then, are required to go beyond simply condemning prohibition because it has coexisted with increases in drug use and drug use harms. They must offer a credible explanation of how exactly prohibition has contributed to these increases and how a non-prohibitionist alternative regime could have avoided the increases and, most importantly, how it could now improve the existing situation.

However, the fact that potent socio-cultural and economic forces may be nurturing and driving the drugs counterculture does not nullify the basic criticism that prohibition has failed to deliver on its own declared aims. Prohibition presents itself as the final solution to the drug problem knowing full well that drug use is a complex phenomenon shaped by the broader cultural context. Prohibition's failure to eliminate or even lower illicit drug use is not rendered excusable by the fact that cultural factors are important influences on drug use. To suggest otherwise would be to suggest that prohibition is entirely irrelevant because no social policy can, in the face of cultural forces, be expected to impact on the prevalence of drug use. If prohibition is ineffectual and irrelevant, then there can be no rational grounds for maintaining such a policy, because it creates so many independent, serious harms of its own.

A tougher prohibition?

However, prohibitionists have another, at least superficially plausible line of defence to the charge that prohibition fails to achieve its core aims, since they can argue that prohibition has failed only because it has not been pursued with sufficient vigour and commitment. They can point to the success of alcohol prohibition in states such as Saudi Arabia, where Islamic Sharia law is strictly enforced and backed by draconian, often quite brutal punishments. Indeed, this kind of hardline thinking appears to have inspired the progressive escalation, over more than two decades, of the severity of the Irish criminal justice response to drug dealer crimes. The existence of societies, which are largely alcohol free, lends some support to the prohibitionist belief that the creation of a drugs free world is a real possibility, not an idealistic pipe-dream and to the belief that tough law enforcement is required.

This prohibitionist argument has much in common with familiar, right-wing arguments on crime, which typically place a naïve faith in the effectiveness of punishment. According to this hardline view, if punishment fails to curb crime, then the best solution is to ratchet up the severity of punishment. At one level this is an unanswerable argument. The hardliner, who is prepared to inflict extremely harsh, disproportionate penalties for relatively trivial offences, including permanent incapacitation through life imprisonment or the death penalty, can always convincingly argue that an ineffective punishment fails not because punishment is the wrong approach, but because the current level of punishment is not tough enough. The hardliner is prepared to increase the severity of punishment until it is guaranteed to provide effective specific deterrence, that is until it ensures that the punished offender will not reoffend. Three-strikes-and-out laws are inspired by this kind of logic. Under these laws, a repeat offender, even one who commits only minor crimes that do not normally attract long prison sentences, can be sentenced to 20 years' imprisonment or even life imprisonment if convicted on a third occasion for such a minor offence. The U.S. has introduced such laws along with mandatory minimum prison sentences for possession of drugs, even small, personal amounts of cannabis. This has led to a huge expansion in the number of prisoners in the U.S., which currently stands at 2.2 million, probably the highest incarceration rate in the world.

Whatever effect this hardline approach in the U.S. has had in terms of specific deterrence of punished individuals, it has had a minimal effect on general deterrence, since it has very obviously failed to impact on the prevalence of drug use. This is partly because the clandestine, generally private nature of drug use means that most drug users face only a very small risk of apprehension and so are not deterred by the example of the severe treatment of others. As Jacoby and Gramckow state, 'it is apparent from experience so far in the war against drugs that arrest, conviction and incarceration rates are inadequate measures of success in reducing the incidence of illegal drug trafficking, drug use or related crime. Numerous studies have indicated that only a very low percentage of drug sales and other crimes committed by drug abusers resulted in arrest.'[3] In other words, the U.S. approach, which is unacceptably repressive and punitive by most European standards, is not nearly repressive enough to ensure abstinence from illicit drugs.

In fact, at least in relation to Western democracies, the hardline argument is entirely disingenuous, since fairness, respect for the privacy and freedom of the individual, and proportionality – that punishment should fit the crime – are key and indispensable principles of the rule of law, on which these societies are based. Draconian repressive regimes are, of course, theoretically and practically possible and not uncommon in countries with totalitarian or theocratic systems. However, the democratic principles underlying the rule of law in Western countries or, whenever a government attempts to undermine them, the democratic electoral response to their violation place strict limits on how far governments can go in toughening the criminal justice and penal response to drugs. In Western democracies, these limits will come into play long before a prohibition regime can become harsh enough to guarantee the compliance and abstinence of the populace.

In short, the argument that an untrammelled, uncompromising and, if necessary, relentlessly harsh prohibition has not been tried is indeed true, but it is an unconvincing defence of prohibition's failure to reduce the use of drugs. Such a draconian prohibitionist experiment would not be compatible with the nature of modern, developed democracies. It could not be tolerated in a pluralist, human rights-based society, which values individual freedom and diversity and where the rule of law is paramount and secular.

Moreover, drugs prohibition has from its initiation been on principle compromised and softened by its compassionate recognition of the addict as a medical patient, deserving of sympathy and support. In developed Western nations, as I have shown in Chapter 2, *strict medical rationale* harm reduction has been an intrinsic element of prohibition from the start and there has never been any possibility of a solely disciplinarian approach. A more hard-line approach would, inevitably, also be undermined by the inconsistencies of prohibition in contemporary Western society, particularly its inbuilt tolerance of alcohol and its widespread dependence on medically prescribed mood-altering substances. In short, the prohibitionist argument that prohibition has real credibility, because there are societies which make prohibition work, must be dismissed, since, in the developed Western nations like Ireland, there is an absolute, principled requirement to attenuate prohibition in order to make it compatible with the core values of democracy, especially the rule of law, and with a compassionate concern for the sick.

Both prohibitionists and anti-prohibitionists rely on the law

On the other hand, prohibition is sustained, even in the face of devastating critiques like that from Transform, in large part because of a perfectly natural and understandable public faith in the law and in the capacity of citizens to conform to the law. Modern society is not viable without a very broad-based conformity to the law and to a plethora of explicit and implicit rules, regulations, conventions and etiquettes.

Creating rules and regulations, some backed by criminal sanctions, is what modern governments do. The instinct of government, faced with the risk of harm to individual citizens, the economy or the social fabric, is to legislate – to regulate and, if necessary, to outlaw and criminalise certain activities. To recognise this is to recognise the seemingly natural, inexorable progression of governments towards prohibition. It is to recognise that a government, confronted by the harm that drugs can cause, but wishing to avoid the criminalisation of drugs, would need to overcome the deeply ingrained habit of resorting to criminal punishment to prevent behaviours which risk serious dangers. Such a government would have to refrain from using the most powerful weapon in its social engineering armoury – the criminal law.

The extent of both self-conscious, deliberate conformity and automatic, inadvertent conformity to laws, rules, conventions and other explicit and implicit codes within society is astonishing. In Ireland, for example, even incorrigible criminals drive on the left and no longer smoke in public buildings. In fact, the introduction of the smoking ban in public places in Ireland was remarkable for its immediate success and for the degree of near-universal compliance it quickly achieved without the need for heavy-handed law enforcement or, indeed, for more than a handful of prosecutions. As such it might be regarded as a case study in how prohibitionist approaches can be successful.

In fact, the real mystery is why mobilising the criminal law and allied forces of social conformity can effectively eliminate the harm of passive smoking in public places – a harm driven by an addiction – but appears powerless to achieve anything similar in the case of drug-related harms. It is relevant that the success of the law in the case of the Irish smoking ban was partly due to the fact that it was used to construct a different social landscape with respect to the etiquette of smoking – one which had the support of both the majority of smokers and non-smokers and which thus did not rely primarily on the deterrent effect of law enforcement. It is also crucial that use itself was not under direct attack and the freedom to smoke on the streets and in the home or designated hotel rooms remained sacrosanct. The success of the smoking ban, therefore, should not be taken as encouraging proof that the law can be successful against drug use, but rather that it can be successful in forging more prudent and careful forms of drug use, so long as the freedom to use drugs is recognised.

In fact, opponents of prohibition, even those who believe there is a human right to use drugs, rarely support a completely laissez-faire situation with respect to drugs, but, on the contrary, advocate harm reduction and some form of regulation of the supply of drugs and of the access of minors to drugs. In other words, even anti-prohibitionists are forced to rely on the law and regulation. It is clearly necessary for these anti-prohibitionists to spell out in some detail the kind of non-prohibitionist legal and regulatory framework which would provide for sufficient legitimate access to drugs, however dangerous these drugs may be, so that the trade in drugs does not fall into criminal hands. This requires a genuine commitment to access and freedom of choice but at the same time this access must be balanced by countervailing legal restrictions which limit drugs access to adults, and by associated policies which ensure the greatest possible impact for harm-reductive measures. The huge diversity in drugs, in the ways of taking drugs and in the harmful effects of drugs mean that the model of alcohol regulation, while useful as an example of the maintenance of quality control and of keeping the distribution of a quite dangerous substance out of the hands of criminals, is of limited relevance. Clearly, the opponents of prohibition must devise a workable scheme of regulation, which achieves, in much more difficult circumstances, something like what is currently achieved by the non-prohibitionist regulation of alcohol.

Opponents of prohibition, however, must first explain why, within prohibitionist regimes, the criminal law and its associated, powerful, informal social conformity pressures are and will continue to be ineffective against the drugs culture. In the next section I suggest a theoretical explanation for the manifest failure of prohibition to impact on the prevalence of drug use.

Given the many unverifiable assumptions in the debate on illicit drugs, the many conflicting interpretations and the paucity of objective or conclusive findings, sweeping claims that prohibition should be abolished because prohibition causes more harm than it prevents are simplistic and unwarranted. In the next chapter, I will analyse and examine in some detail both the effects of prohibition and the effectiveness of current harm reductionist mitigation of the ill-effects of prohibition. The evidence, particularly the Irish evidence, on these issues is critical to any conclusions about the success or failure of Irish prohibition and about the need for alternative non-prohibitionist approaches. I will pay particular attention to distinguishing the specific negative effects of prohibition, that is those which are not attributable to drug use itself or to other factors unconnected to prohibition, and to identifying the real potential of a non-prohibitionist regime to deliver net gains and prevent or ameliorate the kind of problems caused by prohibition.

An explanation for the futility of prohibition

Prohibition: a failed system of elimination, control and propaganda

The most obvious and damning failure of prohibition, as obvious in Ireland as elsewhere, is its failure to stem the rising tide of drug use and the spread of a pro-drugs culture. Prohibition sets out to rid the world of illicit drugs, but has actually presided over and perhaps even facilitated an enormous growth in the use of illicit substances. In 2003, half way through the UN 10-year action plan to entirely eradicate illicit drugs, 85% of member nations of the UN reported a stable or increasing use of drugs in their territories.[4] In June 2006, an EU memorandum stated that 'drug consumption and mortality are at unprecedented levels and show little sign of coming down'.[5] Even if prohibition itself contributes little or nothing to the growth of the drugs culture, it is undeniable that prohibition has proven to be disastrously ineffective at the task of controlling, let alone eliminating, the use of illicit drugs.

The Irish evidence, based on surveys, treatment statistics, and the number and size of drug seizures, is unequivocal. Opiate and poly-drug use is still very high and spreading to provincial areas and the use of 'recreational' drugs, such as cannabis, cocaine, ecstasy and other stimulants, and 'magic mushrooms' has grown phenomenally over the last 25 years and is now commonplace throughout the country. In some sectors of youth and young adults, 'recreational' drug use is today perceived as quite 'normal'. Tellingly, despite increased Garda activity and success in the interdiction of drugs since 1996, the Furey

and Browne[6] study suggested that more users in 2000/01 (76%) were able
to source their drugs from the local drugs market than in 1997 (46%). It is
evident that even the recent more active, organised and focused system of drug
supply control, which has benefited from improved intelligence and better
links with foreign police forces and which annually involves the seizure of tens
of millions of euros worth of drugs, has not been able to impact significantly
on the availability and price of street drugs. The Garda Síochána themselves
suggest that they intercept 10% or less of the drugs circulating in the country.
They do not claim that this proportion is increasing, even though they are
seizing more and more drugs.

It is also evident that prohibitionist propaganda, despite its belliger-
ence, fear-mongering and occasional, sanctimonious moralism, has failed to
convince a substantial minority of the populace. In particular, it has failed to
win over the hearts and minds of young people. Despite the use of the most
powerful weapon at society's disposal, the expression of disapproval through
criminalisation – involving the threat and actual implementation of punishment – more and more children and young adults experiment with or regularly
use illicit drugs in disregard of the law and with apparent lack of concern for
the stigma that attaches to drug use.

Human nature and mood-altering substances

I have argued that the dismal failure of the prohibitionist message is undoubtedly linked to its inherent self-contradictions and hypocrisies, particularly its
specious attempt to distinguish 'good' alcohol and prescribed mood-altering
drugs from 'bad' illicit drugs and in its inexcusable failure to distinguish
between dangerous and less dangerous drugs or forms of drug use.

Four further factors, which relate to 'internal' aspects of biological and socio-
culturally constructed human nature rather than to 'external' social and legal
systems, may play an important role in prohibition's undeniable dual failure
– at persuasion through propaganda and at control through law enforcement.
These are: 1) the relatively intractable nature of human appetitive behaviour in
respect to change of mood and consciousness; 2) natural human curiosity and
desire to explore in order to understand and gain mastery over our environment; 3) the innate sense of and constant search for autonomous agency and
the associated sense of unique ownership of bodies, thoughts and feelings; and
4) reactance, the automatic psychological reaction to constraints on freedom
of action. These four factors and the relations between them are key, on the
one hand, because they provide a theoretical and empirical grounding for the
view that it would be expedient to recognise the human right to use drugs,
and, on the other, because, along with the incoherence and hypocrisy of the
prohibitionist message, they offer a plausible explanation for why prohibition
does not and is unlikely to work in the case of drug use.

Human appetitive behaviour includes eating, drinking and sexual activity –

physiologically driven behaviour, which is necessary for the survival of the individual or the species. These behaviours are the most socially conditioned and controlled of behaviours, precisely because they are so fundamental, powerful and undeniable that they possess immense potential for social disruption and interpersonal conflict. These drive-related behaviours are extensively and sometimes bizarrely shaped and restrained by cultural taboos, codes, conventions and etiquettes; but, they must nonetheless always find relatively convenient forms of approved or unapproved expression or the individual and species would not survive.

There have been many attempts to constrain and direct the instinctive, need-driven behaviours, particularly sexual behaviour, through the criminal law. For example, there have been laws against having sex at all (particularly for certain age groups), prostitution, homosexuality, and sexual relations between people of different races. Needless to say, these efforts to constrain sexuality have in the long run been disastrous failures. These laws have failed to prevent sex between teenagers, prostitution, homosexuality and sex between people of different races. In addition, these prohibitionist sexual laws have often created a raft of new social problems.

The use of mood-altering substances is an appetitive behaviour, although it is one that, unlike eating, has to be 'discovered' by the individual, is not always discovered, and is not necessary for survival. Certain types of drug dependence can even be regarded as forms of physiological drive that are as hard to stamp out or suppress as the other drives. It is believed that powerful drugs such as opiates, which induce tolerance and physical withdrawal effects as well as highly pleasurable effects, can change individual physiology to such an extent that they create an artificial drive, which can be as strong as or even stronger than the thirst, hunger and sex drives.[7] Even though such drug use is an acquired habit and clearly contingent on social setting and on individual choice, once dependence is established, it has the characteristics of an overpowering physiological drive. This kind of drug dependence profoundly shapes motivation and redefines the individual's physical, psychological and moral sense of self.

Prohibition has long recognised the compulsive nature of the appetite for drugs and especially the immense difficulty of breaking an addiction without assistance. Prohibition from the start incorporated medical treatment for addicts. The continuing significant presence of *strict medical rationale* approaches within prohibition is proof of prohibition's recognition of the special status of an uncontrolled or poorly controlled appetite for drugs. However, the notion of drug use as an appetitive behaviour is also relevant to non-addicted, initiatory or experimental drug use. Andrew Weil[8] has gone so far as to posit an 'innate human drive to experience periodic episodes of non-ordinary consciousness'. Drug use, according to Weil, is just one of various ways we have to satisfy this drive.

The use of mood-altering substances is not essential to life like the intake of water and nutrition, but, on the other hand, it is almost as difficult to resist as these fundamental drives, partly because it satisfies so many basic psychological needs, including the need to explore new sensations and experiences and the need to establish and exercise autonomous control over one's own experience. The human desire to change how one currently feels is obviously a ubiquitous, inevitable and persistent aspect of experience. It is mundanely and quite naturally served by frequent resort to mood-altering substances or experiences. We are all on a 'hedonic treadmill'[9] and however blessed we are with reasons to be happy, we do not stay happy (or interested or comfortable or excited or satisfied) for very long. Boredom, discontent and other forms of disagreeable affect inevitably intervene and provide ceaseless cause to seek altered mood.

Consequently, while there may be relatively few intravenous drug users in Irish society, the vast majority of adults use one or more of the following mood-altering substances and are to various degrees dependent on them: alcohol, tobacco, cannabis, other 'recreational' drugs such as magic mushrooms, ecstasy or LSD, caffeine, sleeping pills, anti-depressant or anti-psychotic tablets, tranquillisers, stimulants or opiates. Many of the (usually healthier) minority who avoid such 'foreign' substances will be found to be adrenaline or endorphin junkies, addicted to behaviours such as meditation, sex, jogging, gambling or extreme sports, which provide a 'natural rush'. Weil also mentions the proclivity of children for spinning or whirling – an activity, which he believes is aimed at changing the child's consciousness. There is also widespread use of music to alter and manage mood, seen most dramatically in young, iPod-wearing people, who like to live their lives to a constantly changing sound-track.

It is, of course, crucial that drug taking mostly leads to states of altered consciousness which are inherently pleasurable. The desire to alter one's mood is essentially a desire to improve one's mood and the urge to alter one's consciousness is also normally motivated by the promise of positive, exciting and delightful sensations, perceptions and insights. Taking mood-altering substances involves the incorporation of substances into the body, where they have a special impact on the central nervous system. As far as the user is concerned, this action is motivated and strongly reinforced by the pleasure the process gives.

In relation to this induced pleasure, *optional* mood-altering substance use is similar to *necessary* eating and drinking. The fact that we find necessary survival activities, such as eating, drinking and sex, pleasurable is an evolved part of our biological nature. We are programmed by evolution to take pleasure in what we must do to survive and reproduce. As soon as early humans discovered that eating certain substances or drinking certain liquids happened to be especially pleasurable – because it energised them, eased pain or gave them a sense of elation, release, well-being or broadened consciousness – continued use was inevitable. There never was any question of not using these pleasure-giving substances, even though, quite quickly, their use became ritualised and carefully choreographed by social codes and customs in order to control and reduce the self-evident dangers of intoxication.

These mood-altering substances, by the accident of chemistry, not only mimic or interfere with the action of naturally occurring neurotransmitters in the brain, but also provide the kind of rewarding experiences that we regularly and often desperately seek. There is, therefore, a powerful synergy between the inherited physiological basis for experiencing pleasure and the recurrent psychological demand for stimulation and mood change. As the psychopharmacologist Jarvik has written:[10] 'dopaminergic and opioid receptors (and probably others) in the brain's reward centres represent an ever-present source of demand' for mood-altering substances. In other words, the appetite for mood-altering substances and experiences has a natural basis in universal subjective experience and in human physiology. The demand is in us all, just waiting to be awakened, and our frequent bouts of boredom and other forms of discontent ensure that most people will awaken and indulge at least some of the appetites for mood-altering substances, which are available to us.

The taste for physical and psychic pleasure or stimulation and for a different perspective on reality is not an appetitive behaviour on a par with the need for water and nutrition, but it does not fall far short. Addiction is a kind of artificial drive and brings its own set of exceedingly potent physiological and psychological imperatives. As Jarvik points out, an artificial drive for certain drugs, such as cocaine, is especially dangerous because cocaine unlike the drive for food, water or sex 'does not turn itself off'. Experimental animals will self-administer cocaine or similar stimulants incessantly and obsessively until they kill themselves through starvation caused by their neglect of eating.[11] The satiety mechanism, which regulates our internal reward system in respect of food, water and sex and tells us when we have had enough, appears to be bypassed by those drugs that operate directly on the brain's reward centres. However, the key point is that, even in the absence of dependence that creates an artificial physiological drive, there is a powerful inclination to take pleasure-giving and mind-expanding substances, which itself has a natural physiological basis, is self-reinforcing and is influential long before drug dependence is established.

Crucially, we have an intense interest in and appetite for substances and experiences that make us feel better or just different, even when we do not *need* them. Our relationship to mood-altering substances is, of course, in large part culturally constructed – after all, considerable technical knowledge is required for the production of substances such as alcohol and cocaine. Indulgence in mood-altering substances is also not an irresistible appetite. Nevertheless, there is overwhelming empirical evidence to suggest that the appetite for mood-altering substances is an indelible facet of human nature which cannot be stamped out.

Contemporary theories of human motivation emphasise, amongst other factors, the central importance of curiosity – our urge to explore, expand on our experience, and build up various new competences[12] and self-determination[13] – our unending search to maximise our personal autonomy and control. The urge to explore and experience new sensations, including the desire to alter our mood or consciousness, then, is according to contemporary theory a natural, universal aspect of human psychology. The urge to explore is particularly strong in the young and will push many towards experimenting with mood-altering substances. This natural human curiosity works in tandem with the desire to alter mood to promote drug use, especially in the young, who quite frequently experience very intense dysphoric states, like boredom and sadness, which they yearn to escape.

The sense of autonomy and the desire to exercise autonomy are distinct motivational forces, which can be distinguished from the urge to explore and control. The sense of autonomy and exclusive ownership is especially assertive in the arenas of subjective, conscious experience and the body. The human individual has a natural claim to dominion over his or her own body and even more fundamentally over his or her own thought processes, feelings, choices and sense of identity. Even the galley slave, whose body is rigorously disciplined and cruelly misused by others, retains a stubborn capacity, indeed an inalienable freedom, to silently hate and curse his masters.

We all have a sense of autonomous agency, a feeling that we have sole responsibility for certain of our choices, however restricted our actions are in reality. We also have a sense of unique, sole ownership of our bodies, perceptions and experiences. To a degree we are all solipsists, who believe we are unique centres of consciousness, for whom the cosmos is nothing more than the sum of our own subjective perceptions and experiences. At some level we recognise that we can only know the world through our unique perceptual apparatus and that there is no other way to experience the world. With this realisation comes a deep-seated, unyielding sense of sovereignty over our bodies and minds.

Given this profound psychological reality, it is not surprising that we normally resent and resist uninvited intrusions into the preserve of internal personal control and strive to maximise self-determination. In fact, we typically make strenuous efforts to maintain and, indeed, enlarge our independent influence over everything that happens to us, and, failing this, as we inevitably do, we absolutely insist on our irrevocable power to decide on how we think and feel. It is predictable, then, that many people, especially young people, will consider their own bodies and minds their special preserve, a unique area over which they alone hold absolute sway, whatever anyone else, including parents, churches and the legislature, might say.

The fourth relevant factor which, in interaction with the natural appetite for altered mood, the urge to explore, our sense of autonomous ownership of our bodies and subjective experience and the incoherence and hypocrisy of the prohibitionist message, makes many people impervious to prohibitionist laws and disapproval is the psychological process of reactance. This is defined as a motivational state aroused whenever freedom is threatened or lost.[14] Reactance can be regarded as the other side of the coin of the search for autonomy.

It describes how we react when faced with the loss of autonomy. In essence, the theory of reactance states that if our freedom of action is restricted, this will usually serve merely to increase the attraction of what has been denied to us. Reactance is our motivation to reestablish our freedom and the most direct way to reestablish a freedom is to exercise it.

Research has shown that reactance, involving increased preference for the threatened behaviour and increased exercise of it, grows in proportion to both the importance and extent of the freedom denied and the magnitude of the pressure to comply. The 'war on drugs' epitomises a situation designed to provoke extreme reactance. For young people growing up, as Irish youth are, in a society suffused with mood-altering substances, especially alcohol and prescribed drugs like valium, Ritalin and Prozac, the legal and social strictures against illicit drugs are highly likely to provoke reactance. The level of reactance is liable to be very high because 1) the pressures to comply are extreme; 2) all forms of illicit drug use, whether dangerous or not, are forbidden; and 3) the use of mood-altering substances (broadly defined) is obviously important and attractive to almost everyone and especially to the young.

The young are curious and eager to expand their personal experience and they are particularly aware and protective of their ownership of their bodies and their control over their thoughts and emotions. They usually have a sense that what they do with their bodies is their own business only. The young also have a profound need to define their unique personal identity and to somehow prove their independence from parents and family.[15] All these essentially psychological and developmental factors combine to make utter disregard for 'hypocritical' prohibitionist laws and propaganda the norm within a significant sector of teenagers and young adults. In this context any gearing up of the prohibitionist message or toughening of the laws is likely to be seriously counterproductive, stiffening the resistance of many and making the 'forbidden fruit' more attractive in their eyes.

Many young people will resist the attempts of even clearly well-intentioned parents, teachers, priests, legislators and law enforcers to tell them what to do with their bodies, minds and lives[16]. They will ignore them on issues like drugs, because they believe that they are encroaching without warrant on an intensely personal, private domain. Unless there is a convincing case that their actions will victimise others, people tend to implicitly believe that they have an inviolable prerogative to do whatever they like with their own bodies. This clearly includes sampling the physical and psychological pleasures that are available to them and may even include, for a minority, purposefully hurting themselves or carelessly putting themselves at serious risk.

It is an ironic and tragic aspect of human nature that our motivation to change our mood, to explore and to make autonomous choices, can so easily lead us into forms of physiological, psychological, economic and social dependency, such as drug addiction, that eventually enslave us and severely narrow our interests and capacity for choice.

These points about the human predisposition to explore, to exercise autonomy and to experience reactance in response to constraints on freedom and how these predispositions interact to promote actions that satisfy the innate desire to alter mood and consciousness should not be confused with the related but conceptually distinct issues of risk- or sensation-seeking and rebelliousness. Undoubtedly, teenagers are often keen to take risks and are sometimes attracted to activities precisely because they carry substantial risk or because they signify rebellion against adult authority. Risk itself, including the risk of being caught doing something forbidden, can become a major source of excitement – a key element in activities such as joy-riding, underage drinking or drug-taking.

The attraction of risk is undoubtedly tied up with the search for identity and the need to assert autonomy. However, while teenagers differ from all other age groups in their willingness to take risks, individuals also differ significantly in terms of their temperamental predisposition for taking risks or sensation-seeking. Teenagers are far more likely to experiment with drugs than the elderly, but equally a temperamentally impulsive, sensation-seeking teenager is far more likely to experiment with drugs and to progress to more dangerous forms of use than the normal teenager. Risk-taking is, therefore, an important issue in regard to drug use, but the key point being made here is that the universal human motivations to explore, develop autonomy and resist restrictions on freedom, especially the freedom of subjective experience, not only promote the use of mood-altering substances but also ensure that many people will regard such use as an intensely personal matter for which, in the final analysis, only they themselves can legislate.

The right to use drugs

The previous section has presented an argument not just that drugs prohibition is a largely futile enterprise, at least in the contemporary Irish context, and that much anti-drugs propaganda is counterproductive, but that the human right to use drugs can be recognised for sound, evidence-based reasons, which relate to the realities of human psychology and physiology. It is important to recognise that the right to use drugs can be based on a scientific understanding of human nature as well as on a reasoned legal rationale or on a purely philosophical notion of freedom. Indeed, the case for the recognition of a person's right to use drugs without interference from the state, so long as they are not infringing the rights of others, is greatly reinforced by the joint consideration of the current analysis of human nature and motivation alongside Mill's libertarian credo and specific legal arguments. These three strands of argument are mutually reinforcing and together make a very powerful case.

In fact, a strong legal case can be made for a human right to drug use within the U.S. legal framework. One of the most fundamental rights is to bodily integrity and this surely entails, in Husak's words, 'the right to determine what happens in and to one's body'.[17] The U.S. Declaration of Independence speaks of an inalienable right to 'life, liberty and the pursuit of happiness'. Szasz[18] points out that, because of this, the early twentieth-century system of alcohol prohibition in the U.S. required an amendment to the U.S. Constitution. The irresistible inference is that the Constitution and Bill of Rights confer a right to self-medicate as one sees fit.

The unenumerated right to privacy, which is widely recognised, is also highly relevant to the argument. Indeed, in the U.S., the Alaskan Supreme Court (in *Ravin v State of Alaska*) has ruled that the right to privacy encompasses the use of marijuana in 'a purely personal, non-commercial context in the home'. In his written opinion, Chief Justice Rabinowitz[19] made the following interesting remarks:

> In view of our holding that possession of marijuana by adults at home for personal use is constitutionally protected, we wish to make clear that we do not mean to condone the use of marijuana. The experts who testified below, including petitioner's witnesses, were unanimously opposed to the use of any psychoactive drugs. We agree completely. It is the responsibility of every individual to consider carefully the ramifications for himself and for those around him of using such substances. With the freedom which our society offers to each of us to order our lives as we see fit goes the duty to live responsibly, for our own sakes and for society's. This result can best be achieved, we believe, without the use of psychoactive substances.

The philosophical, legal and 'human nature' arguments interlock to create a cogent and coherent rationale for recognising the right to use drugs. The human nature arguments are especially important because they demonstrate how laws, such as the current prohibitionist laws, which strain against deep-rooted aspects of our physiological and psychological nature, are destined to flounder and stir up stubborn resistance.

At present, the state is totally opposed to recognising a right to use illicit drugs, because it has already arrogated to itself the right to stamp out all such drug use. The justification for this approach is based mainly on two propositions 1) that all illicit drug use is wrong and dangerous and 2) that some drug users cause harm to others and to the social fabric. The first proposition, as will be demonstrated in Chapter 9, is clearly false and the second, clearly true. However, as the current analysis argues, the state's attempt to stamp out all illicit drug use has been and will continue to be futile. Because all drug use is not particularly dangerous or harmful and because much of it is not as dangerous and harmful as the use of licit substances like alcohol, the state's prohibitionist effort is not just futile, but misguided and hypocritical.

Of course, it is perfectly feasible to recognise the right to use drugs, yet at the same time deploy the criminal law against the criminal harms, which are caused by a minority of drug users. Nevertheless, the recognition of a right to use drugs would be highly controversial, because it implies accepting that people have a right to harm themselves or risk harming themselves. However, this right is accepted in the case of deliberate or incidental self-harm that does not involve illicit drugs, including the self-harm from the use of licit drugs. Actions that harm or put others at risk, such as stealing to pay for drugs or driving while intoxicated, would continue to be subject to criminal sanctions.

Given the (not necessarily true) assumption that drug use involves self-harm, the right to use drugs can be regarded as similar to the right of a young man or woman to self-harm by making small cuts on the arm. Indeed, it is about as sensible to prohibit drug use as it would be to criminalise this unfortunate but quite common form of self-harm.[20] It is certainly possible to implement criminal laws that punish or promote the physical restraint of self-harmers, but because the self-harmer has a profound belief that what they choose to do to themselves is their and only their business, the criminal law approach will never prevent this kind of self-harm. Societal disapproval and the threat of the criminal law will not impinge in the least on those who are at a place in their lives and in their own minds where self-harm seems the appropriate action. Attempts at physical restraint are, in fact, likely to have a paradoxical result and provoke reactance and more intense (and more covert) self-harm behaviours. We recognise this and treat self-harmers with respect and sympathetic assistance, not punishment. Surely, the same response would be appropriate for those who self-harm through drug use.

The obvious conclusion is that it is far better for society to accept that, as in the case of self-harm, it has neither the responsibility nor the right to interfere directly with the physical act of drug use or with the personal choice to use drugs. Instead, the most reasonable approach for society to these 'risky' or harmful drug choices appears to be to concentrate, in the individual case, on providing help and assistance to those currently making self-harmful choices. In the general case, the focus should be on 1) remedying underlying problems that lead to destructive choices or behaviours, and 2) providing the kinds of education, honest persuasion and non-coercive intervention, which have real potential for minimising the harm to self and others caused by misguided choices about drugs.

Perhaps the historically recent process of decriminalisation of homosexuality provides a better analogy than self-harm for the purpose of illustrating the futility of drugs prohibition and the importance of recognising a right to use drugs. Until relatively recently, in fact 1969 in the U.K. and 1993 in Ireland, it was a crime to engage in homosexual activity. The criminalisation of homosexuality was both an expression of the moral disapproval of the majority and an attempt to repress and eliminate all homosexual behaviour. This attempt did not and could not possibly succeed because it involved the constraint of a natural, elementally powerful appetite with deep roots in both human physiology and psychology. Current, more enlightened views, at least in most Western secular democracies, now recognise people's human right to the expression of their sexuality. There has been a far-reaching, if long overdue, transformation of values, attitudes and laws that has improved countless lives, which would have been blighted under the previous legal regime.

It is clearly possible for society to shift from a position of unambiguous condemnation and harsh repression of an activity to a diametrically opposed position where it is prepared to actively defend the right to engage in that activity and where it regards the right as a fundamental human right. The current widespread, often contemptuous dismissal of the concept of a human right to use drugs should, therefore, not be taken as evidence that there is any inevitability to the denial of a right to use drugs.

Recognising the right to drug use is not defeatist with respect to drug harms

As Rabinowitz's judgment makes clear, to recognise the right to use drugs is not to argue that society can or should do nothing about the drugs problem. The key point is that it is better to focus on the prevention of drug-related problems than on the prevention of drug use itself. I have argued that the current self-contradictory form of prohibition in countries like Ireland, which place a special value on and encourage human rights, the free market and individualism, is bound to fail to win over many people, especially wilful teenagers, because this cultural ethos reinforces rather than curbs the human psychological proclivities for exploration, autonomy and self-managed control of mood and consciousness. Teenagers are keen to prove their independence and establish a sense of identity, and, on the issue of mood-altering substances, many of them will reject social control mechanisms of all kinds and experiment with alcohol and illicit drugs. They will tend to ignore well-meaning health promotional messages as well as the threats of tough law enforcement action.

However, as history and cross-cultural comparison show us, in general terms there is obviously nothing predestined about adolescent drug use. The rebellious, freedom-loving tendencies of teenagers and the powerful attraction of mood-altering substances are only part of a complex picture. Availability, cost, knowledge and know-how, attitudes amongst the peer group and society at large, including attitudes to alcohol and other licit mood-altering substances, general levels of conformity, which differ under different political, economic and religious systems and local cultural meanings all play a significant role and all vary across time and place.

Socio-cultural trends, which influence availability, social attitudes and symbolic meanings, are key determinants. There can be a cycle, as has happened in Ireland, in which a period of near abstinence and a high level of social disapproval of drugs, amongst young and old, is followed by widespread, excessive use and a huge diversity of conflicting attitudes on drugs.

The advocate of a human right to use drugs, who is concerned to justify this policy in utility terms as well as on principle, will be as eager as the prohibitionist to engineer social conditions and attitudes that make destructive forms of drug use rare. In other words, they will be concerned to modify *set* and *setting* so as to minimise harm. The point of difference is that the advocate of

a human right to use drugs believes that harm will be most effectively mini-
mised in our current socio-cultural milieu by policies and programmes that
accept and explicitly recognise a right to use drugs.

The biased language of risk

There is a large body of empirical research on factors that constitute risk for
adolescent drug abuse. For example, Spooner,[21] following an extensive review
of the literature, identified the following risk factors for the development of a
relatively serious drug use problem:

> biological predisposition to drug abuse; personality traits that reflect a lack
> of social bonding; a history of low quality and consistency of family manage-
> ment, family communication, family relationships and parental role-modelling;
> a history of being abused or neglected; low socioeconomic status; emotional or
> psychiatric problems; significant stressors and/or inadequate coping skills and
> social supports; inadequate social skills; history of associating with drug-using
> peers, rejection by prosocial peers due to poor social skills; a history of low
> commitment to education, failure at school; a history of anti-social behaviour
> and delinquency and early initiation to drug use.

Some, though not all of these factors, point to potentially helpful forms
of intervention, which can contribute to the prevention of serious adolescent
drug problems. Most of these factors can be classed as individual-centred,
biological, psychological and social characteristics, which relate as much to
set, aspects of the individual's general neediness and specific susceptibility
to drugs, as to *setting*, aspects of the individual's culture and social, family
and peer group environment, which make him or her more vulnerable to the
dangers of drug use. To argue that the state should not interfere with the
individual adult's ability to choose to use drugs is clearly not to argue that
no efforts should be made to reduce the prevalence of *set* and *setting* factors
that incline an adolescent towards drug use and especially towards dangerous
forms of drug use.

However, the explicit acknowledgement of the normal and unexceptionable
nature of the appetite for mood-altering substances and new experiences is an
important support for the recognition of a human right to drug use. There are
physical, psychological and social motors that drive our appetite for the use of
mood-altering substances but this appetite is not necessarily perverse, self-destructive or excessively self-indulgent. One of the problems of the risk factors
approach to adolescent drug use is that it almost inevitably portrays drug use
as deviant, wrong and harmful. This is an unwarranted linguistic and rhetorical
bias, which results from the combined influence of the prohibitionist mindset
and the language of risk.

The identification through empirical research of various risk factors for
drug use reinforces the prohibitionist mindset and appears to provide it with a
rational evidential basis. The inevitable, patently sensible focus of research is on

harmful outcomes – that is on the forms of drug use, which it is in everyone's interest to prevent, because they are damaging to the user, his family, community and the wider social fabric. But this self-confirming negative outlook is highly selective and begs the prohibition question. It ignores the large number of people who derive some form of benefit from drug use without incurring significant costs.

The risk factor approach, with its focus on measurable determinants, also tends to objectify the adolescent and so fails to do justice to the adolescent's own subjective understanding of his motives for using drugs. Research that asks young people why they use drugs, such as that by Novacek et al.,[22] surveying a large number of young people in the south-western U.S, has found that adolescents, in their own view, use drugs in order to belong, to cope, to feel pleasure, to be more creative and to handle feelings of aggression. It is clear that motivation in this area is highly complex and is not fully explained by reference to regrettable forms of neediness or susceptibility in the adolescent or his environment. There are strong, almost purely social or symbolic motives for using drugs, for example to assert one's maturity or to establish acceptance by the peer group. These and other motives, such as the desire to expand one's experience and develop one's sense of creativity, can, from the individual's point of view, be construed as mainly positive and constructive.

The influential study by Shedler and Block,[23] which followed up 101 children longitudinally from pre-school to age 18 years of age, is an important corrective to the risk factors mindset which privileges an entirely negative view of drug use. Shedler and Block classified the 18 year olds in terms of their psychological adjustment and according to whether they were frequent drug users, experimenters, or abstainers. There were 29 abstainers, 36 experimental users, 20 frequent users and 16 remaining subjects who could not be reliably classified as belonging in a single group.

The drug use profile of the sample was similar to that found in large-scale national surveys of U.S. adolescents. Adolescents who had engaged in some drug experimentation (primarily with marijuana) emerged, on the researchers' measures, as the best adjusted of the three groups. Adolescents who, by age 18, had never experimented with drugs were, in comparison with the experimenter group, anxious, emotionally constricted and lacking in social skills. Those who used drugs frequently were, in line with the risk factors analysis of Spooner and others, maladjusted, showing a 'distinct personality syndrome marked by interpersonal alienation, poor impulse control, and manifest emotional distress'.

Shedler and Block were able to correlate these findings on drug use with a wealth of data gathered on the sample from early childhood. They found that relevant psychological differences between the three groups were present in the earliest years and related to quality of parenting among other things. Their most important conclusion was that problem drug use is a symptom, not a cause, of personal and social maladjustment. This led them to argue that 'current efforts at drug prevention are misguided to the extent that they focus on symptoms, rather than on the psychological syndrome underlying drug abuse'.

In other words, Shedler and Block are in agreement with the thesis I have advanced – that it is a mistake to attempt to prevent drug use, which is neither intrinsically wrong nor on balance always harmful nor in practice preventable, at least when using reasonable and humane methods. In a minority of cases, adolescent drug use is a symptom of underlying personal and social maladjustment. This maladjustment is a precursor of drug use, not the result of it, but, predictably, inclines a person to more drug use and more harmful forms of drug use. The preventative effort should be focused on this group and aimed either at avoiding their maladjustment, which has its roots in early childhood and temperament, or, failing this, at identifying the maladjusted adolescents and providing them with specific assistance in avoiding harmful drug use.

Summary

The anti-prohibitionist critique is so devastating that one must wonder how prohibition retains any support and credibility. Three plausible, partial explanations for prohibition's endurance despite failure are: 1) that the drugs culture, which prohibition has failed to halt, may be the inexorable and unavoidable result of changing cultural forces; 2) that a truly tough system of prohibition can work, but has only been attempted in totalitarian states; and 3) that governments almost by definition attempt to control dangers by regulation and, when lesser forms of regulation prove ineffective, they tend to turn to the criminal law. Any non-prohibitionist system, concerned to minimise the harms of drug use, would also be reliant on the law, including in certain areas, such as supply to children, the criminal law.

Part of the failure of prohibition is surely due to the inherent contradictions of the prohibitionist position, but a strong case can be made that prohibition's failure is also due to the fact that it is attempting to stamp out a very intransigent, natural appetitive behaviour within a social, economic, political and legal system (in Western democracies), which tends to empower and encourage the psychology of autonomy, exploration and individual freedom. Humans have a powerful, psychological appetite for altered mood and for novel experience, which finds almost irresistible fulfilment in the use of mood-altering substances. Humans constantly strive after autonomy and have a strong sense of inviolable ownership both of their bodies and their subjective experience. This means that people, especially the young, will often respond with strong reactance (resistance) to attempts to prevent them doing what they want with their own bodies and their own consciousness.

Laws that struggle against powerful natural forces will always be ineffectual and socially troublesome. It, therefore, makes good sense to recognise a human right to use mood-altering substances. This does not entail encouragement of drug use – in fact, every effort can still be made to reduce the prevalence of *set* and *setting* risk factors that predispose an adolescent towards dangerous forms of drug use. Recognition of the right to use drugs is the rational response to the futility and unjustifiability of state interference in the personal choice to use mood-altering substances, so long as this use is not infringing the rights of others.

The risk analysis approach, which dominates the discourse on drugs, has an inbuilt bias against drug use that is unwarranted and should be resisted. Shedler and Block's important study has indicated that problematic drug use is primarily a symptom of underlying physiological, psychological and sociological causes (in *set* and *setting*), and that adolescents, who use drugs in a moderate fashion, appear to be better adjusted than those, who never use drugs. It is a mistake to attempt to prevent drug use as such; rather, the main preventative effort should be focused on the maladjusted group, who are predisposed to dangerous forms of drug use.

Notes

1 Transform: Drug Policy Foundation (2005) *After the War on Drugs: Options for Control*, report available at http://tdpf.org.uk.
2 Murphy, T. (1996) *Rethinking the War on Drugs in Ireland*, Cork: Cork University Press.
3 Jacoby, J. and Gramckow, H. (1994) 'Prosecuting drug offenders' in (eds MacKenzie, D. and Uchida, C.) *Drugs and Crime: Evaluating Public Policy Initiatives*, Thousand Oaks: Sage.
4 Trace, M., Roberts, M. and Klein, A. (2004) *Assessing Drug Policy Principles and Practice*, Drugscope and the Beckley Foundation.
5 EU memorandum MEMO/06/249 (26 June 2006) *The EU Policy in the Drugs Field: Present Priorities*, Brussels. The memo also estimated that in any given month 1.5 million Europeans take cocaine and 12 million take cannabis, of whom 3 million take it on a more or less daily basis. Twenty per cent of treatment requests are now related to cannabis, placing it second only to heroin. Ecstasy, produced in Europe, is now the second most common drug after cannabis. According to the European Monitoring Centre for Drugs and Drug Addiction, in some Member States up to 8% of young people take it on a regular basis.
6 Furey, M. and Browne, C. (2003) *Opiate Use and Related Criminal Activity in Ireland 2000 & 2001*, Templemore: Garda Research Unit.
7 Bejerot, N. (1972) 'A theory of addiction as an artificially induced drive', *American Journal of Psychiatry*, 128, at 842–846; Bejerot believes that while drug abuse may be a symptom of psychological or social disturbances, when addiction is established, it has the strength and character of a natural drive. He considers drug dependence to be an artificially induced drive developed through chemical stimulation of the pleasure centres in the brain.
8 Weil, A. (1972) *The Natural Mind*, Harmondsworth: Penguin Books, at page 20.
9 Brickman, P. and Campbell, D. (1971) 'Hedonic relativism and planning the good society' in (ed. Appley, M.) *Adaptation Level Theory: A Symposium*, New York: Academic Press.

10 Jarvik, M. (1990) 'The drug dilemma: manipulating the demand', *Science*, 250, at 387–392.

11 Aigner, T.G. and Balster, R.L. (1978) 'Choice behaviour in rhesus monkeys: cocaine versus food', *Science*, 201, at 534.

12 White, R. (1959) 'Motivation reconsidered: the concept of competence', *Psychological Review*, 66, at 297–333.

13 Deci, E. and Ryan, R. (1985) *Intrinsic Motivation and Self-determination in Human Behaviour*, New York: Plenum.

14 Brehm, J. (1966) *A Theory of Psychological Reactance*, New York Academic Press.

15 Psychological research suggests that the search for autonomy in the second decade of life is focused initially on establishing independence from parents and family and is often negotiated by the teenager going through a period of compliance with peer group values. For example, Steinberg, L. and Silverberg, S. (1986) ['The vicissitudes of autonomy in early adolescence', *Child Development*, 57, 4, at 841–851] state that 'for most boys and girls, the transition from childhood into adolescence is marked more by a trading of dependency on parents for dependency on peers, rather than straightforward and unidimensional growth in autonomy'.

16 Petraitis, J., Flay, B. and Miller, T. (1995), 'Reviewing theories of adolescent substance use: organizing pieces in the puzzle', *Psychological Bulletin*, 117, 1, at 67–86, state that 'experimental substance use is more common among adolescents who are socially non-conforming, independent, critical, alienated, or rebellious' and cite more than a dozen studies that support this contention.

17 Husak, D. (1992) *Drugs and Rights*, Cambridge: Cambridge University Press.

18 Szasz, T. (1994) 'The ethics of addiction' in (ed. Comber R.) *Drugs and Drug Use in Society*, London: Greenwich University Press.

19 Chief Justice Rabinowitz, Supreme Court of Alaska 537 P.2d 494 (27 May 1975).

20 According to the National Parasuicide Registry Ireland [Annual Report 2003 Cork: National Suicide Research Foundation] almost 2,500 cases of deliberate self-cutting were recorded at Irish accident and emergency units in 2003.

21 Spooner C. (1999) 'Causes and correlates of adolescent drug abuse and implications for treatment', *Drug and Alcohol Review* 18, 4, at 453–475.

22 Novacek, J., Raskin, R. and Hogan, R. (1991) 'Why do adolescents use drugs. Age, sex and user differences', *Journal of Youth and Adolescence*, 20, 5 at 475–492.

23 Shedler, J. and Block, J. (1990) 'Adolescent drug use and psychological health', *American Psychologist*, 45, at 612–630.

8

The failure of Irish prohibition

Prohibition as a cause of crime and injustice

Ineffectual criminalisation of 'inherent' drug crime undermines respect for the law

While prohibition in Ireland has failed obviously and drastically to reduce the use of illicit drugs and prevent the growth of the now almost globalised, pro-drugs, youth counterculture, its role as an independent, material cause of drug-related criminal, health and social problems remains a matter for careful empirical investigation. The use of the criminal law to prevent drug use appears to have backfired, but the actual and specific role of prohibition in the creation of crime and other harms is a complex and contentious matter.

It is, however, undeniable that prohibition creates a raft of new 'inherent' drug-related crimes, both user and dealer crimes. For example, it creates the new crime of possession of illicit drugs. In this way prohibition inevitably criminalises a large number of otherwise law-abiding citizens. But, as we have seen, Irish prohibition, in spite of its strident 'war on drugs' rhetoric, has been quite tentative and sparing in the prosecution and punishment of drug possession for personal use. Unlike in the U.S. where many people are imprisoned solely for possession of small amounts of relatively harmless drugs such as cannabis, Irish prisons are not filled with people convicted for the 'inherent' drug crime of possession. This is mainly because the system is not particularly zealous or successful in the discovery of crimes of drugs possession and because it treats the user offenders whom it does prosecute quite leniently. However, even if the criminalisation of a multitude of otherwise law-abiding citizens remains largely a matter of symbolic disapproval rather than concrete punishment, and even if only small numbers of people actually have their lives disrupted by the harsh and stigmatising sanction of imprisonment for possession of small amounts of drugs, it would be foolish to underestimate the harm caused to the social fabric by prohibition's intrinsic crime creation process.

Undoubtedly, in Ireland, the major problem is the damage caused to the prestige and standing of the law itself, rather than the harm done by needlessly criminalising and punishing individuals. When a large segment of the population regularly, casually and unashamedly flouts the drugs laws, as they persistently do in Ireland, this signals the insidious spread of a mocking disregard for the law. It reflects a widespread cynicism, suspicion and hostility towards the law and law enforcement agents. Drug laws, especially those that outlaw relatively harmless, 'recreational' drug use, which many people consider a matter of personal choice, tend to alienate people and undermine their identification with and confidence in the legitimate forces of law and order and in the laws these forces seek to uphold. It is manifestly detrimental to the social fabric when prohibition laws drive a wedge between ordinary citizens and the police and erode the willing consent of the people to being policed. This is a largely unremarked but very significant cost of prohibition in Ireland.

Nadelman's costs of prohibition

In a frequently cited article, Nadelman[1] described a number of additional costs of prohibition, which broadly relate to the criminal justice system or justice issues. In the case of the U.S., the collateral, downstream costs of prohibition are particularly obvious and grave. They include geopolitical problems related to U.S. interventionist, drug interdiction policies in countries across the globe, the corruption of politicians and law enforcement officials in the U.S. and in producer and transit countries, a crisis in the U.S. court and prison systems, pernicious effects on human rights regimes in producer countries, the erosion of the civil and due process rights of U.S. citizens, and a serious aggravation of the pre-existing biases of the U.S. criminal justice system against the poor and members of racial minorities.

Afghanistan is currently a potent symbol of the failure of prohibition policies at a global level and of the interconnection between drugs interdiction and chaotic theatres of war or insurrection.[2] Reports in late 2006 indicated that a bumper heroin crop, originating in the Helmand province of Afghanistan, was flooding into the West. Despite the significant presence of British troops in this province – troops engaged, according to British Army sources, in the toughest fighting faced by that army since the Korean War – the Taliban are resurgent in Helmand and have facilitated local farmers in the growing and indeed processing of the opium poppy. A great irony is that the U.S. has in the recent past provided massive funds to a then 'friendly' Taliban specifically in order to eliminate heroin production from Afghanistan.

On 4 January 2007, press reports covered Operation Tijuana, involving 3,300 soldiers, federal police and navy seamen, which was launched by the Mexican President Filipe Calderon in response to a year of drug gang violence that left more than 2,000 dead throughout Mexico. Tijuana is a small border city close to San Diego and is an important smuggling route into the U.S. for both marijuana and cocaine. The San Diego tram system has a major terminus just short of the border and there is much everyday traffic between the two cities. In 2006, almost two dozen law enforcement officers and almost 300 others were killed by drug gangs in Tijuana, but the reports claimed that President Calderon's action was prompted mainly by the need to respond to corruption and incompetence amongst the local and state police. On 6 January, the Tijuana local police walked off the job, in response to orders from Mexican federal police to some of its members to turn in their weapons in connection with homicide investigations. That same day the mayor of Tijuana admitted that state and city police were being compromised by 'narco-traffickers', because government salaries could not compete with the rewards offered by the drug dealers. This corruption and violent anarchy so close to the U.S. border is, of course, tied to the massive demand for drugs from Americans, which continues despite the decades of increasingly rigorous prohibition.

As a direct consequence of the 'war on drugs', recent decades, in which figures for theft and violent crime in the U.S. have been static or declining, have witnessed a more than quadrupling of the number of people imprisoned in the U.S. The number of U.S. prisoners now stands at over 2.2 million. This means that the U.S. has the highest proportion of its population incarcerated of any country in the world, at least amongst countries for which reliable statistics are available. This 'incarceration binge' has involved massive public spending on prison places and has greatly increased the ongoing costs of prisons to the detriment of other public services, such as health and education. However, the prison system is still overwhelmed and continues to suffer the serious ills of overcrowding and inadequate facilities. In California, the problem is so acute that, in 2006, Governor Schwartzernegger instituted a programme – which met with little initial success – of exporting Californian State prisoners to Arizona and other distant states where privately owned and managed prisons had spare capacity and offered better facilities and somewhat less inhumane conditions.

According to Husak,[3] the U.S. actively supports corrupt, authoritarian regimes which have a dismal record on human rights 'for no other reason than their alleged willingness to join the fight against drugs'. Direct U.S. supply control actions or U.S.-sponsored actions often entail a fierce assault on the human rights of vulnerable individuals. A recent report to the U.S. House of Representatives Subcommittee on the Western Hemisphere by Joy Olson[4] stated that about 47,000 people were displaced in 2005 (in Colombia) after their coca and legal food crops were destroyed by fumigation. Olson concluded that 'aerial eradication is not simply an ineffective policy, it is a cruel one' and that 'we have made poverty and forced migration out of desperation a standard result of U.S. policy'. Olson also concluded that U.S. drug policy in the region had promoted the adoption of harsh anti-drug laws there that are at variance with 'basic international norms and standards of due process and undermine already tenuous civil liberties'.

The Association of the Bar of the City of New York,[5] in an influential report, argue that the pursuit of a 'drug-free' society has resulted in 'a panoply of intrusions into the lives of United States citizens', intrusions which amount to a significant erosion of constitutional rights. They conclude that 'the Bill of Rights is in danger of becoming meaningless in cases involving drugs', due to the fact that exemptions made for drugs cases by the Supreme Court have diluted the citizen's protection against unwarranted searches, evictions, forfeiture of property and double jeopardy prosecutions. In more recent years, of course, the concern of civil libertarians has been deflected from these issues, because the right to privacy and to the presumption of innocence, among other fundamental rights, guaranteed by the U.S. Constitution, have been subjected to many severe assaults in the name of President Bush's new war, the 'war on terror'.[6] However, the strain in the relationship between civil liberties and prohibition is inevitable. As Husak points out: 'since illicit drugs are easy to conceal and involve consensual transactions that typically occur behind closed doors, police have been forced to resort to unusual and questionable tactics to enforce criminalization'.

On the issue of racial discrimination, which is hugely salient in the U.S., Husak[7] points out that surveys and official figures indicate that about five times more whites than blacks and Hispanics in the U.S. use illicit drugs, but that, nonetheless, blacks and Hispanics constitute about 62% and whites only about 37% of all drug offenders committed to state prisons. He asserts that 'prohibition would have vanished long ago if whites had been sent to prison for drug offences at the same rate as blacks'. In other words, the 'war on drugs' in the U.S. facilitates an inherently racially biased system of law enforcement of drug offences, with inevitably pernicious effects for American society.

Nadelman's costs and Irish prohibition

Many of these appalling, collateral costs of prohibition are not especially relevant to Ireland: for example, the costs connected to the U.S. role as self-appointed 'global policeman' and those connected to the very evident racial bias of the U.S. system and its strong preference for criminal sanctions, which are, arguably, totally disproportionate. However, in all conscience the Irish prohibitionist state and the Irish prohibitionist or, for that matter, the ordinary citizen cannot be indifferent to the horrific harms suffered by innocent people or small-scale, peasant drug crop farmers in developing countries like Mexico, Peru and Colombia. These countries have become major casualties of the U.S.-promoted, global 'war on drugs'. However, the Irish government, while not a decision-maker or active participant in the oppression of people in drug producer countries, is uncritically supportive of the U.S.-backed 'war on drugs' and thus, to a not inconsiderable extent, complicit in it.

On the other hand, three of the problem areas discussed by Nadelman have clear, if culturally specific, parallels in Ireland. These are the increased reliance on imprisonment; the erosion of fundamental rights; and the intensification of the negative impact of socioeconomic inequality on people processed by the criminal justice system. The cost of the 'war on drugs' to Irish society has been significant in terms of both the ever-increasing punitiveness of the criminal justice system and the weakening of the legal protections against miscarriages of justice and abuse of state power. The opiate drugs crisis and the way the government has responded to it have also undoubtedly intensified the social exclusion of elements of the Irish underclass through the means of the criminal justice system. This is a serious problem because it exacerbates a preexisting situation in which an egregiously high proportion of prisoners, compared for example to the situation in the U.K.,[8] come from the lowest echelons of society.

The average daily number of prisoners has grown inexorably along with the drugs problem in a way undoubtedly linked to the increasing severity of the Irish 'war on drugs'. The number of prisoners increased from 1,140 in 1979 to 2,108 in 1990 and to about 3,200 in early 2007. This rate of increase, amounting to a near trebling of the prison population, is one of the highest in Europe in this period. Reflecting the growing punitiveness of the system, this rapid growth has occurred despite a fluctuating trend and overall moderate growth in serious crime. The number of Headline crimes recorded in 2002 was 106,415, which is the highest number ever recorded, but which represents a mere 4% rise over 1983, when there were 102,387 recorded indictable crimes, and a 66% rise over 1979, the year when the opiate epidemic began and when there were 64,057 such crimes. By comparison the growth in prison places between 1979 and 2002 was 180%. The number of committals to prison under sentence in the 1970s was about 3,000, and in 2002, a little over 5,000, indicating an increase of about 66%. This is in line with the increase in crime rather than prison places. The opening of a 400-place remand prison in 1999, mainly to house drug-related offenders refused bail, has also made a major contribution to the growth of the prison population. However, the far greater increase in the daily average number of prisoners than in committals shows that sentences and pre-trial custody have not just increased in number but have also significantly increased in length. More people are being sentenced to prison or being refused bail and they are spending considerably more time in custody.

Mandatory minimum sentences for drug dealers, increased sentence length and, since the 1997 Bail Act, the use of preventative pre-trial custody account for much of the growth in the prison population. While this growth cannot be attributed to the influence of prohibition in any simple or direct way, especially since few 'inherent' drug crimes are punished by imprisonment, there can be little doubt that prohibitionist law enforcement and the 'war on drugs' rhetoric have made a major contribution to the increased punitiveness of the Irish system. A shrill, political debate on crime and punishment predominates in Ireland and is obsessively focused on the evils of drug gangs. This debate is characterised by condemnatory, zero-tolerant sentiment and premised on an unjustified faith in the effectiveness of imprisonment and tough law enforcement. While imprisonment undoubtedly has a temporary incapacitative effect, it appears to have little deterrent and reformative value and may, instead, simply serve to harden prisoners and confirm them on the criminal path. A recent study points to unusually high levels of recidivism in Ireland, showing that 27% of ex-prisoners are reconvicted within 12 months of release and more than 50% within two years.[9]

More importantly, few in the greatly expanded population of Irish prisoners are major criminals who profit from the drugs trade or the other perpetrators of 'systemic' drug-related crime such as gangland assassination. The Irish prisons are still, for the most part, full with drug users, who have been convicted for their 'economic compulsive' property crimes. Even the people convicted of drug offences attracting the 10 years' mandatory sentence tend to be minor players – easily exploited, hapless 'mules'.[10] For example, in March 2007, Judge Desmond Hogan in the Dublin Circuit Court sentenced a young, unemployed Polish woman with a sick child to 7 years for importing €147,000 worth of cocaine into Ireland. This woman's fee for smuggling the cocaine was a paltry €700. The judge commented that the woman had been motivated by poverty and duped into doing this crime by others who took advantage of her domestic situation. Many of the convicted 'drug dealers' now suffering the harsher punishments imposed under the banner of the Irish 'war on drugs' have a similar profile.

After a number of general elections in which the main political parties have framed the crime problem chiefly in terms of the menace of drugs gangs and have vied with each other to promise more prison places, more gardai and a strengthening of police and prosecutorial powers, there now appears to be an almost uncritical acceptance of the benefits of the hardline approach. Little attention is paid to the continuing ineffectiveness of imprisonment and to the actual effects of the harsher criminal justice approach on the majority of people sent to prison, who are relatively minor, non-violent, property offenders. Nor is much attention paid to the system's failure to impact significantly on its supposed main targets – the drugs barons and their enforcers. The latest National Plan proposes to increase prison places by more than 15% over the next few years. This proposal has not been subjected to critical analysis or supported by hard evidence on the need for or benefits of more prison places. This proposal and the hardline ideology that spawned it have gone almost unchallenged in the popular and political discourse.

In fact, the 'war on drugs' rhetoric and the bifurcation approach, which enables a separation of victimising criminal drug dealers from their less seriously criminal drug-using victims, have been crucial to the current supremacy within Irish politics of a right-wing, hardline mindset on crime and punishment. The same factors have been instrumental in the significant erosion of legal protections for suspects at a time when numerous scandals have exposed miscarriages of justice and abuse of police powers.

The tough 'war on drugs' legislation of successive Irish governments has selectively eroded the due process rights of drug dealer suspects by curtailing the right to silence and by increasing police powers of detention and search. The restrictions on the right to bail were also primarily introduced to tackle drug-related crime. Political rhetoric, which likens drug crime to terrorist crime in terms of its threat to the stability of the state, has been used to ease the way for legislation which applies restrictions on the fundamental rights of suspect drug dealers in a way formerly thought justified only in the case of political terrorists. The Criminal Assets Bureau approach has allowed the state the advantage of a reversal of the burden of proof and a lowering of the level of proof from 'beyond reasonable doubt' to 'balance of probabilities'. This hardline approach to criminal procedure and fundamental rights, which has been justified by the supposed invulnerability of drug dealers and by the extreme threat they are said to pose, has clearly also acted as a bridgehead for the erosion of the rights of all citizens. The Criminal Assets Bureau very quickly turned its attention to types of crime and tax evasion, which had no relation to the drugs trade. The more restrictive bail laws were from the start applicable to all suspects.

Fears that the selective curtailment of the rights of drug dealers would eventually apply more broadly to all suspects have been strongly confirmed by the latest anti-crime measures proposed in February 2007. These measures, which were quickly contrived by the then Minister for Justice, Michael McDowell, in response to a spate of drugs gang murders in late 2006, include the extension to all suspects involved in 'arrestable crimes' of restrictions on the right to silence and of longer periods of interrogative detention. They also include more severe sentencing, especially for repeat gangland crime, and more restrictions on the right to bail. The Law Society issued a statement on 27 February 2007 stating that 'it is clear from the heads of Bill that it is proposed to reverse principles which have over centuries stood the test of time ... there is a great danger to the rights of citizens if this legislation is rushed into law'.

The Irish Human Rights Commission[11] are clearly concerned that the changes to criminal procedure and police powers carry a risk of serious injustice even when their application is restricted to drug dealers. They have criticised the provisions of the Criminal Justice Act 2006 which relate to mandatory minimum sentences for drug dealers, arguing that 'they may undermine the discretion of the judiciary to ensure that the sentence imposed is in line with the principle of proportionality, and to ensure that a fair balance is struck between the particular circumstances of the commission of the offence and the relevant circumstances of the person sentenced'. They also suggest that the €12,700 figure which triggers the mandatory sentence should be adjusted for inflation and that an independent assessor, not the Garda, should value the amount of drugs involved. They recommend that the prosecution be required to prove intent – 'that the accused had reasonable grounds to believe that the drugs in his or her possession were worth €12,700 or more'. The Commission were also unsure 'how a drug offenders register will be an effective, necessary or proportionate response'.

An alarming aspect of the many changes to criminal procedure which impact on due process rights and the presumption of innocence is that they have been introduced almost without protest from the public and opposition parties in the Dail. Equally alarmingly, most of these measures have been adopted without evidence for their actual practical value. In fact, it appears that very little use is made of new provisions such as extended police detention for interrogation and restrictions on the right to silence. There is little evidence to suggest that these changes have been efficacious in the investigation and prosecution of serious drug criminals. The 'war on drugs' rhetoric helps generate the perception of a crime-plagued society and successfully exploits the consequent climate of fear and condemnation to the extent that people become forgetful of or apathetic about the need for checks and balances on the powers of the state. Successive Ministers for Justice have relied on 'rebalancing' the criminal justice system to the advantage of the police and prosecution as a means of signalling to the voting public that the government is tough on crime. These 'tough' measures may well convince some of the electorate; however, unfortunately, they are more likely to produce miscarriages of justice and lead to more authoritarian and arrogant policing than to bring serious criminals to justice.

The U.S. 'war on drugs' has played a significant role in aggravating the impact of an already discriminatory criminal justice system on the Afro-American and Hispanic minorities. A similar process has occurred in Ireland though it is not so obvious since the Irish underclass is not racially distinct; nor is the process as marked since Irish prohibition rarely uses imprisonment as a sanction for the mere possession of small amounts of illicit drugs. Surveys of prisoners emphasise the high concentration amongst the incarcerated of young, unemployed, under-educated males from the poorest and most marginalised sections of Irish towns and cities.[12] The narrow focus of Irish criminal justice on the mainly property crimes of this group is also demonstrated by the very small numbers of people imprisoned for the kinds of crime which are committed by the more privileged and those who hold positions of trust, such as embezzlement, occupational theft, tax evasion, bribery, fraud and domestic violence. Many programmes, initiated or expanded since 1996, have advanced the cause of social inclusion and have offered genuine opportunities to drug-using offenders from deprived backgrounds to rebuild their lives and avoid crime. However, the expansion of the prison system and the increasing harshness of sentencing have undoubtedly escalated the burden of punishment and intensified the alienation of the marginalised young men who continue to use drugs and commit crime. Insofar as the system tends to focus unfairly on the crimes of the deprived, it is reasonable to infer that the injustice of the Irish system has also deepened. Bifurcation allows lenient and sympathetic treatment for the compliant drug-using offender who takes advantage of methadone maintenance and other supports and avoids crime. But it also encourages hardened and more punitive public and judicial attitudes towards the persistent, petty, drug-using offenders, who spurn the chance for a more ordered life and so seem to ally themselves with the demonised drug barons, whom the system ostensibly targets.

Prohibition's causative role in 'ordinary' crime

In relation to 'non-inherent' drug-related crime, studies indicate that there has been and continues to be an enormous amount of drug-related 'economic compulsive' crime in Ireland. Some of this crime is confrontational and quite violent. This crime is not ignored or treated leniently, but is, on the contrary, often punished by imprisonment. The problem may have abated in the years between 1996 and 2000, in large part due to the expanded methadone maintenance programme and the increased use of imprisonment, but historically it is clear that the arrival of widespread 'hard' drug use substantially increased the scale and seriousness of the crime problem in Ireland.

Over the five years of the original heroin epidemic, between 1978 and 1983, there was a remarkable increase of 38,000 per annum in officially recorded crimes of theft. Robberies almost tripled, larcenies increased by about 20,000 per annum and burglaries soared from 18,900 to 35,800 per annum in this short period. This growth was on top of a steadily rising curve of crime, but was nonetheless dramatic and unprecedented. A decade and a half later, the Keogh[13] study demonstrated that, in 1996 and 1997, opiate users were responsible, at least in Dublin, for the vast majority of robberies and burglaries and many other kinds of theft. It is obviously reasonable, then, to attribute a great deal of the property crime of the last quarter century to the opiate epidemic, which was mainly restricted to marginalised communities of Dublin.

However, it would be entirely unreasonable to attribute this 'economic compulsive' crime to prohibition as such. Much crime could have been avoided, if the opiate epidemic had been avoided. But it is by no means clear that an absence of prohibition would have prevented the opiate epidemic. Prohibition did not, in any obvious way, cause the heroin epidemic, though it may have contributed to its arrival and to the strength of its grip on vulnerable communities. As I have argued, the young people of the poor, disadvantaged, chronically crime-ridden communities of Dublin were for various reasons particularly susceptible to the opiate drugs culture. They may well have succumbed to opiate use regardless of the legal status of drugs. It is undeniable that many would have become involved in acquisitive crime, even if there had been no opiate epidemic.

On the other hand, it is obvious that the prohibition regime, though it cannot be blamed for the opiate epidemic and was not a necessary precondition for it, contributed to and exacerbated aspects of the epidemic. In the late 1970s heroin had hardly any presence in Ireland and was in most circles an unknown quantity. Heroin initially had to be pushed at the youth in Dublin's vulnerable, underclass communities. The illegality of heroin facilitated the pushing process by inevitably involving criminal dealers, who were utterly unaccountable, ruthlessly exploitative and driven only by financial motives. These criminals naturally cloaked their activities in secrecy, which gave them a head start in the battle for hearts and minds and, consequently, a substantial advantage over parents, educators, health services and other possible sources of wise counsel.

The criminal pushers were like totally unchallenged snake oil salesmen, who could talk up the positives and downplay the negatives of heroin to gullible, eager and easily led youngsters. Secrecy enabled the pushers to sell their product as an exciting 'forbidden fruit' to young people almost totally ignorant of heroin and its effects. Crucially, these young people were ignorant of the tolerance process, which quickly establishes a physiological need for more and more of the drug, thereby greatly inflating the cost of a habit. They were largely ignorant of the physical withdrawal syndrome, which underpins the habit-forming power of opiate use and of the numerous risks to physical and mental health. Caught up in the excitement of what was initially seen as a life-enhancing experience, young users themselves soon became apostles for heroin, doing the pushers' work for them by creating conformity pressures and generating demand amongst their peers for the new craze. In short, prohibition, by promoting silence and secrecy around drugs, greatly facilitated drug pushers and cleared the way for opiate drugs to rapidly gain a powerful grip on vulnerable communities. It is reasonable, then, to blame prohibition for an indirect and essentially unquantifiable contribution to 'economic compulsive' drug-related crime through its facilitation of the opiate epidemic in Dublin's disadvantaged communities.

The prohibited nature of drug use also contributed to the increase in crime by lowering the threshold for involvement in acquisitive crime for young people in deprived, drugs-ridden districts. As a greater proportion of each succeeding age cohort in these marginalised areas became involved in drugs, so a greater proportion became persistently and seriously involved in crime. While these localities had always produced young people who got into trouble with the law, they also produced many who successfully managed to avoid serious criminality. With the spread of drugs it became much harder to avoid persistent offending. Indeed an ever-increasing number became locked into a life of crime, mainly because of their drug involvement. The fact that drugs were criminalised eased the drug user's path into 'economic compulsive' crime. Since, by using opiates, one was already labelled criminal and subject to quite punitive laws and severe social stigma, the incentive to avoid other types of crime was substantially diminished. This was especially the case for youngsters who had no available legitimate source of funds and who were surrounded by peers who had no compunction about committing acquisitive crime to finance a drug habit.

Most obviously, however, prohibition contributes to the extent of 'economic compulsive' crime through its inflationary effect on the cost of drugs to the consumer and through the consequent acceleration of acquisitive crime to pay for drugs. Prohibition raises prices by creating artificial scarcity and forcing the trade into a criminally controlled, black market. This price inflation reflects the organisational and physical difficulties and the legal risks attached to the production, importation and distribution of banned substances. It reflects the very real dangers posed by rival criminals operating in this lawless domain. But it also reflects the obscene levels of profit, which the totally unregulated, monopoly-holding traffickers and dealers are free to take in the market. This market covers a wide range in terms of the felt need for the product, from luxury, lifestyle choice (for the occasional cocaine user) to absolute physical and psychological necessity (for the compulsive heroin addict). The end result of inflationary pressures is that an opiate habit can cost hundreds of euro a week. In order to fund what can quite quickly and easily become an insatiable, desperate habit, some opiate-using offenders will commit an astonishing amount of acquisitive crime, far more than the normal non-drug-using offender.

The contribution of prohibition to 'economic compulsive' crime, through raising the cost of drugs and through increasing the numbers willing to pay for their habit through crime, while real and substantial, is possibly not as clear-cut as the contribution of 'hard drug' use per se. After all, a compulsive opiate habit is likely to be relatively expensive even in a free or regulated market without prohibition. Crime will always be an attractive option for those who have no legitimate source of funds but suffer desperate cravings for a drug. However, the remarkable decline in crime following 1996, especially in the areas of larceny, robbery and burglary, and the evidence from the users surveyed by Furey and Browne,[14] shows that the provision of free opiates can have a stabilising effect on the lifestyles of drug-using offenders and can reduce their involvement in crime. Although there are other relevant factors, such as the decline in unemployment and the increase in the use of imprisonment, this decrease in crime, following the easing of some of the effects of prohibition through methadone maintenance, tends to confirm the significant role of prohibition in the increased incidence of drug-related acquisitive crime. It lends considerable credence to the view that a legal, regulated market in drugs would not be as conducive to drug-related acquisitive crime as prohibition, especially if it included free supply of opiates to recognised addict users.

The issue of causality is much more straightforward in relation to 'systemic' crime. It is incontrovertible that most drug-related 'systemic' crime is fuelled directly by the opportunities for illegal gains created by prohibition and would not occur if there were no prohibition. As previously mentioned, by current Garda estimates, prohibition places a colossal €1 billion monopoly in the hands of criminals. Prohibition has created previously undreamt-of opportunities for the criminally inclined. It has provided easy money and the prospect of a glamorous, affluent lifestyle. Prohibition has opened up to those predisposed to crime new criminal routes to success and to the respect of their peer group. It has placed a new premium on the toughness of the 'hard man', on deviousness and on criminal leadership ability.

The rise of this underworld industry from a negligible level in the 1970s has had a drastically corrosive and corrupting influence in Ireland. It has fostered

the growth of scores of gangs, of varying levels of organisation and sophistica-
tion. These gangs tend to share a ruthless indifference to the harm their drug
trafficking causes and a callous disregard for the sacredness of human life. The
breakup of some of the large, relatively well-organised gangs in the late 1990s
appears only to have ushered in younger, more brazen and disorderly gangs.
The level and nature of current drug gang-related violence indicates that these
new gangs are even more volatile and violence-prone than their predecessors.

The dozens of gun murders of recent years, including brutal assassinations
by hired professional killers, may not all be directly connected to drug gang-
related activity. However, many of them do relate to turf wars, debt enforcement, punishment of informers and other types of intimidation and coercion.
In this illegal domain, there can be no recourse to the law for the settlement of
disputes. There are many occasions when large rewards are at stake and when
there are obvious opportunities for cheating and betraying trust. It is almost
inevitable that in the absence of the normal legal constraints and civilised
checks and balances, there is resort to violence and intimidation as the final
arbiter.

It seems clear that some of the recent Irish gun murders relate to purely
personal or family issues, often involving retaliation for initial slights or
perceived acts of disrespect, which would often appear relatively trivial to an
outsider. There have been a number of situations in Dublin, Limerick and
elsewhere, where full-scale feuds with a prolonged cycle of tit-for-tat revenge
killings have developed. While it is not inconceivable that this sort of problem
could have arisen in the absence of the criminal drug gang culture, it is telling
that almost all the groups involved in these feuds are in the drug trade.

It is undeniable that the relatively recent growth of an American ghetto-style
gun culture amongst young criminals and the associated devaluation of human
life are part of a climate, new to Ireland, which has coevolved with the criminal
drug trade over the last 25 years. There is an intimate symbiosis between drug
trading and violence, now frequently exemplified by the phenomenon of guns
being imported alongside drug consignments as an integral part of the deal.
As the profits of drug dealing have increased, so have the attendant risks and
so has the tendency to resort to extreme violence in order to evade detection, protect gains and maintain control over markets. Increasingly severe law
enforcement action against traffickers and dealers, including stronger police
powers, longer sentences and confiscation of assets, rachet up the pressure and
intensify the paranoia and volatility of drug gangs. Haller[15] has made the point
that 'ironically enough, one of the effects of policies to deal harshly with drug
dealers may have been to increase violence within heroin and cocaine markets
and thus increase the degree to which drug dealing has been controlled by
men willing to kill for profit'.

Of course, wherever there is systemic violence, paranoia is never far from
the surface. Once extreme violence, such as murder or torture, is used in even a
loosely organised system such as the drugs underworld, an insidious, progres-

sive cycle of increasing violence tends to emerge. Fear, desperation, rage, and the thirst for revenge add to a paranoid spiral in which the level of violence continuously escalates. The sense of threat and vulnerability can lead people to preemptive strikes – to getting in their retaliation first. All the while, participants become increasingly inured to the use of violence and increasingly nonchalant about imposing their will and securing instrumental gains through extreme violence. It is very difficult to step away from or reverse this extremely negative process. An unfortunate side-effect is that the police are not immune to this paranoid spiral and, in reaction to the escalation of criminal violence, inevitably become participants in a parallel arms race.

In short, it is reasonable to lay the blame for much of the current gang-related violence and intimidation at the feet of prohibition. Prohibition is not a sufficient explanation for this complex subculture, which has emerged slowly over the last two decades and now has a major international dimension, but prohibition was a necessary precondition for it. The huge profits available from drug trading, profits ultimately made possible by the prohibition regime, have propelled the growth of what, 20 years ago, would, in the Irish context, have appeared to be an utterly alien and unimaginably vicious criminal subculture.

It is ironic that this creature of prohibition – the brutal, brazenly lawless drug gang subculture, which is now so widespread in the poorest districts of Irish towns and cities – is probably one of the principal barriers which prevent informed, dispassionate discussion about dismantling prohibition. The murder, feuding, intimidation, glorification of guns, money laundering, smuggling, degradation of neighbourhoods etc., which have become routine for drug gangs, present such a challenge to law enforcement and the ordinary citizen that legalising the trade in drugs has become almost unthinkable, as if it can only be taken to signal victory for the gangs and a licence for them to continue on their ruthless way. However, dismantling prohibition, albeit slowly and carefully, may well be the only viable long-term solution. It certainly does not entail ignoring or failing to punish the wide variety of serious crime committed by drug gangs. However difficult it might be, the abolition of prohibition probably offers the only realistic prospect of finally defeating the gangs by eroding their financial and power basis, which has been created by and still depends on prohibition.

Prohibition as a cause of social and health harms

There are a myriad of drug-related social, psychological, health and economic harms. Plainly, most of these harms, which can include early death, the burden of severe mental and physical ill-health and the anguish caused to loved ones, are, at the most obvious level, the result of drug use itself. An established addiction, especially one involving intravenous use of opiates or other 'hard' drugs, exposes the addict to numerous health risks and can have a devastating effect on the personality and mental and social functioning of the addict, transforming his or her motivational system, work habits, sense of values, and family and social relationships. Opiate drugs in particular can have a drastic effect on the physiology and psychology of the dependent, long-term user, altering his or her appetites, judgment and priorities and profoundly affecting lifestyle and how he or she interacts with others and the world.

A well-established, IV addict lifestyle is often chaotic and irresponsible, in large part due to the effects of continued drug use and drug dependence on the personality and character of the individual, rather than to the immediate pharmacological effects of the drug. Such a lifestyle almost invariably entails criminal involvement and usually entails disruption of employment, education and harmonious relationships with the addict's family of origin, their own partner and children and the wider community. Quigley,[16] in a recent study of 332 mainly heroin users attending a community-based methadone treatment service in Dublin, reports that 80% of the males had a conviction and all clients had left school early, while histories of domestic violence, familial sex abuse, teenage sex work, debt, single parenthood and deliberate self-harm were commonly reported. Of course, some of these adversities predated and possibly contributed to drug misuse. Quigley concludes that treatment services 'need to address the endemic and collective nature of addiction processes in the poverty context'. This is a salutary reminder of the complex interactions between *drug, set* and *setting* and, in particular, of the very significant contribution to destructive drug use and other negative outcomes of the individual's family and socio-cultural context.

The addict lifestyle also often leads to the abandonment of health-enhancing practices, such as sport, exercise and balanced diet, and to the far-reaching problem of homelessness. These various adversities and failures to safeguard health and social status tend to accumulate and to promote and exacerbate each other. There is an unfortunate convergence whereby the increasing recklessness and desperation generated by problematic drug use greatly increase the chances of succumbing to the mounting hazards incurred by more dangerous and dependent drug use. This vicious synergy inexorably increases the risk of damage both to the addict and to his or her dependents and wider circle of contacts.

However, while destructive, uncontrolled forms of drug use are clearly the chief danger and main producer of health and social harms, it is reasonable, as we shall see, to conclude that the prohibition regime itself plays a significant role both as a direct cause of specific avoidable risks and, more broadly, because it promotes a climate, in which rash, unsafe behaviours and negative outcomes are far more likely.

Overdose deaths and drug-use-related illnesses

As the U.S. National Academy of Sciences[17] wrote in 2001: 'No responsible analysis of the harmful consequences of drug use can ignore the possibility that many of the harms of drug use are either caused or augmented by the legal prohibition against these drugs and its enforcement. Many (but not all) overdoses occur due to the unknown purity and potency of illegally purchased drugs.' It is a major tragedy that much drug-related mortality and morbidity results from the lack of any kind of reliable quality control of the drugs traded in the unregulated black market and from the consequent ignorance of users about the actual chemical composition of the drugs they are taking. There is an obvious danger of accidental overdose posed by the lack of quality control and by the total absence of reliable information on drug purity. In addition, severe harms such as the loss of limbs, liver damage and septicaemia can be a direct result of the dilution of drugs with adulterants, a practice that criminal dealers pursue in order to enlarge their profits.

Moreover, the inevitable instability of the suppressed black market in drugs means that change in the composition, purity and potency of drugs is the norm and that, therefore, accidental overdose and toxic reactions are ever-present risks. Although certain progressive countries like the Netherlands have introduced quality control testing of stimulant drugs at raves as a form of harm reductionism, even such restricted forms of drug quality monitoring appear to be anathema to the Irish system of prohibition.

Due to the total lack of regulation and quality control in the illegal drugs market, users regularly ingest or inject substances of unknown composition, which are often contaminated with toxic substances. Many drug-related deaths and injuries in Ireland are directly attributable to the user inadvertently taking an excessive or toxic dose. A study of inquests in the Dublin region[18] found that there were 84 opiate-related, unintended deaths between mid-1998 and mid-1999. Most of the deaths involved poly-drug users, 87% had two or more drugs identified toxicologically and three quarters were officially classified as the result of 'drug dependence'. Indicating the extent to which overdose deaths are continuing despite the methadone programme, 45 of the deaths involved use of methadone and, in 15 of these cases, the client had been receiving prescribed methadone according to official guidelines. These cases imply that many clients of methadone programmes do not restrict themselves to quality-controlled drugs provided to them under medical supervision, but continue to use street drugs.

According to a Health Board study[19] there were 119 drug-related deaths in Ireland in 2000, up from 43 in 1995, the year before the sudden, very significant enhancement of harm reductionist interventions. There was a decline to 91 deaths in 2002; yet, while deaths in Dublin may now be decreasing, the study shows they are increasing in the rest of the country, rising from 4 in 1995 to 35 in 2002. Even in Dublin, where there is by far the greatest concentration of treatment and harm reductionist services, deaths are running at a far higher level than in the pre-1996 era.

A study by Byrne[20] of 332 opiate-related deaths recorded by the City and County Coroner's Office between 1998 and 2001 indicated that a hugely disproportionate share of this death toll occurred in drug-ridden, deprived areas. Byrne found that over 90% of those who died resided in the officially designated local task force areas. Byrne also discovered that 26 (or 8%) of all deaths occurred amongst people who had just been released from prison. This suggests that these were what is commonly termed 'hot shot' overdoses. These are overdoses caused by people taking an amount of a drug which would not previously have been dangerous for them, but which was now lethal because they had lost physiological tolerance for the drug over the period of relative deprivation in prison.

The frequency of 'hot shot' deaths reminds us that awareness of risks and knowledge of physiological and other processes, such as the growth and diminution of tolerance, and the willingness to act on such knowledge are also crucial factors in the prevention of overdose deaths. This is an aspect of the causation of overdoses that cannot be ascribed directly to the lack of quality control of drugs caused by prohibition. However, the failure of the prison system to provide effective education and alert prisoners to these serious risks can in part be blamed on the prohibitionist climate prevailing within the prison system.

The unavailability to consumers of reliable information about the content or purity of drugs – information which might save lives – is a direct result of the covert, illegal nature of the trade, which in turn is created by the prohibitionist legal framework. Prohibition also rules out, for legally *proscribed* drugs, the kind of strict surveillance and testing which ensures that medically *prescribed* drugs meet health and safety standards and are provided in carefully calibrated doses. The more enlightened version of prohibition of recent years, whatever its harm-reductive gains, clearly cannot deliver an effective, comprehensive system of quality control of drugs and cannot provide users with reliable information about the content and quality of the drugs they use. This means that many Irish users will continue to die or fall ill from overdoses or toxic contaminants. In short, one of the strongest arguments for the abolition of prohibition is that the regulation and quality control of 'hard' drugs is totally impossible without an effective process of decriminalisation, which succeeds in wresting the drugs trade out of criminal hands and fully regulating it.

Other negative health effects of prohibition

The spread of certain blood-borne diseases like HIV and hepatitis through the sharing of infected needles and syringes, is undoubtedly facilitated by prohibition. As the National Academy of Sciences writes, 'the sharing of contaminated syringes is largely a consequence of the artificial scarcity created by their illegality'.[21] The relatively uncompromising system of prohibition in Ireland before 1996 substantially increased the health harms associated with intravenous drug use by ensuring that IV equipment would not be readily available, except to bona fide health workers. Prohibition promotes the occurrence of disease, abscesses and other injuries not only because it encourages the sharing of inadequately sterilised equipment, but also because, owing to the ubiquitous threat of law enforcement intervention, intravenous drug use is often furtive, hurried, inexpert and unhygienic.

The criminalisation of recreational drug use and prohibition's false message that all drugs and forms of drug use are equally bad is also thought to escalate social and health drug-related harms by encouraging progression to more serious drug habits. Although it is impossible to quantify these effects, it is clear that prohibition places cannabis, ecstasy and other 'soft' drug users in a criminal ambiance and within the orbit of influence of the criminal drugs trader. This unhealthy situation, allied to the influence of misleading prohibitionist propaganda, blurring differences between different drugs and forms of use, may make experimenting with other more dangerous drugs and forms of use more likely. Certainly, the Dutch experiment with the decriminalisation of cannabis, which attempts to reverse this situation, appears to have successfully separated much of the cannabis market from the criminal black market in other drugs, and thereby, while keeping cannabis use at a relatively low level, reduced the number of cannabis users progressing to heroin use.

The inflated price of illegal drugs, caused mainly by prohibition, also plays a role in exacerbating drug-related harms. The need to fund the next fix causes some people to sell sex for money or drugs, thus exposing themselves and others to infection by sexually transmitted diseases. The high price of drugs can also encourage some users to progress to the most cost-effective ways of using drugs, which are usually the most dangerous. For example, they might graduate from smoking or snorting drugs to intravenous use in order to get the 'biggest bang for their buck', thereby greatly increasing the risk of illness and injury. Within controlled environments, like prison, prohibitionist law enforcement is thought to encourage some inmates to substitute heroin for cannabis because the lesser bulk of the former drug makes smuggling easier and detection harder and, in prisons where there is mandatory drug testing, because cannabis remains detectable for longer than heroin.

Very significantly, a prohibitionist, law enforcement-focused approach means that a thick pall of ignorance hangs over the very communities where susceptible young people enthusiastically and uninhibitedly embrace the most dangerous forms of drug use. In disaffected, socially excluded communities, prohibition forges anti-authoritarian drug countercultures, in which mindless indulgence and reckless sensation-seeking flourish. In such countercultures young people fall prey to drugs with hardly a thought given to health risks and with no appreciation whatsoever of the predictable social, economic and psychological effects for the individual of growing tolerance to heroin and eventual compulsive opiate addiction. Prohibition breeds secrecy, anti-authority attitudes, and a climate of ignorance, fatalism and recklessness, which in its turn greatly increases the risks and actual harms of drug use.

The concealment around drug use, which is necessitated by prohibition, promotes ignorance of the risks of dependency and of the various health risks associated with intravenous use, encourages misleading myths about drugs, cloaks drug use in a glorifying mystique and endows drugs with a potent symbolism. For some young people in drugs-ridden communities, drug use can become just another rite of passage into adulthood, another test of courage and daring. Daring to break the law, daring to take heroin, daring to inject are equal forms of display of daring that earn the respect and admiration of peers and definitively prove maturity. The mindless bravado and nonchalance of the exciting early period of drug use often endure beyond the initiation stage, to the extent that dependent long-term users, who are beginning to suffer health problems and to represent a serious risk to others, are slow to take up available treatment services and to adopt the recommended safe use and safe sex protocols. Criminal involvement and the criminal climate created around drugs by prohibition also lead many users to have a suspicion of all authority and to avoid contact with treatment and support services, however non-threatening these might be.

The legacy of pre-1996 Irish prohibition

Ireland's own peculiar version of 'cops plus docs' prohibition can, then, be partly blamed for much of the devastation caused to individuals, families and communities by drug use, especially opiate use, from the late 1970s to the late 1990s, when eventually something approximating an appropriate scale of effective harm reductionist and social justice driven interventions began to materialise. The earlier, more one-sided Irish emphasis on law enforcement was very deleterious and resulted in a merely cosmetic presence for the 'docs' element and prevention programmes in Irish drugs policy. Health, rehabilitation, educational and preventative services were poor or non-existent – with predictably dire consequences for opiate drug users.

In the late 1980s and early 1990s, evidence suggested that the sharing of IV equipment was a major cause of new HIV infections in Ireland. Of the 363 HIV positive cases reported by 1985, 221 (or 61%) were IV drug users.[22] In 1988 and 1989 almost precisely half of all new HIV cases were IV drug users. Probably reflecting the impact of needle exchange (first introduced in 1988) and other harm reductionist programmes, in the period 1994 to 1998 the number of new HIV cases who were IV drug users fell to an average of 22 per annum from a peak of 82 in 1992. For the years 1994–98, injecting drug users constituted less than one fifth of the total of newly diagnosed HIV cases. However, because of the arrival in Ireland in recent years of substantial numbers of sub-Saharan African immigrants, many of who are HIV positive, statistical comparisons have become more complex, particularly with respect to the issue of the relative contribution of different routes of infection. Nevertheless, as we shall see in the next section, alarmingly, since 1998, there has been a surge of new HIV infections amongst IV users.

Of the total of 691 full-blown AIDS cases reported in Ireland to the end of 1999, 280 (or 41%) were IV drug users. While AIDS and HIV have received most public attention, there are many other illnesses associated with the unsafe and unhygienic drug-taking practices, which are in part caused by prohibitionist constraints on access to equipment, information and services. According to the Health Protection Surveillance Centre,[23] studies indicate that the hepatitis C epidemic in Ireland is 'mainly occurring in injecting drug users and is strongly associated with sharing syringes or other drug paraphernalia'. In general, research data suggest that a large majority of Irish IV drug users are positive for hepatitis C.

The criminal justice system has played a particularly pernicious role in the creation and spread of drug-related harms. The early, strong prohibitionist emphasis of Irish policy led to the failure to establish both a custodial treatment centre and effective non-custodial treatments for drug-using offenders. It also led to utterly inadequate treatment facilities for prison inmates. Combined with the system's tendency to imprison drug users only for their non-drug crime and to then largely ignore their addictions, this predominantly 'cops' approach meant that the prison system rapidly became a scandalously damaging location, where drug-related harms, such as hepatitis, HIV, suicide and overdose became highly concentrated. The National Steering Group on Deaths in Prisons[24] reported that there were 11 drug-related deaths in Irish prisons between 1990 and 1997, through overdose or choking on vomit. A 1999 survey[25] of a large representative sample of prison inmates found that 38.5% of all Irish prisoners were infected either with hepatitis B, hepatitis C or HIV. Infection rates were much higher in Dublin prisons and 72% of IV drug users entering the prison system were found to be positive for hepatitis C.

The Director of Prison Medical Services expressed his frustration with the failures of the prohibition-oriented system in his 1999 report.[26] He stated: 'for a considerable number of years previous reports have lamented the failure to adequately address the problems associated with drug abuse among the prison population. The ongoing lack of adequate therapeutic resources allocated to tackling the problem within prisons has become more marked in the context of the large amount of resources being devoted to addressing the problem in the general community, most specifically to those communities which are particularly affected by drug abuse.'

The prison system, co-opted to serve the needs of the Irish system of prohibition, inevitably became the epicentre of the drugs culture in Ireland, playing a major role in the spread of pro-drug attitudes, seriously dangerous forms of drug use and extremely unsafe practices. According to Allwright et al.'s representative survey,[27] 21% of all prisoners who had ever injected drugs first injected drugs in prison. The very institution, prison, which was intended to be the main instrument of general and individual deterrence from drug use, became a hothouse environment, nurturing destructive drug use, unhealthy patterns of behaviour and wildly pro-drug attitudes, which were destined to inexorably spread out from the prison to the prisoners' home communities.

Meanwhile, in the 1980s and early 1990s, prohibitionist attitudes at a political level helped ensure, as Minister Pat Rabbitte[28] finally admitted, that vulnerable communities were left bereft of any meaningful level of assistance. The crucial role of social conditions, especially relative deprivation and inequity, in the generation of both crime and destructive drug use was in theory officially recognised, but until 1996 a preference for law enforcement solutions was allowed to override any inclination to introduce effective social justice driven measures.

Shamefully, the prohibitionist outlook, with its firm focus on drugs interdiction, law enforcement, punishment and deterrence, also meant that for many years the responsible health and other authorities, including the political establishment, could easily evade their duty to respond constructively to the opiate epidemic by claiming that law enforcement was the best way to solve all drug-related problems. The false hope of achieving a drug-free world was allowed to cloud issues and undermine harm reduction and social justice approaches. It is now obvious that Irish prohibition's early promises to solve drug-related problems were empty and served mainly to divert attention and funds from potentially far more effective and constructive approaches.

The effectiveness of post-1996 harm reductionism

Of course, the negative effects of prohibition, which went largely unchecked before 1996, constitute the precise territory of interest to harm reductionists. The harm reductionist approaches, such as needle exchange, education and methadone maintenance, which have been greatly strengthened since 1996, have undoubtedly had a meaningful impact. Clarke et al.,[29] writing in 2001, describe the massive improvement of services, reporting that 'drug treatment services have expanded from 3 locations to over 50 in the last 5 years, with their annual budget increasing ten fold to €22.2 million in the same period'. They also report that needle exchange programmes in Dublin increased from 3 to 13 in the years following 1996. It seems safe to assume that, by pushing back the boundaries of prohibition and enhancing treatment and preventative interventions, the new focus on harm reductionism has substantially alleviated the burden of drug-related harms, especially insofar as those harms are generated or exacerbated by prohibition.

However, despite gains made by the pragmatic prohibition system of recent years, it is still probable that a full-bodied approach to harm reduction, unencumbered by a prohibitionist legal framework, could achieve far more. The ideology and structure of Irish prohibition continue to hamper harm reductionist efforts and still block many potentially beneficial projects, like safe injecting rooms and needle exchange within prisons. To this extent then, there is still considerable harm-reductive ground to be gained by the abolition of prohibition. Furthermore, the continuing and indeed reinvigorated prohibitionist commitment to the suppression of the drugs trade, which is part of the 'balanced' policy of supply/demand reduction, keeps the drugs business firmly in criminal hands. This perpetuates the secretive, drugs counterculture, which continues to promote reckless and ignorant attitudes, anti-social behaviours, unsafe practices and negative outcomes.

Public health and drug user health gains and their limits

Nevertheless, the wider availability of sterile IV equipment and of medically prescribed opiates and society's somewhat more tolerant attitudes towards drug users, which help integrate drug users and gain a hearing from them for messages about preventative practices, have all been important and have, to a degree, promoted more stable and healthy lives. Harm reductionism has lowered the risk of disease and illness for some drug users and probably also the risk of spread of disease to other users and non-users. There is now Irish research which corroborates these conclusions. The first Irish follow-up study of the effectiveness of a syringe exchange programme by Cox et al.[30] reports that these 'programmes can be highly effective as a public health initiative'. They report a reduction in heroin use and significant reductions in the lending and borrowing of injecting equipment.

The results of the Research Outcome Study in Ireland (Rosie[31]), the first national, prospective, longitudinal drug treatment outcome study, also indicate the positive impact of harm reductionist approaches. The study followed up, for a year, 305 opiate users entering various treatment modalities, including methadone maintenance, detoxification and abstinence-aimed programmes. As well as showing significant reductions in the level of criminal involvement, the study reported that the proportion claiming to be abstinent from drugs increased from 7% at intake to 27% at end of Year 1. The proportion reporting continued injecting drug use reduced from 46% at intake to 29% at end of Year 1. The number of days on which non-prescribed 'hard' drugs were used and the amount of such drugs used both generally declined. At follow-up, the users reported a reduction in 5 of 10 physical health symptoms and 7 of 10 mental health symptoms. These are significant gains and it is reasonable to conclude that the investment in harm reductionist approaches mean that prohibition is now contributing less than it formerly did to the creation of drug-related harms.

However, other research findings and underlying trends place even this modest claim in some doubt. Despite the fact that the enhanced harm reductionist approaches since 1996 appear to stabilise the lives of many problem drug users, significantly reduce crime and help a minority to become abstinent, there is mounting evidence that they are far from fully effective at eliminating unsafe practices and halting the spread of disease. Many opiate users expediently exploit the availability of prescribed methadone but continue to use heroin intravenously, usually along with a wide variety of other drugs. In the Rosie study more than half of injecting users were still injecting after a year of treatment. According to the National Drug Treatment Reporting System,[32] 476 of 1,894 current IV drug users (28.8%) undergoing treatment in 2000 were currently sharing equipment. This was only a marginal improvement over 1996 when 30.8% of 1,492 current IV users in treatment were continuing to share.

Many studies confirm the disappointing result that even people who are accessing needle exchange or methadone maintenance programmes continue with unsafe practices. For example, in 2001, Smyth et al.[33] reported that very many IV users in treatment continue to borrow syringes and take other risks to their own and other people's health. They found that 70% reported recent syringe sharing and that 87% shared other drug-injecting paraphernalia. Cox et al. found that 24% of 360 people attending for syringe exchange had used borrowed equipment over the previous 4 weeks and that just under 30% of them had continued to do so during the 3 months of attendance at the service. More than 10% of the 275, who claimed not to have borrowed equipment at entry to the service, admitted to borrowing during the 3 months' follow-up period. Only 38% of the group were careful to use condoms and only 73 of the 222, who were not, had adopted condom use at the 3 months' follow-up.

The more recent figures on HIV infection[34] are starkly discouraging. Statistics clearly indicate that in the late 1990s there was a marked reduction in the number of new HIV cases attributable to IV drug use. This undoubtedly reflects the impact of harm reductionism in that period. However, from 1998 the trend was reversed. In 1998 there were 26 cases; in 1999, 69 cases; and, in 2000, 83 cases. The incidence of new cases fell in 2001, quite dramatically to 38, but has since increased to 50 in 2002; 49 in 2003; 71 in 2004; and 66 in 2005. The most recent figures are not far below the pre-1996 peak figure from 1992, which was 82, and more than three times as many as in the immediate post-1996 years. Long[35] analysed these figures using a rolling 3-year average, which has the effect of smoothing out the year-to-year fluctuations, and concluded that there is 'a true increase in the number of cases'. This raises the very real possibility that expanded needle exchange and methadone maintenance programmes have had only a temporary beneficial effect in this area and that the ready availability of clean injecting equipment and condoms is no longer, if it ever was, sufficient to ensure safe practice.

Unfortunately, the discouraging Irish figures confirm the pessimistic conclusions of an important meta-analytic study[36] of a large number of international evaluations of methadone maintenance programmes. This important study concluded that methadone maintenance 'has a moderate effect in reducing illicit opiate use and drug and property-related criminal behaviours, and a small to moderate effect in reducing HIV risk behaviours'.

The continuing spread of disease amongst IV drug users is even more obvious with respect to hepatitis. A study,[37] published in 2001, well into the period of enhanced harm reductionism, reports on a survey of methadone maintenance clients and found that of those tested for individual viruses, 5.1% were positive for hepatitis B, 78.8% for hepatitis C and 16.7% for HIV. In a more recent paper Smyth et al.[38] report that, in Dublin, about 66% of IV drug users undergoing treatment have hepatitis C infection and inform us that this is high by international standards. These authors report that most of their subjects had a short history of injecting drugs and so it can be presumed that they have become infected during the period of enhanced harm reductionist activity. They also found that those users who reported closer social relationships with other IV drug users were at greater risk of infection. They suggest that this raised risk may be associated with inadvertent sharing of equipment through carelessness or confusion as much as with deliberate sharing.

Clarke et al.,[39] concerned by the apparent evidence for the growing ineffectiveness of harm reductionism and by the continual emergence of new generations of young, ignorant and rash drug users, suggest that 'recent health education regarding HIV transmission, safer sex practices and safer needle sharing activities has become poorly prioritized ... prevention must take a rejuvenated and multidisciplinary approach, akin to the publicity campaigns of the early 1990s, emphasizing both sexual and needle sharing risk practices'.

In order to reduce harm through the adoption of safe practices, it is obviously necessary, in addition to providing access to sterile equipment and condoms, to educate, raise awareness, persuade and motivate. The negative recent Irish results indicate that there are probably strict limits to what can be achieved by harm reductionist interventions working with a population of users with ingrained habits of careless behaviour, which have been acquired in a furtive drugs counterculture shaped by prohibitionist imperatives. Such a culture persists under the current Irish prohibition regime, despite its concessions to harm reductionism, and it is particularly detrimental because of its major impact on young new drug users. The criminal drugs culture is still a potent force, which promotes dangerous injecting use, while simultaneously insulating enthusiastic new opiate recruits from potentially life-saving educational and health messages, at least for the first few crucial years.

Demand reduction

An important epidemiological study[40] of alcohol and drug use in Ireland's second city, Cork, and of counties Cork and Kerry is particularly useful because it was an 8-year follow-up of a near identical study undertaken in the watershed year, 1996. This study period coincides almost exactly with the first 8 years of the new compromise regime of harm reductionist prohibition. This was a quota-controlled household study with randomised starting points and involved 1,512 respondents, aged between 15 and 44 years. Between 1996 and 2004, there was a doubling of the use of cannabis to a lifetime prevalence rate of 32%, with 7% of the sample reporting current use (within the last month).

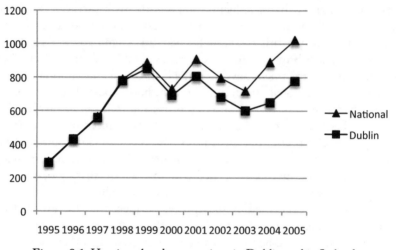

Figure 8.1 Heroin-related prosecutions in Dublin and in Ireland
Source: Garda Annual Reports

The reporting of lifetime use of cocaine increased more than five fold, from 1.1% to 6% over the same 8 years. Lifetime use of crack was 2% and of stimulants, including ecstasy, 10%, with the former increasing about seven-fold and the latter doubling since 1996. Lifetime use of opiates had doubled to 2% with current use increasing from 0.3% to 1%. Lifetime use of any drug was 41% in the city area and 30% in the two county areas, but the rate of increase had been greater in the more rural districts. This is powerful and incontrovertible evidence that, in regard to demand reduction, the new compromise system of prohibition is not winning the 'war on drugs'.

Meanwhile in Dublin, many young people are still being recruited into injecting use. The annual report of the Merchant's Quay Ireland project for 2005[41] reports that their service was used by 450 new, injecting users in that year. An increasing trend is apparent, since this figure was up by 6% on the previous year. The report also points out that, because there is often a considerable time lag between initiation of IV use and accessing treatment services, many of these young, new users engage in unsafe practices in the interim period.

Perhaps most alarmingly, in recent years, opiate use has spread out from the cities to small provincial towns, such as Portloaise, Arklow and Athlone. As Figure 8.1 illustrates, the proportion of prosecutions involving heroin, which arise outside Dublin, has increased significantly in recent years. These towns now have numbers of opiate users, which indicate a proportionately greater problem than in Dublin. In 2006, Ireland's leading television current affairs programme, *Prime Time*,[42] broadcast interviews with local GPs from Athlone and Arklow who stated that there were about 300 opiate users in each of the towns, which have populations, respectively, of 24,000 and 12,000.

In 2007, the National Advisory Committee on Drugs produced a report[43] on cocaine use in Ireland, which strongly confirmed the burgeoning drugs culture. They concluded that 'all the indicators point to a continued increase in cocaine use, that this cocaine use crosses all social strata and that the impact is very much experienced nationwide'.

Crime reduction

There are no recent studies which update the Keogh[44] and Furey and Browne[45] studies on drug-related crime. The decreasing trend in crime in the years following 1996, however, appears to have ceased by 2001. The annual crime figures in Table 8.1 illustrate both the sharp decline in the post-1996 period and the reversal of this trend from 2000. The results from the first series of victimisation studies undertaken in Ireland complement the official crime figures and provide an alternative estimate of the prevalence of crime.[46] These studies surveyed a large representative sample of the adult population on two occasions and show a more than doubling of reports of theft from the person (with and without violence) between 1998 and 2003. The proportion of respondents reporting such thefts increased from 2.1% to 4.3%. On the other hand, as Table 8.1 indicates, the number of homicides did not fall after 1996 and have indeed continued at a high level since 1995. The annual figure for homicides includes many drug gang-related killings.

It appears reasonable to conclude that the remarkable reduction in burglary,

Table 8.1 Trend in reported crime – various categories 1979–2005

Year	Indictable crimes	Homicides	Robberies	Burglaries	Thefts	Thefts from person
1979	64057	29	792	19067	39980	3313
1983	102387	33	2178	35826	58283	5665
1990	87658	27	1646	29087	50222	4495
1995	102484	53	2624	32470	57123	7111
1996	100785	46	3357	31394	55041	6983
1997	90875	53	2558	28648	48390	6172
1998	85627	51	1892	26587	46127	5188
1999	81274	36	1304	18060	33524	3374
2000	73276	56	2662	22158	39539	3894
2001	86633	58	1744	24015	45652	4720
2002	106415	59	2939	25602	58180	6144
2003	103360	52	2794	25733	57870	6669
2004	98964	45	2617	24753	55510	5714
2005	101659	59	2341	26400	56364	4674

Source: Garda Annual Reports

robbery and theft, year on year from 1995 to 1999, is at least in part due to the
stabilising effects on drug using, acquisitive offenders of the rapidly expanding
methadone maintenance scheme. But as the figures make clear this period of
significant reduction in acquisitive crime appears to have come to a halt in
2000. Since that year the incidence of these crimes has began to climb back
to the sort of levels prevailing in 1995. This does not necessarily mean that
the same people, who reduced their involvement in crime after joining the
methadone maintenance programme, later returned to crime or escalated their
criminal involvement, though a considerable number may have. There have
been many new recruits to opiate and poly-drug use in recent years, who tend
to avoid treatment for a substantial period and are likely to become involved
in 'economic compulsive' crime.

For a number of years following 1996, crime reduction, attributable to
harm reductionist interventions, appears to have been substantial. Methadone maintenance programmes in particular almost certainly permanently
reduce the aggregate amount of crime undertaken by their clients. However,
it is clear that the most serious and violent forms of 'systemic' drug-related
crime, including murder, have not decreased since 1996. The criminal black
market has continued to flourish and indeed expand and it is very likely that
an increased amount of 'systemic' crime connected with the importation and
distribution of drugs is occurring, though undetected and thus not reflected
in official figures. Some at least of the increase in acquisitive crime since 1999
can be attributed to new drug-using offenders who avoid treatment and to the
continuing criminal involvement of people on methadone maintenance who
have persisted in or returned to using street drugs. The crime-reductive benefits of the post-1996 compromise system of prohibition, then, would appear to
be mainly limited to acquisitive crime and to have been largely exhausted.

The inadvertent negative effects of harm reductionism

An objective appraisal of the current system of prohibition, which works hand
in hand with harm reductionism, must lead to the conclusion that the results
are at best mixed. It is probable that the most substantial benefit has been in
the reduction of acquisitive drug-related crime in the immediate post-1996
years. But, the raised public awareness, galvanised political attention, huge
investment, expanded services and new climate of optimism of the mid-1990s
also led to initial, significant gains in the reduction of health risk behaviours. However, the cumulative evidence now indicates that these may not be
enduring net gains.

Harm reductionists can, of course, point to continuing failures in the
management and provision of services and necessary supports such as public
health promotional campaigns. So, for example, there is criticism of the failure
to set up needle exchange projects in local areas and to provide comprehensive, intensive outreach programmes. In many areas, there are still very long

waiting lists for treatment programmes. 'Nimbyism', that is local resistance to the setting up of treatment centres in a particular neighbourhood, remains a potent force blocking the development of services, especially in provincial towns. There is no doubt that the effectiveness of harm reductionist measures could be increased in various ways, for example through the better integration of services. However, the fact remains that, while the current compromise system of prohibition can no longer be accused of ignoring and thus multiplying the risks of IV drug use, it is far from an optimal solution.

It would not be outlandish, at this juncture, for prohibitionist critics to turn the tables on harm reductionists and suggest that harm reductionism is now causing more harm than it prevents. After all, it is reasonable to argue that the appreciable but limited benefits of current harm reductionist interventions have to be weighed in the balance against the normalising effects of programmes such as methadone maintenance, which, according to the conventional prohibitionist objection, 'send out the wrong message' and tend to increase the general acceptability of drug use and thus potentially increase its prevalence.

Although definitive figures are not available, it is clear that young people are still being recruited into opiate and IV drug use in large numbers. The more widespread physical availability of methadone and injecting equipment in society might play some part, along with changing social attitudes, in the continuing spread of IV opiate use. Of great concern is the fact that young people are initiating IV drug use both in local drug task force areas, despite their very active and well-resourced preventative, educational and treatment services,[47] and in provincial towns, which lack services and the large areas of concentrated deprivation and disadvantage of the kind that played such a key role in the original heroin epidemic in Dublin. The data on provincial towns suggest there may be a spread of opiate use to social classes which had previously avoided it. It also suggests that opiate use is being propagated by a form of social contagion in which *set*, that is factors relating to the susceptibility of the individual personality, such as a proclivity for sensation-seeking, educational failure or emotional maladjustment, may be of increasing significance relative to *setting*, that is social and cultural contextual factors, particularly socio-economic disadvantage, which were so central in the original opiate epidemic.

The provision of free opiates to many thousands of users undoubtedly has an economic impact on the black market in drugs. A certain amount of legally prescribed methadone inevitably becomes available for sale on the black market. The competition from free and traded methadone is likely to place downward pressure on the price of heroin supplied by criminal dealers. This may be part of the explanation for the continuing availability of comparatively cheap heroin. Despite the costs inflicted on criminal dealers by law enforcement, including seizures and confiscation of profits, the profit margins established by criminal dealers are so great that they can substantially reduce prices without endangering the viability of their business. Similarly, the competition from the provision of free methadone may well stimulate a drive by drug pushers to recruit new young heroin users or to spread into new markets such as the provincial towns.

Harm reductionist interventions inevitably normalise opiate use and make it more visible in society, perhaps thereby lowering the barriers to experimentation for those who previously would have been deterred by fear, prudential self-interest or respect for the law or who would simply not have come across opportunities for opiate use in their normal walk of life. If harm reductionist interventions tend to normalise opiate use, they tend to doubly normalise relatively non-problematic 'recreational' use of drugs such as cannabis, ecstasy and even cocaine. If opiate use is now in one sense 'acceptable', surely it is no longer possible to object to non-problematic use of 'recreational' drugs. 'Recreational' drug users can now argue that their drug use should be tolerated and should not be a matter of concern for the law, because heroin addicts are no longer harassed by the law but, on the contrary, supplied with opiates by the government itself.

The ultimate aim of prohibition is to reduce the prevalence of all illicit drugs and to curb the growth of the drugs culture. It is, therefore, reasonable to suggest that, from the prohibitionist perspective, the new system of relatively peaceful coexistence between prohibition and harm reductionism may, indeed, be seriously counterproductive, because it fosters the growth of social attitudes and social conditions which promote the spread of 'recreational' drug use and, also probably, of 'hard' drug use, while failing to eliminate the unsafe practices of many IV drug users.

Of course, while prohibitionists might argue that what is required is a return to stricter prohibition and tougher law enforcement approaches, this is no longer a viable political option. The compromise with harm reductionism has not solved the problems of prohibition, but this cannot be regarded as an endorsement of prohibition, which has already been proven to be a disastrous policy. A return to more rigorous prohibition is unthinkable, on the one hand, because it would involve the abandonment of harm reductionist programmes of limited, but clear and appreciable, benefit and, on the other, because it would involve the knowing, cynical adoption of policies which would definitely increase health risks.

Summary

Opponents of prohibition must be careful to distinguish the harm caused by the system of prohibition from the inevitable harm of drug use itself. A first problem, which is conclusively attributable to prohibition, is that it creates a raft of new drug-related crimes and so criminalises many citizens, most of whom are law-abiding apart from their drug use. In Ireland, unlike in the U.S., very few drug users are sent to prison merely for drug-using crimes, such as possession for personal use. In Ireland, the kind of disproportionate harm and stigma caused to drug users by easy and frequent resort to incarceration is generally avoided. Similarly, the immense financial and operational burdens of a prison system, which is ever-expanding in order to accommodate mere drug users, are also avoided. Nevertheless, criminalisation of a large proportion of the population, even if it is largely nominal, is a serious problem, because it creates strain between citizens and the authorities and because unenforceable or unenforced laws bring the law itself into disrepute.

While few people are imprisoned for mere possession of small amounts of drugs, the prison system has expanded enormously since the arrival of opiate use in Ireland, mainly in order to hold people involved in drug-related, acquisitive, 'economic compulsive' crime. The criminal justice system has become harsher throughout the period of the 'war on drugs'. This is apparent both in the greater use of imprisonment and in the many new restrictions on fundamental legal protections for an accused. These measures have been mainly targeted at drug dealers but there is evidence of a creeping erosion of civil liberties and a strengthening of police powers, which weaken the position of all citizens in their dealings with the state. These serious costs of the 'war on drugs' have been suffered without proof of counterbalancing gains, since very few of the new measures, apart from the Criminal Assets Bureau, have proven effective against serious drug criminals.

Ireland, as a fully compliant signatory to global prohibition, cannot simply ignore the harm, in terms of poverty, hardship, corruption, violence and political disorder, caused by the U.S.-inspired programme of supply control in many drug-crop-producing third world and developing nations. Nor should Ireland excuse itself entirely from culpability for the many human rights abuses perpetrated in the name of the 'war on drugs' by the U.S. and its political allies in drug-producing countries. In Ireland itself, the 'war on drugs' has increased the already marked and unfair concentration on the criminal wrongs of the poorest sectors of society. The 'war on drugs' has also probably exacerbated the social exclusion of those people in the Irish underclass and in the new immigrant minority groups who happen to get caught up in drug use.

Another problem of prohibition is acquisitive crime undertaken to pay for drugs. It is reasonable to attribute a very large proportion of the property crime of the last quarter-century in Dublin to the opiate epidemic. However, it would be unreasonable to attribute this crime mainly to the system of prohibition itself rather than to opiate drug use. Prohibition did not prevent the opiate epidemic, but nor did it directly cause it. The opiate epidemic almost exclusively hit deprived, marginalised communities, which contained many people who would have been involved in property crime, regardless of their drug use. Intravenous opiate drug use creates desperate cravings for the next fix, can have a drastic effect on people's value system and can cut people off from ways to make legitimate income. Opiate drug use itself can, therefore, make crime far more likely. However, the fact that drug use was criminalised by the prohibition system probably eased the path of the opiate drug user into 'economic compulsive' crime, including many who, despite their background, might otherwise have avoided crime.

Moreover, prohibition clearly facilitates the pushing of heroin by inevitably involving criminal dealers, who are driven entirely by financial motives and utterly unaccountable. These criminals cloak their activities in secrecy and so are able to recommend the joys of drug use but at the same time keep people ignorant of dangers, such as the tolerance process, the physical withdrawal syndrome and the numerous risks to physical and mental health. While prohibition did not cause the opiate epidemic, it involved pushers and users in the surreptitious spread of drug use, allowing ignorance and myth to play an influential role. Prohibition in this way enabled opiate use to rapidly gain a firm grip on Dublin's most marginalised communities and to spread in a wanton and dangerous manner.

The totally unregulated monopoly created by prohibition is a direct influence on acquisitive crime. Criminal drugs traders, because they are free to, inevitably choose to make obscene profits. Because this profit-taking makes drugs unnecessarily expensive and because of the rapid growth of tolerance to opiates, an opiate habit quickly develops to the point where it costs hundreds of euro a week. This level of expenditure forces many users into inordinately prolific, property crime. In addition, prohibition was and remains a necessary precondition for the violent gang culture which now thrives in Ireland. This gangland lifestyle, fuelled by the immense profits of an illegal drugs trade probably worth in excess of €1 billion a year, has evolved over 25 years and has now embraced a vicious gun culture reminiscent of prohibition era Chicago or modern American ghettos.

Most drug-related social and health harms are the direct product of problematic drug use and particularly of dangerous and reckless forms of drug use, such as sharing syringes and needles. However, prohibition ensures that there is a lack of quality control of drugs traded in the black market. The unknown purity of heroin and the contaminants mixed in with various drugs are direct, though not the sole, causes of most of the overdose deaths and many of the injuries and illnesses associated with drug use. Prohibition promotes social and health drug-related harms in a myriad of ways, such as making clean syringes scarce and scaring people away from treatment and educational services. Perhaps most importantly, prohibition forges criminal, anti-authoritarian drug countercultures, which breed the kind of ignorance, fatalism and recklessness that greatly increases the risks and actual harms of drug use.

The stricter form of prohibition in place in Ireland prior to 1996 made a substantial contribution to serious health harms such as the spread of HIV and hepatitis C. The failure of the criminal justice and health systems and the political system generally to rise to the challenges of drugs meant that the prison system became the epicentre of a virulent pro-drugs culture, notable for its embrace of reckless hedonism and mindless risk. Since 1996 there has been massive investment in forms of harm reductionism that are specifically designed to ameliorate the harms caused by prohibition – for example, needle exchange which tackles the previous problem of restricted access to clean syringes. While harm reductionism initially appeared to impact significantly on crime and social and health harms, more recent evidence suggests that these positive effects may be waning. Moreover, harm reductionist approaches are still seriously hampered by the prohibitionist legal framework and by prohibitionist social attitudes. A case can be made that the normalising effects of harm reductionism have strengthened the drugs culture in Ireland and increased the prevalence of drug use generally. The post-1996 pragmatic prohibition has certainly failed to halt recruitment to IV heroin use and failed to eliminate risky drug-related behaviours. Also, over the last 10 years, cocaine use and recreational drug use generally have become increasingly common and are now by no means restricted to specific classes or groups of people or areas of the country.

Notes

1 Nadelman, E. (1989) 'Drug prohibition in the United States: costs, consequences and alternatives', *Science*, 245, at 939.
2 For an interesting Irish perspective on these issues see King, P. (2003) *The Politics of Drugs from Production to Consumption*, Dublin: Liffey Press.
3 Husak, D. and de Marneffe, P. (2005) *The Legalization of Drugs*, New York: Cambridge University Press at page 94. This book is co-authored but it is in two separate sections, which are the unique work of in turn Husak and de Marneffe.
4 Olson, J., Executive Director, Washington Office on Latin America, *Addicted to Failure*, report before U.S. House of Representatives Subcommittee on the Western Hemisphere (30 March 2006).
5 Special Committee on Drugs and the Law (1994) *A Wiser Course: Ending Drug Prohibition*, New York: Association of the Bar of the City of New York.
6 For a description and analysis of the erosion of legal safeguards in the U.S. see *Assessing the New Normal* (2003) New York: Lawyers Committee for Human Rights.
7 Husak, *The Legalization of Drugs*.
8 O'Mahony, P. (1997) *Mountjoy Prisoners: A Sociological and Criminological Profile*, Dublin: Stationery Office.
9 Institute of Criminology, UCD (2006) *A Study of Offender Recidivism in Ireland*, Dublin: University College Dublin.
10 O'Malley, T. in a paper presented to the National Conference of Prosecutors (Dublin, 19 May 2007) described his study of a series of 100 trials of drug dealers stating that 65% were small-time dealers making less than €1,000 from a transaction and only 5% could be considered major dealers making substantial profits. Nonetheless similar long sentences were imposed for markedly different offences in terms of the value of drugs involved and the level of participation of the accused.
11 Irish Human Rights Commission (2006) *Observations on Additional Proposals for Amendments to the Criminal Justice Bill 2004*, Dublin: IHRC.

12 For an overview see O'Mahony, P. (2000) *Prison Policy in Ireland: Social Justice versus Criminal Justice*, Cork: Cork University Press.

13 Keogh, E. (1997) *Illicit Drug Use and Related Criminal Activity in the Dublin Metropolitan Area*, Dublin: Garda Headquarters.

14 Furey, M. and Browne, C. (2003) *Opiate Use and Related Criminal Activity in Ireland, 2000 & 2001*, Templemore: Garda Research Unit.

15 Haller, M. (1989) 'Bootlegging: the business and politics of violence' in (ed.Gurr, T.) *Violence in America Vol.1*, California: Sage.

16 Quigley, P. (2002) 'Family and community burdens of addiction: case-mix analysis at a new community-based methadone treatment service', *Drugs: Education, Prevention and Policy*, 9, 3, at 221–231.

17 U.S. National Academy of Sciences, *Informing America's Policy on Illegal Drugs: What We Don't Know Keeps Hurting Us* (2001) Washington, D.C.: U.S. National Academy of Sciences.

18 Ward, M. and Barry, J. (2001) 'Opiate-related deaths in Dublin', *Irish Journal of Medical Science*, 170, 1, at 35–37.

19 Long, J., Lynn, E. and Keating, J. (2005) *Drug-related Deaths in Ireland 1990–2002*, Dublin: Health Research Board.

20 Byrne, R. (2001) *Opiate-related deaths investigated by the Dublin City and County Coroners 1998 to 2000*, Dublin: Addiction Research Centre, TCD.

21 U.S. National Academy of Sciences, *Informing America's Policy on Illegal Drugs*.

22 The figures are from Kelly, G. and Clarke, S. (2000) 'Has there been a turning point in the numbers of AIDS and HIV antibody positive cases in Ireland?', *Irish Journal of Medical Science,* 169, 3, at 183–186.

23 Health Protection Surveillance Centre, Annual Report for 2004, Dublin: Department of Health and Children.

24 National Steering Group on Deaths in Prisons (1999) Report Dublin: Stationery Office.

25 Allwright, S., Barry, J., Bradley, F., Long, J. and Thornton, L. (1999) *Hepatitis B, Hepatitis C and HIV in Irish Prisoners: Prevalence and Risk*, Dublin: Stationery Office.

26 Director of Medical Services for the Irish Prisons Service (1999) *Report*, Dublin: Department of Justice.

27 Allwright et al., *Hepatitis B, Hepatitis C and HIV in Irish Prisoners*.

28 Rabitte reports (1996) *First Report of the Ministerial Task Force on Measures to Reduce the Demand for Drugs* and (1997) *Second Report of the Ministerial Task Force on Measures to Reduce the Demand for Drugs*, Dublin: Stationery Office.

29 Clarke, S., Keenan, E., Bergin, C., Lyons, F., Hopkins, S. and Mulcahy, F. (2001) 'The changing epidemiology of HIV infection in injecting drug users in Dublin, Ireland', *HIV Medicine*, 2, 4, at 86–89.

30 Cox, G., Cassin, S., Lawless, M. and Geoghegan, T. (2006) 'Syringe exchanges: a public health response to problem drug use', *Irish Medical Journal*, 99, at 7.

31 Cox, G., Comiskey, C., Kelly, P. and Cronly, J. (2006*) ROSIE Findings 1: Summary of 1-Year Outcomes*, Dublin: National Advisory Committee on Drugs.

32 *Trends in Treated Drug Misuse in the Republic of Ireland 1996–2000* (2003) Dublin: Health Research Board.

33 Smyth, B., Barry, J. and Keenan, E. (2001) 'Syringe borrowing persists in Dublin despite harm reduction interventions', *Addiction*, 96, 5, at 717–727.

34 Health Protection Surveillance Centre, Annual Reports, Dublin: Department of Health and Children.

35 Long, J. (2006) 'New data on the Incidence of HIV', *drugnet*:Ireland, 19, at 24, Dublin: Health Research Board.

36 Marsch, L. (1998) 'The efficacy of methadone maintenance interventions in reducing illicit opiate use, HIV risk behaviour and criminality: a meta-analysis', *Addiction*, 93, 4, at 515–532.

37 Fitzgerald, M., Barry, J., O'Sullivan, P. and Thornton, L. (2001) 'Blood-borne infections in Dublin's opiate users', *Irish Journal of Medical Science*, 170, 1, at 32–34.

38 Smyth, B., Barry, J. and Keenan, E. (2005) 'Irish injecting drug users and hepatitis C: the importance of the social setting of injecting', *International Journal of Epidemiology*, 34, at 166–172.

39 Clarke et al., 'The changing epidemiology of HIV infection'.

40 Jackson, T. (2006) *Smoking, Alcohol and Drug Use in Cork and Kerry, 2004*, Cork: Department of Public Health, Health Service Executive South.

41 *MQI Annual Report for 2005* (2006) Dublin: Merchant's Quay Ireland.

42 RTE's *Prime Time* programme (26 September 2006).

43 National Advisory Committee on Drugs (2007) *An Overview of Cocaine Use in Ireland: II*, Dublin: Stationery Office.

44 Keogh, E. (1997) *Illicit Drug Use and Related Criminal Activity in the Dublin Metropolitan Area*, Dublin: Garda Headquarters.

45 Furey and Browne, *Opiate Use and Related Criminal Activity*.

46 *Quarterly National Household Survey: Crime and Victimisation in 1998 and 2003* (2004) Dublin: Central Statistics Office.

47 Smith et al. (2001) 'Syringe borrowing'.

9

The seductive folly of prohibition

Answering the three key questions

At the beginning of Chapter 7, I posed three questions. The first question was: Has prohibition as a legal framework succeeded? After almost 100 years in the U.S. and over 30 years in Ireland of quite rigorous repression of illicit drugs, it is blatantly obvious that prohibition has utterly failed to achieve its most important objectives. The raison d'être of prohibition is to prevent all illicit drug use and, therefore, as a necessary step, to avoid the growth of positive attitudes towards drug use amongst young people. However, the prohibition regime has actually overseen and, very probably, actively contributed to a remarkable increase in drug use and to ever more widespread attitudes favourable to drug use.

Prohibition was a necessary precondition for the creation of the current viciously violent and obscenely wealthy drugs gang culture in Ireland. Prohibition has also significantly accelerated the rate of growth of predatory acquisitive crime. Prohibition has directly contributed to or seriously aggravated many health and social harms. The answer to the first question, then, is unequivocal. Prohibition as a legal framework has not succeeded. On the contrary, it has failed catastrophically in its own terms.

The second question asked whether the current 'cops plus docs' compromise in Ireland between prohibition and harm reductionism is working. The answer to this question cannot be nearly as definite, but it is clearly in the negative. While the new coalition of prohibition and harm reductionism can be reckoned a partial success and while it is probably, in harm-reductive terms, an improvement on the more one-sided prohibition that preceded it, there are considerable grounds for the view that the current, more 'balanced' approach is disappointing in its results and falls far short of expectations. The compromise approach reduces some harms, but often only marginally or temporarily. On the other hand, there is evidence that the current approach is creating or contributing to new harms. The inherent flaws and severe disadvantages of the new pragmatic form of prohibition are becoming increasingly apparent and are seriously alarming and discouraging.

However, it is reasonable to whole-heartedly endorse one aspect of the new approach, an aspect which is not strongly connected to prohibitionist ideology and so was not dealt with in the previous chapter. This is the new level of investment in actions that alleviate deprivation and social marginalisation. Given the causal role of deprivation and social exclusion in both crime and more destructive forms of drug use, the introduction, as part of the new compromise between prohibition and harm reduction, of relatively large-scale social justice and social inclusion driven projects in education, training for employment, the enhancement of social housing estates and youth facilities is hugely significant.[1] In fact, a strong case can be made that social inclusion programmes have a positive potential for the reduction of drug-related harm of all kinds, irrespective of the shape and direction of drugs policy. This is to suggest that these programmes are so crucial and potentially so powerful that they will be beneficial whether or not prohibition remains the fundamental framework.

Leaving aside these very welcome developments in the area of social inclusion, which are warranted for all sorts of reasons apart from the prevention of drug misuse, a measured evaluation of the current compromise between prohibition and harm reductionism must conclude that, despite its limited successes, it is by and large a dysfunctional arrangement. It is failing to deliver on both prohibitionist and harm reductionist goals. Astonishingly, given the utter failure of prohibition in its own terms and the increasingly obvious deficiencies of the current 'cops plus docs' compromise, the political and popular support for prohibition appears undiminished.

The third question posed in Chapter 7 was: is there now a case for a radical change in drugs policy, for the total abolition of drugs prohibition? The manifest failures of prohibition, described in the last chapter, might seem to render the answer to this question a foregone conclusion. But this is far from the case. In fact, the prohibitionist establishment in Ireland and elsewhere has a very blinkered and sanguine view of the evidence against prohibition and tends to shrug off all criticism. This impunity of prohibition to attack needs to be understood and addressed since it is a serious impediment to radical change in drugs policy.

But the case for radical change cannot be conclusive in a situation where the effects of abolition remain largely speculative and untested. The ill-effects of prohibition are well known and obviously grave, but we must be reasonably sure that they can be removed by abolition before embracing that approach. Commitment to abolition is a moral, political and practical matter of the highest moment and in making the case for abolition due regard must be paid to all the evidence. It is necessary to weigh potential risks and benefits in the balance and radical change cannot be justified unless substantial net benefits can be reliably anticipated. The final chapter of this book will summarise the case for abolition based on analysis of the relevant facts and on a realistic assessment of how abolition might unfold. It will also outline what these considerations tell us about the kind of abolition that is required.

However, before proceeding to this task, I believe it is necessary to address in some depth prohibition's defences and its imperviousness to the powerful evidence of its own failure. The obliviousness of prohibition to counterevidence is in itself an important phenomenon and a daunting barrier for the abolitionist. If the anti-prohibitionist argument is not heard, it cannot prevail, however cogent and persuasive it might be. Like some of the more successful political leaders, prohibition appears to be Teflon-coated. It is necessary to scrape holes in prohibition's Teflon shield in order to get even the most irrefutable criticisms to stick. This chapter will examine and critically analyse the seductive power of prohibition and its impunity to even well-founded attack. I will first examine the faith-based nature of prohibition and then go on to critique, in turn, the key assumptions of this faith, the prohibitionist exploitation of the concept of drug-related harm, the other rhetorical defences of prohibition and its counterattacks on abolition. Finally, I will examine and call into question some further strategic advantages of prohibition, which underpin its current dominance, as well as the specific defences available to Irish prohibition since the introduction of extensive harm reductionist approaches in 1996.

Prohibition as a faith-based belief system

Barbara Tuchman has described how enormous prior investment in an enterprise together with the incurring of mounting losses can, paradoxically, propel people, organisations and nations to ever greater commitment to a hopeless, failing cause.[2] The more costly the cause and the more obvious the failure, the blinder people become to reality and the more willing they are to expend ever greater resources to prove the rightness of their cause. People, especially powerful people who might lose face, are extremely reluctant to accept the 'appalling vista' that the whole endeavour to which they have made such a major commitment might be a futile, wasteful, dreadful mistake. Prohibition has failed catastrophically and appears to be just such an expensive and mistaken, hopeless cause. As Szasz remarks, 'the failure of [prohibitionist] measures to curb the 'drug menace' has only served to inflame our legislators' enthusiasm for them'.[3] The 'war on drugs', despite its ever-increasing economic, social and human costs, is still pursued, especially in the U.S., with eagerness, self-righteousness and apparently unshakeable self-belief. The group psychology of expensive failure – the stubborn loyalty to a lost cause – accounts for some of prohibition's blindness to counterevidence. Even more important, however, is the fact that prohibition has become a self-confirming ideology, a fundamentalist belief system, which routinely ignores all alternate views of drug problems.

At present, in Ireland, the anti-prohibitionist case is not heard or is prematurely dismissed, without proper examination. Similarly in the U.S., Nadelman reports that repealing the drug prohibition laws is an option that is 'repeatedly and vociferously dismissed without any attempt to evaluate it openly and objectively.'[4] The abolitionist view is often rejected out of hand and ridiculed as the absurd ramblings of professional dissenters, drug-heads or misguided cranks. Prohibition, it appears, has wrapped itself in what philosopher Daniel Dennett[5] has called a 'veil of systematic invulnerability to disproof'. Dennett used this phrase to describe forms of religious belief, but there can be little doubt that the kind of prohibitionism, espoused by the U.S. government, the UN and, in a somewhat diluted version, the Irish government, has many of the hallmarks of an extreme, fundamentalist system of faith.

Faith, according to Richard Dawkins,[6] is belief without adequate evidence – a deep, unwavering commitment to a particular set of propositions, generated and sustained more by the satisfactions of faith itself than by objective evidence. Faith self-constructs a near impregnable citadel of belief. The faith-based character of prohibition is demonstrated by its extraordinary indifference to disproof and its utter conviction in its own truth, regardless of the evidence. These characteristics are typical, indeed definitive, of belief systems, which rely on the power of faith. Many religions and absolutist political creeds, like Soviet Marxism or Maoism, demand faith and insist on the unchallengeable authority of their own holy writ. Prohibitionism appears to share this unquestioning, credulous attitude towards its own assumptions.

Also typical of the faith-based approach, is the confident assertion by prohibitionists that prohibition is self-evidently correct and merely a matter of common sense values. In its uncanny capacity to prevail despite disastrous failure, prohibition appears to possess the monolithic stature of an immutable law of nature or of a fundamental truth. Another familiar characteristic of faith-based systems, exemplified in prohibitionism, is the tendency of the faithful to disregard the views of the non-believer. The faithful regard faithfulness as a virtue in its own right, distinguish friend from foe by where they stand on key articles of faith, tend to cling together and despise unbelievers. They even tend to question the right of the non-believer to hold or express views, which conflict with their 'holy' doctrine. Accordingly, in Ireland, we have seen prohibitionists becoming increasingly intolerant of the expression of anti-prohibition views.[7]

Perhaps the clearest proof that prohibitionism wears a 'veil of systematic invulnerability to disproof', however, is to be found in prohibition's tendency to engage with people through emotion rather than reason. This is especially obvious in prohibition's 'war on drugs' rhetoric. The faith-based nature of prohibition is highly conducive to the development of an emotive, 'war on drugs' rhetoric. As in a genuine war or in the religious war against evil, the 'war on drugs' deploys a rallying rhetoric, which identifies and demonises the enemy and demands the loyal, unquestioning support of all believers. In particular prohibition provokes, manipulates and exploits anxiety, fear and self-righteous anger.

In the 'holy war' against the evil of drugs, there is little room for rational argument and mere criticism can easily be counted treasonable heresy. The critic of prohibition is often portrayed as a traitor to the cause and regarded as deservedly silenced, because he or she perversely offers solace to the self-evident enemy. This rhetoric is fuelled by the passion and moral certainty generated by faith and the rhetoric in its turn reinforces faith and further inflames emotions. Impassioned, 'war on drugs' rhetoric, then, plays on emotions and typically succeeds in creating a deep, but unexamined emotional attachment to the idea of prohibition as a morally sanctified doctrine. At the same time it engenders a closed, irrational mindset, which totally rules out any possibility that prohibition might be mistaken.

The first important step, then, towards a more rational drugs policy must be a less emotional and less absolutist way of thinking and talking about the problems posed by drugs. This first step requires the prohibitionist to set aside the powerful, but ill-founded and misleading 'war on drugs' rhetoric. It requires him or her to step outside the preprogrammed mindset of the prohibitionist faith for long enough to engage in sincere discussion of the merits and demerits of the evidence and arguments. Undoubtedly, in the case of many committed prohibitionists, this is a tall order akin to engineering a religious conversion or, more aptly, to deprogramming a cult member. The problem is not that there is an element of faith in prohibition, since faith will always be a component of any conceptual system, which has implications for how we *ought* to behave and which deals with values as well as facts. Indeed, according to Kuhn,[8] there is even an element of faith in major scientific theories, including those that claim to describe strictly observable material reality. The problem is that the prohibitionist faith has become a self-vindicating, self-perpetuating ideology and is so deeply emotional and so entangled in incoherent 'war on drugs' rhetoric that it mandates the casual dismissal of contrary evidence and sustains an entirely false optimism about the effectiveness of prohibition.

The faith-based, emotionally engaged nature of prohibitionism is a significant part of its seductive power and its ability to establish and maintain political dominance. Drugs issues are difficult, complex and extremely anxiety-provoking. The prohibitionist faith offers considerable emotional comfort and, because it greatly simplifies matters, replaces doubt and moral ambiguity with a kind of certainty. However, by the same token, a highly seductive, faith-based system like prohibition exposes the believer to the folly of ignoring objective evidence. The blindly faithful prohibitionist runs the risk of sacrificing the broader truth for a narrow, questionable 'certainty'. Prohibition's inability to take its own manifest failures seriously is not only a telling sign that it has become a faith-based, 'infallible' ideology, but also the most unfortunate result of this process. That prohibition is a faith in this quasi-religious sense is a major impediment for abolitionists, who cannot rely on an attentive, fair-minded hearing for their arguments.

The immorality of drug use?

Prohibition's basic assumptions and drug-related harm

People's strong faith in prohibition provides it with a virtually impenetrable suit of armour, but prohibition also has many formidable, offensive weapons at its disposal for defence against abolitionist attack. Not least amongst these are the key articles of faith, which establish, in many people's view, a more than credible foundation for prohibition. At the core of the prohibitionist faith and constituting its basic dogma are two ideological assumptions: 1) that the use of illicit drugs is a harmful evil or moral wrong that deserves to be punished with society's strongest weapon, the criminal justice system; and 2) that prohibition can rid the world of the harms and evils of illicit drugs. These are potent, transformative ideas with enormous emotional appeal to almost everyone, who is aware of the appalling damage produced by drug use and wants something done about it. These two core ideas are strongly conducive of faith but also are compelling and seductive in their own right. At one and the same time they launch a law enforcement campaign against well-known wrongs and an emotive, moral crusade against feared evils. In order to pierce the sturdy armour of the prohibitionist faith it is not sufficient to simply point out the folly of a faith that ignores powerful, objective evidence; it is also necessary to critique and refute these two core assumptions, which constitute the fundamental doctrine of prohibition.

The issue of the harm and immorality of drugs is obviously crucial to the debate on prohibition and this issue has many traps for the opponents of prohibition. Prohibition commandeers the fear and moral disapproval aroused by drug-related ills and turns them against drug use itself. At every turn, prohibitionists attempt to blur the line between drug use and the serious ills linked to drug use. Prohibitionists are also at pains to identify any and every health-related harm associated with drug use. Simply by debating the purported harms of drug use, the anti-prohibitionist runs the risk of appearing to concede that, if these harms are proven, then drug use must automatically be deemed wrong and deserving of punishment.

There are undoubtedly drug-related evils, which all right-thinking people would wish to prevent. Drug-related harms constitute one of the most serious scourges of developed societies. Much drug use is not victimless. For example, women who continue to use cocaine (or alcohol) while pregnant can cause physical and neurological damage to their babies.[9] Many drug users make victims of themselves. Or to take another tragic example, in December 2006, the bodies of five young female prostitutes were found in the Ipswich area of Suffolk, England, leaving their families devastated. All of these young women had an opiate addiction and all of them had become sex workers primarily to feed their drug habit. The parents of one of these murdered girls publicly declared that their daughter had been a normal, intelligent girl doing well in life until they had 'lost her to heroin hell'. Who would not sympathise with these parents? Who would not understand, if these parents responded to the horrific consequences of heroin addiction for their daughter – the degradation of selling sex to fund her drug habit and her eventual awful death at the hands of a callous murderer – by urging tough law enforcement action against all illicit drug use? It is unsurprising that many of the victims of drugs and the friends and relatives of victims have a strong prohibitionist outlook.

The ordinary young woman with a bright future, whose drug use led her to prostitution and death, was a victim of drugs but also, crucially, a victim of the far too easily made conflation of drug use with serious drug use harm. Arguably, she was a victim of the system of prohibition that this confused thinking supports. In fact, if drug use had not been criminalised and the pernicious effects of prohibition on the drugs market and on attitudes to and knowledge about drugs had been avoided, the progression into prostitution of a young woman with a heroin addiction and, indeed, her earlier descent into self-destructive dependence on heroin would, perhaps, have been far less likely. It cannot be emphasised enough that all the appalling and morally repugnant harms linked to drug use now occur in spite of the existence of prohibition and, very probably, to some degree, because of the existence of prohibition.

Many difficult questions lurk within the debate on drug harms and I will return to these in a later section of this chapter. In this section, I will deal with the core prohibitionist assumptions that drug use is intrinsically immoral and, therefore, justifiably criminalised and that illicit drug use can be eliminated from the world. The assumption that illicit drug use is immoral is often buttressed by claims about the harms of drug use. These harms are obviously relevant. However, the prohibitionist assumption actually makes the claim that illicit drug use is inherently and always wrong, irrespective of consequences, even when there is little or no associated harm. Before addressing the issue of the harms of drug use, I will examine the basis for the contention that drug use is intrinsically immoral and thus deserving criminal sanction.

The logical incoherence of the idea that illicit drug use is wrong

Prohibitionists constantly blur the lines between harm, morality and legality in an attempt to persuade us that illicit drug is not wrong or immoral because it is illegal, but that it is illegal because it is wrong. For example, President Bush speaking in 2001 said 'legalizing drugs would completely undermine the message that drug use is wrong'.[10] However, the core assumption that illicit drug use is intrinsically immoral is, under the present prohibition regime, untenable on three separate grounds relating to logic, the empirical facts and ethical considerations.

To elucidate the logical incoherence of contemporary forms of selective prohibition, it is necessary to expand the term, 'illicit drugs'. This term is accurately defined as 'those psychoactive, mood- or consciousness-altering substances, which it is a crime to use or possess'. This definition draws attention to the continuity, with respect to their capacity to alter mood and consciousness, between the illicit drugs and licit drugs such as alcohol, nicotine and medically prescribed tranquillisers. Equally, this definition makes clear the stark discontinuity between illicit and licit drugs as in turn prohibited and socially accepted substances. When the terms are spelled out like this the logical nonsense becomes clear. In the conspicuous absence of a convincing calculus of harms justifying the distinction between alcohol (and the other legal drugs) and all the illicit drugs, the continuity between the illicit and licit drugs, as mood-altering substances that act on the brain, totally invalidates the discontinuity in their treatment by the law.

In fact, the decision to criminalise the use of particular mood-altering substances has been and is still an essentially arbitrary political or cultural decision with no real connection to the actual or potential harms of use or to any other rational basis for differentiation. It does not, for example, relate to the psychoactive substance's potential for producing addiction. It is, therefore, reasonable to consider all mood-altering substances as falling into the same moral category. They are either all morally repugnant or all morally acceptable. Societies, which arbitrarily define some mood-altering substances as immoral and illicit, but define others as morally acceptable and legal, are deeply mired in logical incoherence and hypocritical self-contradiction. The fallacious logic and hypocrisy underpinning prohibition's claim that the use of illicit drugs is inherently immoral are critically important because they engender much of the contempt towards drug laws felt by a significant proportion of the population.

Of course, a logically coherent, whole-hearted prohibition is possible. Rare societies, such as the Mormons, have maintained a more logically consistent line on mood-altering substances. Such societies, exercising their internal norm-creating powers, have chosen to declare the use of all mood-altering substances as immoral. The Mormons forbid alcohol, tobacco and caffeine along with all the other mood-altering substances. This logically consistent form of prohibition clearly has legitimacy and credibility within its own culture. However, a similar credibility cannot be claimed for the Irish or indeed for most contemporary systems of drugs prohibition, which turn a blind eye to the fact that alcohol, nicotine and medically prescribed drugs are simply drugs like all others. Of course, the history of the human use of mood-altering substances and the unrelenting nature of the human appetite for these substances suggest that an ascetic, puritanical approach like that of the Mormons is neither viable nor desirable. In addition, the human proclivity for autonomy, personal control over body and consciousness and reactance against constraints on freedom, mean that it is impossible to envisage a successful global or even national system based on the logically coherent, but extremely exacting, 'unnatural' form of prohibition of the Mormons.

There is no excuse for the logical incoherence of the current selective forms of prohibition since the harms that result from drug use are clearly amenable to empirical investigation. It is possible to imagine an evidence-based ordering of drugs, which is carefully constructed on the basis of the relative dangers of the different drugs and their associated forms of use. This kind of ordering would make it possible to determine a meaningful cut-off point between licit and illicit drugs, if not between moral and immoral drugs. A logically coherent, selective prohibition would be premised on the view that some drug use is criminally harmful, but it could not and would not claim that all drug use is intrinsically immoral. Such a scheme offers a basis for a logically coherent and defensible form of selective prohibition. This rationally constructed form of selective prohibition would be a tenable alternative to the uncompromising, total prohibition of the Mormons and to the self-contradictory, incoherent forms of prohibition which currently exist in Ireland and most other jurisdictions.

While in theory a rational and defensible form of selective prohibition is possible, in reality the Irish and almost all other existing systems of prohibition are arbitrary and irrational. They tend to chaotically classify many relatively harmless substances as illegal and some of the more harmful substances, such as alcohol, as legal. Clearly, in any rational, hierarchical ordering by danger, alcohol would inevitably be placed towards the more dangerous pole. Alcohol has very deleterious effects on health, which are in general more serious and certain than the ill-effects of heroin. Alcohol is more addictive than many of the illicit drugs and alcohol's potent ability to disinhibit people and encourage anti-social and aggressive behaviour, is a major contributor to crime and other social ills. Any logically consistent and credible prohibition system that allows alcohol should, at the very least, allow all less harmful psychoactive drugs. By the same token, it should prohibit only those few drugs, which are in various ways more harmful than alcohol.

Either it is morally wrong as a general rule to use mood-altering substances or it is not. Clearly, most societies, despite their prejudices against various drugs, have no real or principled objection to the use of mood-altering substances as such. In logic, these societies should acknowledge the moral neutrality of drug use, which does not harm others. They should cease demonising selected forms of drug use as intrinsically immoral.

The arbitrary cultural and historical basis of the licit/illicit distinction

The core idea that drug use is in itself wrongful is empirically untenable because the use of mood-altering substances is a normal, natural appetite – not an essential, irresistible, life-supporting appetite, but a commonplace, fairly urgent appetite for life-enhancing, pleasurable, relaxing and meaningful experiences. Use of psychoactive substances is in itself a morally neutral and unobjectionable activity. In essence it is also a private matter, which almost always lacks a victimised complainant and, indeed, any victim of any kind other perhaps than the user. Most societies, so far from condemning the use of all mood-altering substances as wrongful, not only accept the appetite for some of them as a normal facet of human nature, but also celebrate it by giving the use of certain psychoactive substances a central place in social life.

In many developed Western nations, alcohol has this accepted, even celebrated role; but different cultures rely or have relied, in a similar way, on other psychoactive substances like cannabis, opium, coca leaf or khat. Wisotsky[11] argues that, despite the fact that coca leaf chewing has been outlawed since 1986 under the UN Single Convention, 'effective coca control in today's world is implausible'. This is largely because 'coca chewing represents a centuries old, revered tradition among the Andean Indians' and is thoroughly socialised in countries like Bolivia. Khat, a similar stimulant leaf to coca, was overlooked by the UN Convention, and is still legal and widely used, often by a majority of the male population in Horn of Africa countries like Yemen. Khat is also currently legal and openly sold in Israel and, under licence, can be imported for personal use into Australia.

Meanwhile, of course, the favoured mood-altering substance of the West, alcohol, is outlawed in strict Islamic countries. As Nadelman states: '"moral" condemnation by the majority of Americans of some substances and not others is little more than a transient prejudice in favour of some drugs and against others'. These cultural variations, determining which psychoactive substances are tolerated and which are taboo, depend on many historical factors, including local product availability, social traditions, folk myths and religious beliefs.

The process underlying the condemnation of some, but the celebration of other, mood-altering substances is clearly analogous to the process by which pork became anathema within Jewish and Islamic culture and the cow became sacred within Hindu society. It is claimed by some religious authorities that pork was outlawed at the express command of God, but it is also very likely that specific historical experiences of death and disease linked to the use of contaminated pork underlie the original emergence of this taboo within specific groups. The main point, however, is that cultural variation in the socialisation of mood-altering substances – the fact that one society's meat is another society's poison – refutes all claims that there is a genuine divide between licit and illicit drugs and that the use of mood-altering substances is or should be seen as inherently wrong. The current superior legal status of alcohol and the global movement to outlaw locally socialised drug use, such as coca leaf chewing, are no more than symptoms of the domineering hegemony of 'first world' values, particularly U.S. values.

The lack of a sound ethical rationale for the illicit/licit distinction

Finally, from the ethical point of view, there is a key distinction between harms against victims, that is harms, which violate the rights of others, and self-inflicted harms that damage only the self. Szasz poses the correct question about the morality and legality of drug use, when he asks 'If we take drugs and conduct ourselves as responsible and law-abiding citizens, should we have a right to remain unmolested by the government?'[12] Nadelman provides a most compelling answer to this query: 'enforcement of drug laws makes a mockery of an essential principle of a free society, that those who do no harm to others should not be harmed by others, and particularly not by the state'.[13]

Almost all activities involve both costs and benefits and the fact that an action has costs is obviously not an adequate ground for invoking the criminal law and punishing the action, certainly if it is only the actor who suffers the costs. The philosopher Husak[14] makes the argument that the criminal law and state punishment should only be used, and are only fully justified when used, against harms that make victims of others. Punishing people in order to protect them from themselves, when they are harming themselves but not others, is, as Mill states in his famous libertarian credo, an objectionable and unwarranted form of state paternalism. To paternalistically punish people for victimless use of drugs is an obvious nonsense and an unacceptable intrusion on personal freedom. It is obviously inappropriate to punish people for using drugs, which are not even harmful or which are not harmful to others and have benefits to the user that outweigh their harms to him or her.

Even the philosopher de Marneffe, who is an opponent of the legalisation of heroin, believes that 'no one wrongs anyone simply by using heroin and no one morally deserves to be punished for doing so'.[15] De Marneffe also states that 'there is nothing inherently wrong with a person's altering his states of consciousness for the purposes of relaxation, enjoyment or self-exploration'. Yet forbidding and punishing single acts of heroin use or other forms of, often relatively safe, illicit drug use, is exactly what prohibition does, albeit in the name of preventing serious harms and wrongs associated with destructive patterns of extended use.

The self-confirming circle from illegal to wrong to illegal

Because they are aware that the selective nature of the prohibition system casts serious doubts on the claimed inherent immorality of illicit drug use, prohibitionists often seek to derive the wrongfulness of illicit drug use from the mere fact that such use is illegal. However, cannabis use is not morally different from alcohol use, except insofar as it is against the law. According to the prohibitionist, this legal fact alone implicates the cannabis user in a form of wrongfulness or immorality. But this prohibitionist argument is circular and vacuous, in effect asserting that illicit drug use is illegal because it is wrong, when in fact it is wrong only because it is illegal.

The wrongfulness of using an illicit drug derives from breaking the drug possession laws and from complicit involvement in an illegal market. There can be no question but that, just as the consumers of child pornography or the receivers of stolen goods provide motivation for the more serious crimes of child abuse and theft, respectively, the existence of willing and eager purchasers of drugs keeps the criminal drug market buoyant. The fact that, on these specific grounds alone, people can reasonably castigate all illicit drug use as wrong, both in the obvious breach-of-the-criminal-law sense and in a limited moral sense (since all citizens have a moral duty to obey the law), is undoubtedly a very useful rhetorical and emotional support for the prohibitionist assumption that all illicit drug use is wrong. It convinces many people. But this wrongfulness is a product of the law and is not an inherent characteristic of illicit drug use per se. Moreover, the morality of the law criminalising drug use is plainly open to challenge.

The criminality of illicit drug use and the limited degree of immorality it implies are both generated by the law. They have no relevance to the question whether the use of psychoactive substances is or is not *intrinsically* wrong. This is a subtle and elusive point, but it is by no means a trivial or pedantic one. The condemnation of an activity as intrinsically immoral or evil on the sole grounds that the law says it is wrong is a confusion of thought, which is exploited by prohibitionists and needs to be resisted.

Crime, immorality and harm are not synonyms and do not map precisely onto each other. Many immoral behaviours are not criminalised and many harmful behaviours are not immoral or indeed crimes. Crimes, although they normally relate to harms, are not necessarily immoral – beyond the inescapable fact that they involve disobedience of the law. Not only is there no equivalence between crime, harm and immorality, but it is also the case that the supposed immorality of certain actions, implied by their criminalisation, is often widely and hotly contested.

A disputed law, which criminalises and punishes behaviour, which many people regard as acceptable and harmless, can itself be attacked as immoral and socially divisive. Many laws have been repealed because they have come to be seen as morally repugnant. Take, for example, the nineteenth-century laws that created totally disproportionate punishments, such as the death penalty for petty theft. In fact, as social values have changed and, most particularly, as the separation of church and state has progressed, many laws that created specific crimes (for example anti-homosexual legislation and laws that punish attempted suicide) have come to be regarded as unacceptable, because, although they are compatible with and derive from certain religious moral codes, they have no basis in the secular, essentially humanist, moral values, espoused by modern pluralist democracies. Illicit drug use is clearly in a similar category, because the legitimacy of the criminalisation of drug use is in serious doubt on the grounds already discussed.

This is not to deny that the law can and does have a normative purpose and that it can be used to shape people's sense of moral right and wrong. Legislators undoubtedly have this expectation for the laws that criminalise drug use. They expect that people will perceive and consent to the moral vision implicit in the law. Law certainly has this kind of authority and it has the capacity to create moral stigma around specific outlawed behaviours, especially if the law is rigorously enforced by punishments, which involve their own independent element of stigmatisation. However, as Finkel and Parrott[16] argue 'the Law cannot reside solely on the ought side of the line, building airy theories divorced from reality – for part of the Law's very purpose is to bridge the gulf between the empirical is and the normative ought. Thus for particular laws to be respected and obeyed by its citizens, their normative ought story must portray human nature with fidelity, by taking men "as they are", in Rousseau's words, rather than by propping up metaphorical fictions or outright myths that citizens reject'. Rawls[17] has made a similar point by stating that what we ought to be depends significantly on what we are.

Quite recently, laws that outlaw incitement to racial hatred have been enacted in many jurisdictions. These laws emerge from a changing societal value system and in their turn help spread and reinforce these new values and substantiate their moral content. However, the critical fact is that the laws that criminalise drugs are self-contradictory, hypocritical and unfair and fail to 'portray human nature with fidelity'. Accordingly, while some people consent to these laws and are influenced by their normative force, many people quite reasonably reject them as misguided, unworkable or even immoral.

The immorality of the drug user's complicity in drug-related violent crime

There appears to be a recent trend in the discourse on drugs for authorities to stress not only the illegality of possessing small amounts of illicit drugs, but also the moral complicity of those who purchase drugs in more serious 'systemic' drug-related crime, including violence and murder. This is obviously a powerful rhetorical device with profound implications, which go beyond simply attempting to establish the wrongfulness of drug use.

In March 2006, District Court Judge Flann Brennan, responding to an accused appearing before him on charges relating to possession of small amounts of cocaine and cannabis, said that 'individuals who dabbled in drugs, even for their own use, were co-operating in the promotion of the kind of drugs culture, which had led to the recent spate of drug-related killings in Dublin and elsewhere'.[18] Similarly, Mr McDowell, the then Minister for Justice, was reported as stating that 'Everyone who consumes any kind of drug, be it cocaine, be it the new crystal meth, be it marijuana or cannabis, anyone who consumes those substances participates in the world of crime and makes the task of the drug gangs more profitable.'[19] In fact, the Minister seemed to be waging a campaign to stigmatise and isolate the recreational drug user. He regularly invoked or tried to create a moral consensus by appealing to individual conscience and the citizen's duty of loyalty to the state. In one of his strongest statements,[20] he said: 'It is not a matter of individual choice or freedom as to whether you take drugs. Every citizen in Ireland holds a duty of loyalty to the state and this entails upholding the criminal law. So, if you do a line of cocaine in Foxrock, you are personally responsible for the murder of someone in Clondalkin or Coolock or wherever. There is no tolerated level of drug consumption in Ireland. The law is the law and it applies to everyone.' There is obviously some truth in the former Minister's remarks, but this intemperate statement seems designed more to appeal to the emotions of the Irish electorate than to faithfully represent the legal and moral facts. Minister McDowell, who is a Senior Counsel and experienced criminal lawyer, surely knows that it is inflammatory and legally untenable exaggeration to suggest complicity, let alone personal responsibility, in murder on the sole grounds of cocaine use.

The complicity of drug users can be contrasted with that of consumers of child pornography. Currently society regards the use of child pornography as a serious offence, usually punishable by imprisonment, even when the offence involves only paying for images downloaded onto a computer. This is regarded as a serious offence because it involves complicity in a business which is dreadfully exploitative and abusive of children. The complicity need not involve any actual consent to the coercion or abuse of children. It has to be admitted that the cocaine user is complicit in a somewhat similar way in the violent, illegal drugs market. It is certainly true that the cocaine user is inevitably breaking the law (against possession) and, like any other lawbreaker, risks the consequences of this. But the link between drug gang murders and the purchase of small amounts of cocaine for personal use is quite tenuous. The level of complicity involved can be likened in its remoteness to the kind of complicity we all share in global warming or in the exploitation of Chinese workers when we purchase cheap Chinese goods. Most importantly, there is absolutely no intent or implied consent to violence or murder involved in the purchase of illegal drugs. The analogy with child pornography is in fact not sound. It is a critical distinction that the viewing of child pornographic images cannot occur without the exploitation and abuse of children, while trade in drugs is by no means necessarily linked to violence. Therefore, any level of complicity in the sexual exploitation of children is widely recognised as intrinsically immoral and as appropriately sanctioned by way of the criminal law. However, many people sincerely believe that the decision to criminalise some mood-altering substances, but not others, is in essence an arbitrary political decision lacking a firm basis in morality.

There is obviously a vital distinction to be made between the criminal law and morality. For example, for a very long time, homosexuality was criminalised in Ireland. By Michael McDowell's logic, when this law was in place and notwithstanding the unreasonableness of the law, the homosexual person's clear duty was one of loyalty to the state, obedience to the law, and effectively a life of celibacy. However, social attitudes and values change and can through the political process profoundly influence laws, rights and freedoms. Today, in Ireland, most people perceive the now historic anti-homosexuality laws as unfair, oppressive and indeed immoral. Most people, looking back from the vantage point of current attitudes, would tend to be entirely sympathetic and understanding towards those who had in the past broken the anti-homosexuality laws. From our present, more enlightened position, their disobedience of the law can indeed be regarded as morally justifiable. In fact, it is essential in a democracy for people to be free to argue openly that any particular law is wrong and should be changed. A credible and cogent case can be made that, like the past laws against homosexuality, the current laws against drug use are wrong and oppressive because they encroach unnecessarily on personal freedom and attempt to stamp out perfectly natural and unobjectionable behaviours.

Quite clearly, hundreds of thousands of people who continue to buy illicit drugs are not much moved by arguments about their complicity in serious crime, but, if they did take them seriously, their logical response would surely be to reverse the burden of guilt by questioning the morality and legitimacy of the prohibition laws. They would turn the tables by blaming the law itself for the involvement of criminals in drug supply and by pressing for the decriminalisation of both drug use and supply. For support, they can point to examples of relatively successful alternatives to a criminalised drugs market, for example in the pre-prohibition era or in the Netherlands, where it is currently legal to cultivate, buy and sell cannabis. These kinds of arguments have sufficient force to overcome most people's scruples and assuage any guilt feelings about their undeniable, if minor, level of complicity in a criminal enterprise. This complicity may rightly be termed immoral but this immorality is entirely about involvement in the drugs market and totally irrelevant to the matter of drug use. The legally constructed, intrinsic immorality of complicity in the drugs market does not render drug use itself immoral.

The fantasy of ridding the world of drug harms

The second major assumption of the prohibitionist creed is that it is possible through prohibition to rid the world of the harms of drug use. This promise of a drug-free world is itself a powerful propaganda weapon, offering, as it does, the only positive, final solution to the drugs problem. The total elimination of drug harms has the appearance not just of a worthy cause but of a profoundly inspirational one, which by comparison makes all other aims, such as harm reductionism, appear paltry and inexcusably unambitious.

The concept of the drug-free world is so seductive that it lulls many people into a convenient amnesia about the inherent contradiction of a world, suffused with often extremely harmful, but legal, medical and non-medical mood-altering drugs, seeking to rid itself of the harms caused by another subset of drugs, which have been more or less arbitrarily defined as illicit. Given society's acceptance of alcohol and other legal mood-altering substances, this aspiration inevitably degenerates into an attempt to create a compliant population, who will use mood-altering substances only in the manner prescribed by the authorities and not in the manner of their own choosing. The existence of authoritarian societies, like Saudi Arabia, which can threaten and constrain their citizens so powerfully that for the most part they refrain from alcohol or drug use, is often used to confer some credibility on the idea of a drugs free world. However, this is disingenuous in the extreme because it ignores the obvious fact that this kind of control is only possible at, by Western standards, a totally unacceptable cost to individual freedoms, democracy, pluralism and the rule of law.

An unbiased consideration of the role that mood-altering substances play in human life inevitably leads us to two conclusions: that a drug-free world (free of all mood-altering substances) is an unrealisable, purely fanciful goal; and that something approaching a drug-free world, that is a world largely free of the currently illicit drugs, could only be attained by the creation of a profoundly unfree, mindlessly conformist humanity, closely supervised by a repressive police state.

The vexed discourse on drug-related harms

Prohibitionists have the considerable advantage of being in a position to count all the harms of drug use and the fear and revulsion they arouse as supportive of their cause. Abolitionists are easily wrong-footed when they argue against the existence of certain supposed drug harms or about the relevance of other drug harms to the criminalisation of drugs. They can appear to be ceding to prohibitionists a monopoly over the fight against drug harms. This is, of course, a travesty because, although a small minority of anti-prohibitionists may wish to see the right to use drugs vindicated at any costs, most support legalisation because they believe this approach will reduce the net harm accruing from drugs.

There are three main categories of actual or supposed drug harms: 1) the calamities of one-off or brief exposure to drug use; 2) the cumulative health harms of extended use; 3) the serious harms linked to addictive and careless patterns of use, such as disease, early death through overdose or suicide, personal degradation, crime, abuse or neglect of others and loss of productivity and motivation. There are two further more subtle harms, which relate to the issues of personal choice, responsibility and self-control and so have a special moral dimension: 4) the harm of starting on the slippery slope (or entering the 'gateway') to ever more serious drug-related harms; and 5) the harm of self-indulgent, self-induced enfeeblement of the will. All these harms can be interpreted, on the one hand, in terms of their impact on the individual user and, on the other, in terms of their impact on others, who might be relatives, victims or, indeed, society as a whole.

There are a number of famous critiques of legalisation, notable among them *Against the Legalization of Drugs* by James Q. Wilson.[21] These critiques tend to focus on drug harms and argue that, from the social policy point of view, it would be madness to abolish prohibition since this would inevitably invite an enormous multiplication and intensification of drug harms. They argue that the risks of legalisation completely overwhelm the kind of considerations raised in the previous section, which show that there is nothing intrinsically immoral or deserving of punishment about the use of mood-altering substances. These prohibitionist critiques tend to take a utilitarian perspective, stressing the tragic consequences of drug use and the probable negative consequences of the abolition of prohibition. They project, somewhat speculatively, that legalisation would inevitably lead to more drug use, which in turn, they are convinced, would lead to more serious drug harms. In fact, there is little hard evidence or theoretical reason to support either of these claims.

However, prohibitionists can rely on a number of cogent and apparently valid arguments, which they believe support their case:

1 There are indeed catastrophic harms, which result from one-off use. The 'hot-shot' overdose death of the IV opiate use is one example. However, there are also rare examples associated with the use of 'soft' drugs. For example, death due to extreme dehydration is known to occasionally result from the use of ecstasy and similar compounds. A temporary toxic psychosis, involving confusion, disorientation and hallucinations, or other frightening psychological syndromes, such as panic attacks, are known to occur following the use of cannabis or a variety of other drugs. There is also some evidence that a relatively brief use of cannabis can help precipitate a 'true' psychotic episode.

2 There are a number of serious cumulative health problems associated with the prolonged use of psychoactive substances. Perhaps the most obvious of these are lung cancer and other lung diseases and cancers associated with cigarette-smoking and possibly marijuana smoking (although the evidence for this is weak), liver and other diseases, including brain damage, associated with extensive alcohol use, memory loss due to chronic, heavy use of cannabis, and destruction of the septum associated with the use of cocaine.

3 The ills of addictive, compulsive use of various drugs, but especially the opiates, are very obvious to everyone. They involve: (3a) a multitude of criminal and non-criminal harms inflicted on others and economic, social, and personal development disadvantages inflicted on self; and (3b) health harms due to self-neglect or unhygienic methods of use. The latter categories include such ills as abscesses, septicaemia, malnutrition, and the contraction of serious diseases, such as AIDS and hepatitis C etc.

4 Part of the seductive attraction of prohibition resides in the simple, irrefutable logic that drug use is necessary for drug related harm. The moral justification of prohibition does not rely solely on the false assertion that drug use is intrinsically immoral. Prohibition can also be morally justified by its aim of total harm reduction through the elimination of illicit drug use. Of course, it is the case that, if illicit drug use could be stopped, then all illicit drug use harms would be avoided.

5   Any relatively serious drug-related harm always has some impact beyond
    the user, either on victims, family or on society as a whole, for example
    through costs to the economy or the burden on the health and welfare
    systems.

6   It is possible to imagine a drug that is so powerful in its psychic effects
    and in its capacity to induce compulsive use that one or two episodes of
    use would lead to a damaging addiction. It is also possible to imagine
    a drug that would almost certainly lead to outrageously aggressive and
    uncontrolled behaviour. It would be sensible and justifiable to outlaw such
    drugs. It is difficult to draw a precise line between drugs, which, like these
    imaginary ones, should be outlawed and those which people should have
    a right to use without interference from the criminal law. Some prohibi-
    tionists claim not only that IV use of heroin and the use of crack cocaine
    are at the level of addictive dangerousness which justifies attention from
    the criminal law, but also that using cannabis carries such a high risk of
    progression to these more dangerous forms of drug use that, in the eyes of
    the law, it should be treated like them.

7   There is a special moral dimension to the use of drugs that induce toler-
    ance and addiction. The initiation period is especially significant because
    in some cases the drug user is ceding control to a drug, at a point when
    they still have control, and, because of this, they are taking a serious risk
    that they will eventually (often quite soon) reach a point where they
    will have little or no control. With typical rhetorical flourish, James Q.
    Wilson[22] argues that drug use (he does not differentiate which type) is
    immoral because it 'enslaves the mind and destroys the soul'. Weil[23] an
    opponent of prohibition, admits that 'anyone who uses a tolerance-pro-
    ducing drug must sooner or later come to terms with his need for larger
    and larger doses to maintain the experience first associated with the drug
    … the individual must somehow stabilise his use in order to keep his life
    from being disrupted by an unstable habit'. Some people manage this
    trick – there are numerous examples of even chronic IV opiate addicts
    living stable, professional lives – but many tragically do not. Certainly, one
    of the most pernicious dangers of the strongly addiction-forming drugs is
    that people often initiate use in a frame of mind, which is totally oblivious
    to or ignorant of the insidious addiction-inducing power of the drug. As
    Samuel Johnson eloquently pointed out, with reference to tobacco: 'the
    chains of habit are too weak to be felt until they are too strong to be
    broken'. Addiction is especially likely to develop, if the user is turning to
    drugs as a crutch or emotional support in a stressful or difficult time. For
    a time, the drug use serves as a beneficial psychological survival mecha-
    nism, but it does not solve the on-going crisis in the person's life and soon
    itself becomes an additional severe problem. It is ironic that people, espe-
    cially young people, are often stubbornly wilful and quite deluded about
    their ability to control drug use into the future and that this delusion

encourages the drug use which undermines self-control and eventually proves the delusion. Their initial perceptions of their level of self-control are reasonably based on the control which they really do exercise at the early stage, but this control gradually dissipates with continued drug use and increasing dependence.

8 Modern inventions, including new types of drug (for the most part initially developed for medical purposes by the pharmaceutical industry) and forms of use, such as injection by hypodermic syringe, have made the socialisation of drug use much more difficult. So, for example, the drug heroin, which is a derivative of opium, is, whether snorted, smoked or injected, a more powerfully euphoric and tolerance- and addiction-inducing drug than opium. Opium is the more 'natural' form of the drug and its use was effectively socialised in Asian and Middle Eastern cultures for centuries. In other words, it is possible to integrate the use of opium into social life without serious negative consequences, but it is hard to envisage how IV use of the more volatile and powerful drug, heroin, could be similarly 'domesticated'. In the same way, the use of cocaine and even more so crack cocaine are, in various ways, far more dangerous than the more 'natural' chewing of coca leaf. In particular, the invention of the hypodermic syringe has introduced a far more dangerous mode of use of drugs, especially heroin, cocaine and amphetamines. Intravenous (IV) use is more dangerous, on the one hand, because it facilitates a more immediate and more intense high and in this way makes addiction more likely, more compulsive and more unstable and, on the other, because it involves health risks connected to lack of hygiene and lack of skill in the delicate art of injection.

9 Prohibition laws clearly fail to deter many people from using illicit drugs. However, they probably do deter some people. The failure to deter substantial numbers is not necessarily incontrovertible proof of their ineffectiveness. In any event, many offences, such as thefts and assaults, continue to be committed despite their proscription by the criminal law, yet this fact does not persuade us that we should repeal the relevant laws and abolish punishment for such offences. Society does not and should not capitulate to offenders merely because they persist in breaking the law.

10 There has to be a fairly high probability that the use of illicit drugs would increase in a society that abolishes prohibition. As Nadelman states: 'legalization implies greater availability, lower prices, and the elimination (particularly for adults) of the deterrent power of the criminal sanction – all of which would suggest higher levels of use'.

These arguments clearly create a minefield through which the opponent of prohibition must tread with great care. However, prohibitionists typically exaggerate the relevance and strength of these points. They do this in the main by sewing confusion about the different types of drug harm and by using a number of invalid arguments to assert that the harms of illicit drug use inevitably outweigh the benefits in the case of every illicit drug and all kinds of use.

Prohibitionist arguments tend to clump drug harms together, confusing the very rare with the common, the dramatic with the trivial, the incremental with the catastrophic, and those that justify the attention of the criminal law with those that do not. Because prohibitionists are uneasy about the glaring self-contradiction of a system that allows alcohol but outlaws cannabis, a common theme of prohibitionist discourse is that there is no 'soft' versus 'hard' drug distinction. This view rests on a fallacious blurring of the distinctions between types of drug harms. Prohibitionists also tend to ignore the critical distinction between harms that are inherent to drug use and harms that are the direct or partial result of prohibition itself. This is clearly illegitimate in an argument proposing that prohibition actually reduces such harms. Prohibitionists, in making the case that the abolition of prohibition would increase total harm, tend to dismiss or forget altogether the independent harms of prohibition. That is they ignore the important gains that can be achieved by abolition in areas other than direct drug use harm. They emphasise the health-related harms, which might (or might not) result from abolition, but ignore such potential major gains as the reduction in the prevalence and power of organised criminal gangs. Finally, prohibitionists ignore the glaring fact that most of the harms they deplore actually flourish under the prohibition regime.

Turning, then, to *Argument 1*, concerning the calamities of one-off use, the first counterpoint is that as a matter of empirical fact these harms are very rare, far rarer than catastrophic harms risked in mundane and totally accepted activities like horse-riding, rugby and hill-walking. As Husak[24] notes, 'we allow people to take enormous risks when they engage in recreational activities that do not involve the use of drugs'. Secondly, many of the calamities are directly caused or exacerbated by prohibition. The lack of quality control of illicit drugs and the paucity of simple precautionary measures, such as the routine dissemination of information on dehydration and the actual provision of water to users of ecstasy, are a result of the prohibition regime. Thirdly, society and the state have a valid interest in preventing these harms, but this interest does not justify criminalising personal choices, because they carry a tiny risk of some calamity. It is wrong to treat the risk of harm as if it were a harm itself. The state's duty is, rather, to fund scientific research that uncovers and elucidates the risks, to inform and warn people about the real risks and to regulate and monitor the quality of recreational and other drugs, which people use.

The cumulative health harms of extended use (*Argument 2*) and the health harms of careless, unsanitary and botched IV use (*Argument 3b*) are far more common and a very serious problem, though by no means an inevitable consequence of extended or addictive use. However, it is again undeniable that prohibition, so far from being the solution to this problem, itself plays a key role in promoting some of these health risks, such as those linked to careless and unhygienic use of injecting equipment.

A recent report[25] emanating from the U.K. Department of Health states that 'drugs are not, of themselves, dangerous, with the risk residing in the interaction between the substance, the individual, the method of consumption and the context of use'. Drugs and forms of use do differ in their potential to engender health harms, dependence and addiction. However, the destructive effects of drug use are almost always long-term, cumulative effects and the result not just of many instances of drug use, but of the complex interaction of drug use and aspects of *set* and *setting* – that is, respectively, the user's personal needs, expectations and vulnerabilities and the socio-cultural context of drug-taking. Some people, because of their personal predispositions and the specific contingencies of their environment, are more likely to engage in immoderate and destructive forms of drug use. This will be true whether or not there is prohibition. The environmental conditions and individual susceptibilities, which make dangerous use more likely, are more justifiable and useful targets for preventative action than the single instances of drug use, which prohibition targets and which might but, more than likely, will not lead to significant harms.

In this context, it is instructive to examine the manner in which society responds to cigarette-smoking. There is little immediate pleasure in the first weeks of smoking. Indeed, perhaps the most important pleasure for the established smoker is in satisfying the essentially self-induced cravings associated with addiction to nicotine. People usually begin smoking for curiosity or symbolic reasons, such as to appear mature. While the novice smoker assures him or herself that they are in control and can take it or leave it, the nicotine addiction quietly establishes itself and creates a whole new set of psychological and physiological motives for continuing to smoke. We now know that this apparently innocuous addiction is actually, in the long run, a major contributor to lung and heart disease and to early death from these and other causes. In short, it is difficult to conceive of a more stupid and wasteful activity than cigarette-smoking and it is obviously imperative to attempt to avoid the development of nicotine addictions. The most obvious way to do this is to prevent people from beginning to smoke – that is to prevent all cigarette-smoking. By extension, prohibition is seen as the appropriate response to all addiction-inducing substances.

However, this line of argument crashes when it runs up against the brick wall of the legality of cigarette-smoking. Moreover, in the developed world at least, cigarette-smoking is being successfully reduced by education, taxation and other persuasive methods, which do not rely on criminalisation. If the right to smoke cigarettes is defended despite the highly questionable cost-benefit balance for the smoker and despite the obvious harms of cigarette-smoking for broader society, how could it be justifiable to criminalise the use of drugs such as cannabis and ecstasy, which have far lower levels of proven risk to health and well-being?

With respect to the social, criminal and other harms raised in *Argument 3a*, it is undeniable that a significant, if relatively small, minority of drug users progress to a level of addiction, which seriously compromises their judgment, reshapes their motivational system and reorders their priorities and values. Such a problematic addiction, for example to heroin, can have a drastic effect on personality and behaviour and can frequently influence a person to the extent that, as well as putting their own health and well-being at serious risk, they regularly victimise others through crime, neglect and irresponsible behaviour. These sobering facts do not, however, justify criminalising the relatively harmless choices of the vast majority of drug users, who do not violate the rights of others. They do not even justify criminalising the use of heroin at an early or indeed at any point, solely because it is a risky personal choice or a necessary precondition for any later progression to damaging addiction. The problematic users who harm others should be tackled by the criminal law for the harms they do to others, but not for the harm they do to themselves.

Despite the eventual negative outcome, which one can confidently anticipate for a substantial proportion of experimenters with a potently addictive drug like heroin, a single use of heroin, in and of itself, is not an inherently wrongful or harmful action and certainly not one that victimises others and so demands the intervention of the criminal law. In addition, it is clear that many drug-related, social and criminal harms are generated or seriously aggravated by prohibition through processes like the hyperinflation of the cost of drugs and the creation of a clandestine, criminal market.

Argument 4 refers to the prohibitionists' ability to exploit the unremarkable fact that drug use is a necessary condition for drug harm. Many people (but probably not the majority of people) do actually refrain from all illicit drug use precisely because they appreciate the risks of addiction and other drug-related harms. Many of these people cannot see why everyone cannot and should not refrain as they do, especially when this would effectively end all illicit drug harms. But many other people, who have an equal right to their opinions and choices, find value in illicit drug use and believe, sometimes mistakenly, but often correctly, that the value they derive from drugs outweighs the risks they take and the harms they inflict on themselves. What is more, almost all activities carry some risk to health and future opportunities and many carry a far greater risk than most drug use. Total avoidance of risk is tantamount to total inaction and is neither a viable nor a desirable option.

Argument 5 refers to the fact that the pains and costs of harmful drug use are spread widely across users, relatives, victims, communities and society. This fact should not be used to cloud the reality that the majority of drug use is as innocuous and inconsequential as the taking of a glass of wine with a meal. The pains and burdens of the ill-effects of alcohol and nicotine use are also widely spread, as are those of other non-drug activities that eventually cause serious harm, such as over-eating or having a high-cholesterol diet. Many 'lifestyle' choices involve activities, which carry long-term cumulative risks or a small risk of immediate catastrophe, but we routinely accept and discount such risks as a mundane part of life and certainly not something that should be controlled by the criminal law. It is as absurd to outlaw cannabis in order to prevent the ills associated with IV opiate addiction as it would be to outlaw the use of wine in restaurants in order to prevent the ills of alcoholism.

Argument 6 suggests that allowing people the right to use drugs will freely permit (but not necessarily encourage) some of them to become addicted. This has to be admitted. *Argument 6* also raises the chimera of a drug, the single use of which guarantees addiction and serious harms. No such drug, which should obviously be criminalised, exists and, in reality, the development of addiction is a gradual process, involving the interaction of *drug, set* and *setting*. A case can be made that IV use of heroin and similarly risky forms of drug use meet the criteria for forms of drug use, which should be criminalised, but any decision to introduce a carefully calibrated form of selective prohibition directed only at risky forms of drug use (as opposed to the present system of self-contradictory selective prohibition) would have to take account of the costs of prohibition and its current failure to impact on the more destructive forms of drug use. Also, it is not justifiable to treat risk as if it were a harm in itself.

The argument that cannabis is a gateway drug to serious addictions, such as IV heroin use, and should be treated similarly by the law is an obvious absurdity, based on a misunderstanding of the facts. When studies examine people who use heroin or other 'hard' drugs, they frequently find a history of prior cannabis use (and indeed of cigarette-smoking and alcohol use). On the other hand, it is also the case that the vast majority of cannabis users (probably far more than 90%) do not go on to use heroin or other 'hard' drugs. There is, therefore, no significant causal relationship between the use of cannabis and the development of a heroin or other serious addiction. The association between 'hard' drug use and prior use of cannabis, alcohol or cigarettes must be explicable in terms of third factors, which are most probably linked to aspects of the *set* or personality of the individual and the *setting*. Likely explanations, which have considerable empirical support are an individual's predisposition to sensation-seeking and curiosity or the contagion related to the social mingling of 'soft' and 'hard' drug users, which is actually promoted by the prohibition regime.[26] The gateway theory, then, does not offer credible support for the view that there are no significant differences between 'soft' and 'hard' drugs and that, consequently, all illicit drugs should be regarded as equally harmful and deserving of punishment.

Argument 7 relates to the especially insidious nature of tolerance- and addiction-inducing drugs. The temptation to adopt a paternalistic form of prohibition is strong and, perhaps, most clearly warranted in respect of drugs such as crack cocaine and IV opiate use, which have a potent capacity for creating addiction. Many people are particularly foolish and deluded in their thinking about the strongly addictive drugs, believing, usually wrongly, that they can maintain control over their drug use. Jarvick suggests that the over-confidence of the beginning user can be explained by 'an optimistic bias or short-time horizon caused by the delay between rewarding reinforcement and the punishing consequences'. These people can appear to need to be protected from themselves.

However, the first point that must be noted is that many illicit drugs have little or none of this addictive potential. The hallucinogens do not create tolerance or patterns of addiction. De Marneffe[27] states that it is hard to find 'any good argument for prohibiting psychedelic drugs (LSD, mescaline, peyote and mushrooms) or the euphoric/empathic drug ecstasy'. He asserts this because these drugs lack significant addictive potential; because it is virtually impossible to overdose on them; because they do not lead to violence; and because they are unlikely to undermine motivation but, on the contrary, seem to have considerable psychological benefits for some people. Cannabis, the most widely used illicit drug in Ireland, has only a limited capacity to create psychological dependence in certain users. The second point is that nicotine is one of the most addictive of substances and alcohol too far surpasses many illicit drugs in this regard. These substances are, of course, legal and adults are free to become addicted to them, if they so choose. The selective nature of prohibition undercuts the argument that drug use should be criminalised because it is addictive just as it undercuts the argument that drug use should be criminalised because it is intrinsically immoral.

A broader point is that it is not appropriate to limit people's freedom and punish them for actions that do not harm others simply in order to save them (and, in the case of users of hallucinogens, which are not addictive, to somehow save other people) from becoming addicted. Addiction to mood-altering substances is in this regard no different to the many habits and automatic practices, originating in voluntary choices, which are frequently regarded by the actor him or herself and by others as regrettable vices. For example, the habit of meanness and miserliness is a common and disreputable vice, but one in itself of no interest to the criminal law. Addiction which does not cause criminal harm to others should similarly be of no interest to the criminal law.

Szasz makes the important point that the freedom to become addicted must not be abused by allowing addiction or intoxication to be used as a legally acceptable excuse for irresponsible and wrongful behaviour. He argues that 'the right to self-medication must entail unqualified responsibility for the effects of one's drug-intoxicated behaviour on others. For, unless we are willing to hold ourselves responsible for our own behaviour and hold others responsible for theirs, the liberty to use drugs (or to engage in other acts) degenerates into a license to hurt others.'

Prohibition's criminal law assault on every act of drug use, including those that carry no substantial risk of addiction, diverts effort from potentially much more effective, persuasive strategies. Prohibition promotes misunderstanding and ignorance by blurring the distinctions between the illicit drugs. The state's interest would be far better served by educational approaches which ensure that everyone knows about the tolerance and addiction-inducing properties of different drugs and about the common psychological traps and delusions, which ease people's paths into addiction. Treatment services, which focus on identifying and helping people beginning to lose control over their drug use, should also be widely available.

Argument 8 emphasises the near-impossibility and the undesirability of socialising the IV use of 'unnaturally' powerful drugs such as opiates or amphetamines. Safe-injecting rooms for IV drug users, which are focused on harm reduction, can hardly be counted as playing an equivalent role to opium dens, which are focused on acceptable forms of enjoyable consumption, in the contemporary socialisation of drugs. In fact, while IV drug use is an extremely foolhardy and imprudent choice under any circumstances, many people are able to integrate such drug use into a safe, stable, productive and law-abiding lifestyle. Many more fail, however, and it is certainly reasonable to argue that social policy through persuasion, but not criminal justice policy through coercion, should be directed at preventing initiation into IV use.

A far more difficult question is whether in a new selective system of prohibition, which permitted the use of alcohol and all currently illicit drugs less harmful than alcohol, it would be right to deploy the criminal law against IV use of the more powerfully addictive drugs. A credible, evidence-based ordering of the harms of drug use could, theoretically, justify a system which grants a general right to use mood-altering substances, but withholds it from a small number of more harmful drugs and modes of use. However, current experience suggests that such an approach would continue to generate very significant prohibition-related ills, such as crime and unsafe practices, which spread serious disease. After all, most of these serious problems are, under the current system of prohibition, most intensively associated with harder drugs and more dangerous forms of use. A much better approach would be to employ every regulatory, educational and persuasive approach short of criminal sanctions in the endeavour to prevent people using the more dangerous drugs and the IV mode of use.

However, speculation about a calculus and ordering of harms is purely theoretical and, regardless of what many prohibitionists claim, does not reflect the current prohibition system. In fact, the self-contradictions and dishonesties of the current system of prohibition almost certainly promote ignorance and misunderstanding and, in the minds of the more vulnerable, minimise the differences between relatively safe and far less safe forms of drug use, thus making progression to more powerful drugs and to IV use more likely.

Argument 9 suggests that the drug laws' lack of deterrent effect is similar to the failure of the ordinary criminal laws, for example those against theft, to deter offenders. The fact that some people are not deterred by the law does not imply that nobody is deterred. Just as their failure to deter everyone does not mean we should abandon anti-theft laws, so the failure of prohibition is not a compelling argument for abandoning anti-drug laws. Of course, prohibition fails to deter perhaps as many as half of the population from at least experimenting with illicit substances – a far greater rate of failure than applies to most criminal laws. In addition, any claim that the approximately half of the population, who do refrain entirely from the use of illicit substances, is mainly motivated by fear of the law is highly dubious. People typically have a variety of other reasons for avoiding illicit drugs.

Another absolutely critical difference is that there is a near total moral consensus about the inherent wrong of theft, murder, sexual assault and other 'normal' crimes, whereas there is a great deal of dispute about the inherent wrongfulness of drug use. Indeed, as I have argued, under the present system of prohibition, the claim that drug use is inherently wrong is untenable. There is no option but to outlaw theft and murder, but outlawing drug use is a policy choice to create a new, 'artificial' wrong.

On purely pragmatic grounds, the deterrent failure of drug laws should give prohibitionists cause to rethink. Fagan,[28] at the end of an extensive study in New York of the re-offending rates of people, who received different types of sentences following conviction for drug possession and drug dealing, concluded that 'drug crimes appear to be intractable, persistent behaviours that are insensitive to the severity of criminal sanction'. He argued that 'the limited effects of incarceration for all types of drug offenders call into question the assumptions about punishment that mandate or encourage prison sentences for drug offenders'. The increasing trade in and use of illicit drugs in Ireland throughout the recent period of ever tougher criminal sanctions and ever greater investment in law enforcement strongly confirm Fagan's sceptical view of the deterrent effectiveness of the drug laws.

It is clear that the desire for drugs frequently outweighs any fear of detection and punishment. In addition, the essentially private and, under prohibition, furtive nature of drug use, undoubtedly, means that the vast majority of instances of drug use go undetected and never lead to arrest or punishment. On these grounds alone, it is hardly surprising that drug laws have so little deterrent effect.

In fact, there is very little reason to believe that the drug laws and law enforcement are the main factors in people's decision to abstain from illicit drug use. Drug and alcohol use goes through regular fashion-led peaks and troughs for various cultural and historical reasons, which are largely unconnected to the criminal law and levels of enforcement. Just as people have reasons for using mood-altering substances, which are insensitive to the threat of the criminal law, so people have reasons for abstaining from illicit drugs, which are stronger and far more influential than fear of the law. It is clear that prudential reasons for abstaining, such as health and economic concerns, fear of loss of control or anxiety about undergoing sudden and intense mood changes, would be just as powerful in the absence of prohibition.

Argument 10 is the final defence, the lynchpin and clincher argument of the prohibitionist faithful seeking to dismiss all the powerful evidence against prohibition. Surely, they argue, making drugs legally available and economically accessible and abolishing the criminal law deterrent can only lead to more drug use and thus to more drug use harm. This is a superficially plausible, 'common sense' argument, which even sways many people who are convinced of the flaws of prohibition. However, there is little empirical support for the view that abolition of prohibition would lead to more use of the currently illicit drugs and certainly no good reason to believe that, even if there were an increase in the use of some drugs, the total costs of drug-related harm would inevitably rise.

In the next section, I will examine a particularly significant version of this argument based on the fear of more drug use and more drug use harms. This is an ostensibly 'scientific' version, which has been advanced by the prestigious and influential U.S. National Academy of Sciences. The Academy has, in its report on the drugs problem,[29] provided a trenchant critique of prohibition. However, the Academy eventually recommends adhering to prohibition with all its faults, mainly because of fear that things could be far worse without it.

The assertion that legalisation would inevitably cause a major surge in drug harms is frequently reinforced with another closely related, 'common sense' argument. This can be termed the 'floodgates' argument and is a neat rhetorical reversal, which turns the tables on the contention that current forms of prohibition are fatally flawed because of their self-contradictory tolerance of alcohol and other harmful legal drugs. How could the legalisation of illicit drugs ever be a wise or rational approach, the argument runs, if, as the facts show, alcohol, nicotine and other legal substances presently create ten times as much harm as the illicit drugs?[30] If the legal drugs are so harmful, how can one suppose that legalising cannabis, heroin and cocaine etc. could do anything but lead to widespread and intractable problems on an equal or greater scale to those now associated with alcohol, nicotine and the other legal drugs?

This is a powerful and at first glance persuasive argument focused on the issue of harm reduction at the aggregate level. Alcohol and nicotine cause much more harm than illicit drugs precisely because they are so widely used. They are widely used because they are legal. If cannabis and heroin were legal, they would similarly be widely used and would thus cause immense harm. In one stroke this argument encapsulates many of the strongest points of the prohibitionist position. It simultaneously purports to demonstrate that legalisation in the case of alcohol and nicotine is itself a failed strategy and to overwhelm theoretical concerns about individual rights by weighing them in the balance against a vision of immense, practical social harm. Implicit in this argument is the idea that, if societies had known what they know now, they would not have legalised alcohol and nicotine. The argument also implies that although the legalisation of alcohol and nicotine is an anomaly, it is far better to live with a little inconsistency and a rather muddled conception of rights than to jeopardise the social fabric.

While the 'floodgates' argument condenses much of the strength and emotional appeal of the prohibitionist position, it is, by the same token, vulnerable to all the telling criticisms aimed at prohibition. Crucially, this argument is based on the presumption that, following the abolition of prohibition, the use of illicit drugs, but most especially the damaging use of more dangerous, illicit drugs, would increase. The next section will examine the evidence for this assumption in detail and show that it is weak and unreliable. In fact, abolition has a real potential to lower the use of the currently illicit drugs and especially the more dangerous forms of use.

Furthermore, the 'floodgates' argument totally discounts the value to individuals of licit drugs like alcohol. Many of the high costs of alcohol use are willingly borne or at least willingly risked precisely because the benefits are substantial and meaningful. The 'floodgates' argument is also ultimately premised on the naïve and, as I have argued, discredited, puritanical view that mankind does not need and can successfully survive without mood-altering substances. In fact, there is no question of Irish society moving towards criminalising alcohol use. The argument also fails to take any account of the harms, which the legalisation of drugs, such as alcohol, actually prevents. Most obvious in this category are the criminal activities associated with a black market in alcohol and the illness and death, caused by a loss of legally enforced quality control. To give just one example, the wider distribution of illegally distilled wood alcohol could have devastatingly lethal effects.

The 'floodgates' argument envisions the spread of the worst kind of destructive drug use, but ignores the critical fact that most drug users take drugs, which actually carry substantially lower risks than alcohol in terms of ill health and regrettable behavioural outcomes. It is quite conceivable that, in a society, which recognised the right to use drugs, many current users of alcohol would transfer their consumer allegiance to one of the safer, newly socialised drugs with a consequent reduction in overall harm. Indeed, users of cannabis and ecstasy have a very strong case for arguing, in response to the 'floodgates' argument, that their generally less harmful drug of choice should be socialised and legalised and not alcohol.

The limited success of Irish alcohol policy in limiting the harms of alcohol use is undoubtedly a useful supporting argument for prohibitionists. Ireland has witnessed a substantial increase in per capita intake of alcohol over recent years. Much of this increase is accounted for by the binge drinking of young people. The average annual Irish intake of alcohol by those over 15 years of age, in 1982, was 8.77 litres of pure alcohol, which was then considerably below the EU average. In 1992, average intake was 11.35 and in 2002, 14.34, which was second highest in the EU and well above the average.[31] A 2002 study by Ramstedt and Hope[32] found that Irish adults had the highest reported consumption per drinker and the highest level of binge drinking in comparison to adults in other European countries. The 1999 international ESPAD study[33] showed that Irish boys and girls aged 16 years are among the highest alcohol abusers in Europe in terms of binge drinking and drunkenness. One in three were regular binge drinkers and one in four reported being drunk ten or more times in the last year. This very marked increase in alcohol intake and these patterns of drinking, especially amongst the young, will almost certainly impact negatively on health outcomes into the future and have already had undoubted ill-effects in the area of behaviour. Many assaults, homicides, sexual assaults and many instances of criminal damage and vandalism in recent years have been directly linked to excessive use of alcohol.[34]

The fact that these problems relate to a legalised substance, alcohol, is certainly a forceful reminder that a laissez faire system of legalisation of illicit drugs, based simply on the recognition of a right to use drugs, is not a viable political or harm reduction strategy. The abolition of prohibition is likely to have a complex effect on drug use – in some ways lowering, in others raising prevalence. However, as the case of alcohol makes clear, cultural factors, encouraging use of mood-altering substances, can easily overwhelm the influence of the law and other restraining factors. These cultural factors can be the predominant influence on prevalence, whether substances are prohibited or not.

However, to recognise the role of cultural factors is not to be defeatist or deny the importance of social policy. If cultural and attitudinal factors can encourage use, they can also discourage it. In particular, education, health promotion, civil law and administrative regulation can play a positive role. It is necessary to acknowledge the complex, dynamic and largely unpredictable trajectory of change in social attitudes and mores and its influence on illicit drug and alcohol use, but it would be wrong to draw the fatalistic conclusion that social policy is utterly ineffectual in this area and that society is a passive and helpless victim of passing fashions and changing values. In fact, the deleterious effects of the recent growth of a youth binge and underage drinking culture in the U.K. and Ireland is largely a result of a specific failure of social policy not of its inevitable, general ineffectiveness. Other European countries, including high alcohol intake countries like France, Spain, Portugal and low alcohol intake countries like Greece and Italy, have socialised alcohol in far more successful ways and have been able to resist the excesses of the binge-drinking culture. These major cultural differences in handling alcohol are, in fact, proof of the considerable potential for harm reduction in social policy both on alcohol and illicit drugs.

In other words, the problem is not that alcohol is socialised (and therefore legal) in Ireland, but the manner of this socialisation. Alcohol has a very central place in Irish social life and is celebrated as an essential component in the 'good life' of *craic agus ceoil*.[35] The pub is often the only available and certainly the most popular social meeting place for Irish people. It is also possible to speculate about more specific causes of the rise in binge-drinking amongst Irish youth. It is likely to be related, among other things, to Ireland's newfound affluence, which provides young people with considerable amounts of discretionary cash; to the intensification of stress and competition within the education system and the work place; to the earlier and more confident assertion of independence from parents; and to media representations that glorify excess and immoderation in many walks of life. However, it is impossible to ignore the social policy response of government. This has been an important component in the cultural change process and it is difficult to avoid the conclusion that the government has been complicit in the rise of the binge-drinking culture. The relaxation of licensing laws in the Celtic Tiger period has permitted a huge expansion in late-night drinking. New nightclubs and superpubs, not just in the large cities but all around the country, attract crowds of young people intent on drinking long and hard into the night. There are other key policy issues, which have not been handled well, including the commercial promotion of alcohol, health promotion, taxation and underage drinking. Indeed, the National Youth Federation[36] has called Irish social policy on alcohol 'probably the worst policy in the world'. Their criticism is based primarily on the government's failure to effectively implement the policy recommendations laid out in the two reports of the strategic task force on alcohol.[37]

The anti-prohibitionist, then, must take the 'floodgates' argument seriously. It is clear from the evidence on alcohol that, even though the abolition of prohibition holds out some prospect of lowering the prevalence of dangerous drug use, it would be extremely foolish to assume that abolition per se will be a panacea and will guarantee a reduction in overall harm. A credible abolitionist position must acknowledge that legalisation alone is an insufficient response. In order for abolition to succeed, it needs to work in tandem with a rigorous, proactive, ever vigilant, harm reductive social policy. This social policy should utilise education, health promotion and civil law/administrative regulation in an energetic and carefully targeted way. However, by definition in a legalised regime, legal regulation should stop short of criminal law sanctions, which are counterproductive and create more harm than they prevent.

The U.S. National Academy of Sciences' view on the abolition of prohibition

The U.S. National Academy of Sciences has offered what can be taken as its response to my third question – whether or not we should abandon prohibition at this relatively advanced juncture in the evolution of the drugs problem. It is worth examining this response in some detail because the Academy is a prestigious and authoritative scientific body which has carefully explored and fully acknowledged many of the flaws and shortcomings of prohibition yet still concludes that prohibition should not be abandoned.

The Academy plays the customary 'fear of the unknown' card, opting for the prohibitionist status quo on what might first appear to be impressive scientific grounds. They state quite reasonably that 'the observation that drug illegality contributes to drug harmfulness is by no means tantamount to endorsing drug legalisation … which is an unproven and potentially risky strategy for reducing drug-related harms'.

In fact, the Academy are inclined to believe on the basis of their examination of available evidence that, in a non-prohibitionist world, following the introduction of proper quality control of drugs etc., the average harm per incident of drug use would decline. However, putting on their scientific hats and relying on an equation originally described by MacCoun et al.,[38] they argue that since *total harm* is the product of *total use* and *average harm per incident* (*total harm = total amount of use* x *average harm per use*), and since *total use* could greatly increase if prohibition were abolished, abolition of prohibition could easily result in greater *total harm*.

However, like most simplistic mathematical models, this equation obscures more than it clarifies. The formulation is fatally flawed because it has inbuilt prohibitionist assumptions. It appears to beg the question of the harmfulness of drugs by not allowing for drug use without harm. It also tacitly ascribes all types of drug-related harm to drug use itself; when, as we have seen and the Academy agrees, some drug-related harms are caused not by drug use but by the action of prohibition itself.

Moreover, the equation treats harm as a constant, which even when it is partitioned retains a consistent relative value. However, in reality there are major qualitative differences betweens harms and harms are not constant or easily comparable. Some drug-related harms are trivial; others are devastating. All these factors make any equation such as *'four times as many instances of a third as harmful drug use totals to more harm than the given original level of harm'* (that is, in algebraic terms, where y = drug use harm and x = the number of cases of drug use, ⅓y4x > yx) merely an uninteresting algebraic tautology with no persuasive value on the question of the abolition of prohibition.

As the Academy agree, proper quality control and full access to education and health services are likely to lead to far safer forms of drug use and are therefore likely to reduce catastrophic harms such as overdose and HIV. Even if the abolition of prohibition leads to more widespread use, and this is by no means certain, it is very probable that the resulting greater volume of 'harm' would be more acceptable because it would consist largely of harms below the threshold of catastrophic damage. There is no reason to believe that abolition of prohibition would lead to a greater prevalence of dangerous, self-destructive forms of drug use. People have many good reasons to avoid such use other than its illegality. Indeed, in a non-prohibitionist world they would probably have many more good reasons due to the greater availability of more open and honest information and to the growth of more mature and responsible attitudes to drugs. On the other hand, there is little to be concerned about in the greater prevalence of prudent drug use, involving the safer modes of use and the safer substances, such as cannabis and the hallucinogens.

In fact, the Dutch experiment with decriminalisation of cannabis makes nonsense of the view that abandoning prohibition would inevitably lead to an explosion of drug use.[39] In the Netherlands, effective legalisation of cannabis has resulted in generally stable, significantly lower use of cannabis than is found in countries where cannabis is prohibited. Very importantly, there is also sound empirical evidence that the decriminalisation of cannabis in the

Netherlands has lead to fewer people progressing from cannabis use to more damaging forms of drug use such as intravenous use of opiates. There is also substantial evidence that the Dutch (admittedly partial and restricted) abolition of prohibition has resulted in less crime and serious disease associated with 'hard' drug use.

Moreover, useful empirical experience with partial legalisation is not restricted to the Dutch experiment with cannabis. The current compromise system in Ireland is very dependent on methadone maintenance, which suspends prohibition to good effect and without the sky falling in or the floodgates opening. Essentially, methadone maintenance is a system, though admittedly quite a restrictive, medicalised one, for the legalisation of opiate use. The important lessons about the potential beneficial effects of legalisation have not been learnt from the methadone maintenance experience, mainly because it is rarely recognised as a form of legalisation.

Much the same can be said about the recent *de facto* legalisation of the trade in 'magic mushrooms', which endured for several years causing relatively little harm, public nuisance or indeed public outrage. Not unexpectedly, but arguably for no good reason, this trade has now been criminalised in accordance with the inherently intolerant, dominant doctrine of prohibition. However, it is clear that when magic mushrooms were 'legal' and readily available from high street shops, this did not lead to massive consumption. The prevalence study *Drug Use in Ireland and Northern Ireland*[40] surveyed households in 2002 and 2003 and reports lifetime and last year prevalence rates. Only 3 people in 1,000 in Ireland (the Republic) had ever used 'legal' magic mushrooms. This compared with 11, 51, and 57 people in 1,000, who had ever used, respectively, cocaine, cannabis and the prescription drug group – sedatives, tranquillisers and anti-depressants.

The Academy's equation, with its narrow focus on quantifiable, drug use-related harms, is also unable to do justice to the inestimable benefits to society of undermining the violent drugs gang culture through the abolition of prohibition. These benefits have no direct quantifiable relation to individual instances of drug use (and are thus not included in the Academy's equation), but they are nonetheless potentially some of the most important gains to be made from the abolition of drugs prohibition.

In short, the Academy's conservative adherence to prohibition and dismissal of radical anti-prohibition approaches is superficial and anything but scientific. It flies in the face of the strong evidence against prohibition they themselves have accumulated. The at-first-glance impressive equation is no more than a vacuous, mathematical dressing up of an uncorroborated and unlikely proposition. Of course, declining yields per acre (declining harm per drug use) can be offset by the farming of more acres (more drug users), but the crucial issue in drug harm prevention is surely the avoidance of the more destructive harms which flourish only in certain soils. Arguably, the most harmful forms of drug use flourish most vigorously in prohibitionist soils.

Further strategic advantages of prohibition

Defending the status quo

Prohibition has two additional strategic advantages – its command of the legal status quo and its role as the engine driving positive action. Prohibition is the entrenched legal framework, nationally and at the global level; so, prohibitionists have the incalculable rhetorical and moral advantage of speaking for the status quo. All nations that are signatories to the UN Convention are obliged to prohibit drugs. This position is regularly and unscrupulously exploited by prohibitionist authorities, from local politicians to high-level UN committees, who cite international law in order to cast a cloak of inevitability about prohibition and to evoke a sense that it is the only viable option. This exploitation deflects attention from the negative evidence against prohibition and helps silence and marginalise critics.

The prohibitionist case is greatly bolstered by the seeming immutability of the legal status quo. International law rigorously mandates the prohibitionist approach. However, as we have seen, the claimed consensus amongst nations is a fiction maintained by the suppression of dissent. The U.S. government and the UN present a united front, which never wavers from strict prohibitionist dogma. In this way they successfully persuade many policy-makers around the world that it is futile to think beyond prohibition. This spurious consensus hides the reality that the current approach is a political choice as open to revision and change as any other political policy.

Supporting the perception that prohibition is the only viable option is the natural tendency for governments and the people to place their faith in the criminal law and in the capacity and obligation of citizens to conform to the law. It is normal to turn to the criminal law to deal with problems which have a major potential for harm and social disruption. The worse the drugs situation has become, the more obvious it appears that law enforcement against drugs is necessary and unquestionably justified. What started with a voluntary (and unnecessary) policy choice to criminalise the use of and trade in drugs quickly became a glaring need to provide a suitably tough law enforcement response to a whole raft of serious, undeniably criminal offences, such as murder, tax evasion, torture and intimidation. It is easy to forget that these crimes arose directly from the newly created illicit drugs trade and that their existence cannot be used as an excuse for the initial criminalisation of the drugs trade. Similarly, the fact that these prohibition-related, systemic crimes deserve punishment does not in any way justify the punishment of drug use per se.

The idea that prohibition is the only viable option is, of course, absurd, since history, anthropology and cross-cultural studies show us that human societies have often, in fact almost without exception,[41] organised themselves in a way that tolerates or even encourages the use of psychoactive substances, including many which we now classify as illicit. The wide diversity of arrangements around alcohol and cannabis in developed Western nations clearly demon-

strates the fact that prohibition is a political choice not somehow an imperative of our biology or of our social, economic and political structures.

Delivering direct positive action

Prohibition also has the enormous advantage of offering and to an extent
delivering direct, concrete and forceful action against violent, ruthless drugs
criminals, who exploit the misery of others and outrage all decent opinion. A
focus on the obvious wrongs of drug pushers and brutal drug gang members
wraps prohibition in a mantle of moral rectitude. This focus both animates and
justifies the simplistic 'war on drugs' rhetoric.

Prohibitionists can highlight a continuously unfolding catalogue of concrete
success in supply control – the frequent large seizures of drugs, the numerous
arrests of dealers and the destruction of drug crops and drug processing plants.
They can point to these events as proof of the effectiveness of their approach
and even anti-prohibitionists must sometimes grudgingly applaud, because
they accept that there are many drugs dealers, who do great harm to others
and deserve to be punished and suppressed. This catalogue of seeming success,
which is dutifully publicised, indeed often trumpeted, by all the newspapers
and broadcast media, serves to keep alive the prohibitionist dream of eliminating drug use. But, support for the prohibitionist fantasy can only be maintained by diverting attention from the immense costs of the law enforcement
effort and from the continuing reality of prohibition's ultimate failure to deliver
a drug-free world or even a world where drug use is not constantly increasing.
The focus on individual law enforcement successes blinds the prohibitionist
faithful to the bigger picture, which depicts only calamitous failure.

The 'war on drugs' rhetoric is rendered more persuasive by the unfolding
narrative of police and customs successes against the drugs trade. In the Age
of Anxiety, when citizens, society and most especially government are increasingly risk averse, it is becoming more and more difficult to do nothing or to
allow oneself to be perceived as doing nothing in the face of real or imagined
risks. Prohibition, with its promise of a drug-free world and its formula for
tough, concrete law enforcement action, is in tune with the risk-averse zeit-
geist of modern developed societies. Modern society is ever more intolerant
and condemnatory of the sources of risk and increasingly eager to intervene,
control and regulate. For many elected politicians keen to prove their creden-
tials as strong, effective leaders, it is impossible to refrain from the 'war on
drugs' rhetoric and to give anything but enthusiastic support to the hard-line
law and order response. The 'self-evidently' good, moral crusade against illicit
drugs provides politicians with an irresistible opportunity for rabble-rousing
(and they hope vote-gathering) polemic.

Post-1996 Irish prohibition and its specific defences

Most of the structural, strategic and rhetorical advantages of prohibition have little or no connection to the reality of prohibition's role in the struggle against drug use harms. However, they tend to be strongly dependent on the exploitation of emotion, blurred definitions and confused thinking. In order to make the case against prohibition, one must first understand these advantages, which so effectively marginalise the anti-prohibitionist argument, and one must expose their hollow foundations. The many published, trenchant critiques of prohibition, such as that of Transform, usually fail to address the reasons for the enduring impunity of prohibition. They fail to get beyond the formidable defences of prohibition and so generally do not have as much impact at the political level or on wider public opinion as they deserve.

I have argued that on close examination the seemingly impregnable faith-based system of prohibition is seen to be riddled with self-contradiction, wishful thinking, cynical obscurantism and faulty logic. However, the picture becomes more complicated when one considers more closely the current Irish system of prohibition, as it has been modified by harm reductionism. For example, it is clearly more difficult to criticise a form of prohibition which is so flexible that it permits the free supply of opiates to thousand of drug users than it is to criticise a stern, uncompromising, more consistent form of prohibition. Many services have now been extended to drug users. These services are sincerely intended to assist them in reducing the harm they might do to themselves and others. It is also clearly more difficult to criticise a form of prohibition which uses the tool of bifurcation to more sharply concentrate law enforcement efforts on suppliers and dealers of drugs than on drug users. Irish prisons are not overflowing with drug users convicted for simple possession. In fact, most Irish drug users go either undetected or ignored and, whenever they are prosecuted for possession, are generally treated leniently with non-custodial sanctions.

The fact that prohibition in Ireland has been turned inside out by the very considerable concessions made to harm reductionism is a major, relatively new factor that confuses critics and deflects politicians and decision-makers from giving serious consideration to the continuing failure of prohibition and to radical alternatives. Current pragmatic prohibition, so the anti-abolitionist argument runs, is itself a radical alternative to strict prohibition and, if this experiment, dedicated as it is to harm reduction, does not work, how can one think that anything more radical could possibly work?

Because of the new rapprochement with harm reductionism, unreconstructed prohibitionists can, without appearing irrational or shaking their own faith in prohibition, candidly admit that prohibition has in the past generated more problems than it has solved. They can admit that, tragically, the past errors of prohibition have left us with a dreadful legacy of death, disease, crime and social disruption. They might even admit that it was folly to take the prohibitionist route in the first place. Nevertheless, they typically remain totally unconvinced by anti-prohibitionist critiques and stubbornly opposed to the abolition of prohibition.

Indeed, recommendations to abandon prohibition, based on the kind of critique of its failure and negative effects that I have presented in this book, tend to be dismissed as naive, irrelevant and utopian. They are summarily rejected because 1) the past negative effects of prohibition cannot be undone; 2) the abandonment of prohibition offers no obvious, immediate solutions to the ongoing, highly complex drug-related problems facing society, especially violent gang culture; and 3), most importantly, because it is now possible to claim that many of prohibition's negative effects are being tackled effectively, or as effectively as possible, through prohibition's more enlightened, pragmatic compromise with harm reductionism.

These are superficially plausible arguments. Prohibition's contribution to the spread of a violent gang culture cannot be undone and the abolition of prohibition will not solve the problem of the current generation of armed violent criminals, whose criminal activities now spread well beyond the drugs trade. Murders, massive tax evasion and many other non-inherent drug-related crimes are so serious that they transcend their connection with drugs and cannot be forgiven or in any way erased simply by abolishing prohibition. Other past negative effects, such as prohibition's contribution to the spread of HIV, also cannot be undone and are currently, to some extent, being obviated through harm reductionism. However, as we have seen in the last chapter, harm reductionism has not been as successful as was hoped and prohibition's continuing, if now somewhat masked, dominance remains a major factor in the continuing failure to effectively minimise the harms of drug use.

The Irish evidence is clear that, under the new compromise system, the prevalence of dangerous forms of drug use and the drugs culture generally continue to grow and flourish and that drug-related harms, especially disease and violent gang crime, are as common or even more common than they were before 1996. However, despite all the concessions to harm reductionism and despite the 'balanced' binary approach of supply/demand reduction, prohibition endures as the prepotent legal framework. In fact, as I have argued, prohibition's many concessions to harm reductionism actually serve to consolidate the underlying political commitment to prohibition. Prohibition is still the agenda-setting ideology, which trumps harm reductionism whenever necessary, and as such it continues to contribute, as it always has done and in much the same ways, to the creation and aggravation of drug use harms.

Against the backdrop of the current activities of drugs gangs, the anti-prohibitionist promise of a future, where social conditions, specifically drug market conditions, would be less likely to spawn ruthless, violent criminals, may appear weak and merely aspirational. However, it would be a serious mistake to allow the inadequacy of the abolition of prohibition as a response to the current crime situation to obscure the genuine potential of abolition to permanently lower the future extent of serious and violent crime across society by removing the drugs trade from criminal hands. In fact, prohibition's belittling of the anti-prohibition argument as utopian is risible in the context of prohibition's blatant failure to deliver on its own utterly unrealistic ideal – a drug-free world.

The fact that the current Irish compromise system has made major accommodations in order to reduce harm, but has achieved only limited success, does not justify the view that the abandonment of prohibition would be merely an intensification of this compromise process with little prospect of making substantially greater improvements in harm reduction than we have already seen. The current Irish system, although it does involve curtailing the reach of prohibition, is not an experiment in even the partial abandonment of prohibition, but is actually a consolidation of prohibition. Indeed, the far more radical complete abandonment of prohibition promises gains of an entirely different order. The next chapter will outline these positive gains, most importantly those that can only be obtained by the complete abandonment of prohibition.

Summary

It is perhaps surprising that prohibition has not collapsed under the weight of evidence that it has failed in its own terms, that is at eliminating or even reducing drug use. However prohibition successfully shields itself from criticism and seems impervious to the undeniable reality of its own failure. Prohibition has attained the status of a faith-based belief system with two main articles of faith – that illicit drug use is wrong in itself and that a world free of illicit drugs is possible. The policy of prohibition parallels the process of addiction itself inasmuch as the increasing costs incurred by prohibition appear to actually increase attachment to the policy, just as the increasing costs suffered by the alcoholic or drug addict can increase emotional attachment to and dependence on alcohol or a preferred drug.

Prohibition's core doctrines have enormous emotional appeal and, by blurring critical distinctions between drug use and drug use harms, between risk and harm, between harms that it is appropriate to punish and those that it is not, and between an intrinsically wrongful action (or an action that is wrong because of its inevitable harmful consequences) and one that is merely defined by law as wrongful, can rely on a number of apparently strong, superficially persuasive arguments. However, the self-contradiction of tolerating and encouraging some mood-altering substances but criminalising others destroys the credibility of the core principle of prohibition – that illicit drug use is an intrinsically evil or immoral activity, deserving of punishment by the law – and is utterly at variance with the promise of a drug-free world. It is the lack of credibility and the hypocrisy of this position rather than its logical inconsistency that are the main problem. This lack of credibility and this hypocrisy have enormous consequences, since they play a central role in hampering prohibition's capacity to control illicit drug use and to win over hearts and minds in the educational and propaganda struggle against dangerous drug use.

The two core doctrines of prohibition should also be rejected because they prop up a narrow belief system that has totally foreclosed on the paradoxical but very real possibility that using the criminal law as a weapon against drug use harms, that is using it to forbid and preempt all illicit drug use, may well create more serious drug use harms than the toleration of drug use.

The discourse on harms is particularly complex and tangled and supplies the prohibitionist with many apparently powerful arguments. Some of these arguments, like the erroneous 'gateway' theory, are aimed at obscuring the differences between 'soft' and 'hard' drugs. This is not only a disingenuous and invalid tactic but also a perilous one. The failure of prohibition, to respond appropriately to the varying hazards attached to different drugs and types of use, contributes significantly to widespread ignorance about drugs, which makes dangerous use of drugs more likely. The prohibitionist discourse on drug harms is premised on the utopian vision of a risk-free life and the false promise of eliminating all health-related drug harms, but it ignores the more credible abolitionist promise of significantly reducing the drug-related criminal and health harms caused by prohibition. Moreover, the harms and risks attached to individual episodes of drug use are of the same or lesser order as those attached to many recreational and lifestyle choices that are routinely accepted and even encouraged. They are not of an order that warrants criminal law sanctions.

The two strongest prohibitionist arguments relating to the harms of drug use focus on 1) the seductive, insidious nature of the addiction process, which entraps many people by exploiting their lack of awareness of or tendency to deny their gradual loss of self-control and 2) the fact that it is difficult to envisage the successful socialisation of IV use of powerfully euphoric and addictive drugs. However, becoming addicted is a protracted process, involving a complex chain of events and lacking any neatly identifiable, responsible action that might justifiably be regarded as a criminal offence. While social policy should be aimed at the non-coercive prevention of damaging addictions, many regrettable forms of addiction are tolerated and, for some mood-altering substances, the adult's right to become addicted is respected. This right should be extended to all addictions so long as the rights of others are not violated. The fact that some forms of drug use probably cannot be successfully socialised is not a valid argument against socialising those that can be. The more dangerous forms of drug use, such as IV use of heroin, should be discouraged by every means short of criminalisation and, where they nevertheless continue to occur, should be partially socialised by providing medically supervised maintenance along the lines of the original 'British model'.

Abolition does not necessarily entail a laissez faire approach to addiction and the more dangerous forms of drug use. On the contrary, the potential benefits of abolition depend on a proactive, preventative harm reductive approach. Under legalisation, education and prevention could be far more effective because they would not be undercut by the dishonesties, confusions and self-contradictions which doom the current prohibitionist approach to failure.

There are few reliable grounds for believing the prohibitionist assumption that legalisation of illicit drugs would lead to a major upsurge in drug use, particularly in the more dangerous kinds of drug use. The Dutch experiment with decriminalisation and other strands of empirical evidence tend to contradict this assumption. People have far stronger reasons for not using drugs than economic cost, limited availability or fear of the law. Abolition may make drugs cheaper and more accessible and it will eliminate the legal deterrent, but personal prudential considerations will still be the dominant influence on people's decisions and will persuade many people to avoid drugs. The abolition of prohibition also promises to enhance people's knowledge and understanding of drugs and the addictive process and thus increase the likelihood of more sensible decision-making about the use of drugs.

Prohibitionists often succeed in diverting attention away from the failures of prohibition and the potential of other approaches by exploiting the public relations advantages of the facts that 1) prohibition is the global legal status quo and 2) that every drug arrest or seizure can be counted as a success for prohibition. It is an inescapable fact, in the current realpolitik, that effective total abolition of prohibition, even within a single jurisdiction, would be impossible without dismantling the reigning global system of prohibition. Although this is a daunting political task, it is not an impossible one. Equally, the everyday public relations successes of the 'war on drugs' in Ireland and elsewhere are clearly delusory and ultimately unable to disguise the overall failure of prohibition.

The failure of the current Irish compromise between prohibition and harm reductionism to stem the growth of the drugs culture and drug-related harms is strong evidence that the curtailment of prohibition is insufficient and that what is required is the complete abolition of prohibition.

Notes

1 The Ballymun regeneration project, for example, is targeted at a formerly extremely disadvantaged and drug-infested area in North Dublin and is claimed as the largest urban regeneration project in Europe. At the launch of the Masterplan for the area in March 1998 the Department of the Environment and Local Government announced government funding of £250 million for the regeneration of housing and facilities.

2 Barbara Tuchman (1984), *The March of Folly: From Troy to Vietnam*, New York: Random House.

3 Szasz, T. (1994) 'The ethics of addiction' in (ed. Comber, R.) *Drugs and Drug Use in Society*, London: Greenwich University Press.

4 Nadelman, E. (1989) 'Drug prohibition in the United States: costs, consequences and alternatives', *Science*, 245, at 939.

5   Dennett, D. (2006) *Breaking the Spell: Religion as a Natural Phenomenon*, London: Allen Lane.

6   Dawkins, R. (2006) *The God Delusion*, London: Bantam Press.

7   In January 2007, as reported in the *Irish Times* (23 January 2007), a prohibitionist group called Eurad called for the creation of a new crime – viz. inciting others to use drugs.

8   Kuhn, T. (1962) *The Structure of Scientific Revolutions*, Chicago: University of Chicago Press.

9   Foetal alcohol syndrome is a well-established and serious problem, but recent research casts considerable doubt on the existence of an equivalent foetal cocaine syndrome, despite the fact that it is claimed to be a widespread and serious problem by many defenders of prohibition. See Frank, D., Augustyn, M., Knight, W., Pell, T. and Zuckerman, B. (2001) 'Growth, development, and behaviour in early childhood following prenatal cocaine exposure', *Journal of the American Medical Association*, 285, at 12.

10 President Bush announcing new head of ONDCP (10 May 2001).

11 Wisotsky, S. (1990) *Beyond the War on Drugs*, Buffalo, N.Y.: Prometheus Books, pages 49–60.

12 Szasz, in *Drugs and Drug Use in Society*.

13 Nadelman, 'Drug prohibition in the United States'.

14 Husak, D. and de Marneffe, P., *The Legalization of Drugs*, New York: Cambridge University Press.

15 De Marneffe, *The Legalization of Drugs*.

16 Finkel, N. and Parrott, W. (2006) *Emotions and Culpability*, Washington, D.C.: American Psychological Society, at page 9.

17 Rawls, J. (1999) *The Law of Peoples*, Cambridge, M.A.: Harvard University Press.

18 Reported in the *Irish Times*, 27 March 2006.

19 Healy, A., '12 murders in first three months of 2006', *Irish Times*, 14 April 2006.

20 Cullen, P., 'Dramatic increase in number of drug offences', *Irish Times*, 28 October 2006.

21 Wilson, J.Q. (1990) 'Against the legalization of drugs', *Commentary*, 89, at 21–28.

22 Wilson, J.Q., 'Against the legalization of drugs'.

23 Weil, A. (1972) *The Natural Mind*, Harmondsworth: Penguin Books.

24 Husak, *The Legalization of Drugs*.

25 Best, D., Gross, S., Vingoe, L., Witton, J. and Strang, J. (2003) *Dangerousness of Drugs: A Guide to the Risks and Harms Associated with Substance Use*, London: Department of Health.

26 Morral, A., McCaffrey, D. and Paddock, S. (2002) 'Reassessing the marijuana gateway effect', *Addiction*, 97, 12; Pudney, S. (2003) 'The road to ruin? Sequences of initiation to drugs and crime in Britain', *The Economic Journal*, at 113.

27 De Marneffe, *The Legalization of Drugs*.

28 Fagan, J. (1994) 'Do criminal sanctions deter drug crimes?' in (eds MacKenzie, D. and Uchida, C.) *Drugs and Crime: Evaluating Public Policy Initiatives*, Thousand Oaks: Sage.

29 U.S. National Academy of Sciences (2001) *Informing America's Policy on Illegal Drugs: What We Don't Know Keeps Hurting Us*, Washington, D.C.: National Academy of Sciences.

30 WHO, Epidemiology and Burden of Disease Team (2001) *The Global Burden of*

Disease, Focus 5, Brief 2, Geneva:WHO.

31 Strategic Task Force on Alcohol (2004) *Second and Final Report*, Dublin: Health Promotion Unit, Department of Health.

32 Ramstedt, M. and Hope, A. (2005) 'The Irish drinking habits of 2002: drinking and drinking-related harm, a European comparative perspective', *Journal of Substance Use*, 10, 2, at 233–283.

33 Hibell, B. et al. (2000) *The 1999 ESPAD Report: Alcohol and Other Drug Use among Students in 30 European Countries*, Strasbourg: Council of Europe.

34 Institute of Criminology, University College Dublin (2003) *Public Order Offences in Ireland*, Dublin: National Crime Council.

35 *Craic agus ceoil* is Irish for 'fun and music'.

36 *Young People and Alcohol* (2006) Dublin: National Youth Federation.

37 Strategic Task Force on Alcohol, *First Report* (2002); *Second and Final Report* (2004) Dublin; Health Promotion Unit, Department of Health.

38 MacCoun, R., Reuter, P. and Schelling, T. (1996) 'Assessing alternative drug control regimes', *Journal of Policy Analysis and Management*, 15, at 1–23.

39 See Leuw, E. (ed.) (1991) ' Drugs and drugs policy in the Netherlands' in *Crime and Justice: Annual Review of Research*, 12, Chicago: University of Chicago Press; *Drugs Policy in the Netherlands: Continuity and Change* (1995) The Hague: Ministries for Foreign Affairs, Health, Justice and the Interior; MacCoun, R. and Reuter, P. (1997) 'Interpreting Dutch cannabis policy: reasoning by analogy in the legalization debate', *Science*, 278, at 47–52; Uitermark, J. (2004) 'The origins and future of the Dutch approach towards drugs', *Journal of Drug Issues*, 22, at 511–532.

40 *Report on Drug Use in Ireland and Northern Ireland* (2003) Dublin and Belfast: National Advisory Committee on Drugs and Drug and Alcohol Information and Research Unit

41 Weil in *The Natural Mind* suggests that only the Eskimos of the far north, who had no access to vegetation, have failed to develop the means of intoxication.

10

The promise of alternative approaches: the possibility of a Kuhnian paradigm shift in the way we think about drugs

The analysis in Chapter 8 of the unique, independent contribution of prohibition to crime and to social and health harms confirmed the catastrophic failure and the horrific costs of prohibition in Ireland and elsewhere. It also indicated that the current compromise between prohibition and harm reductionism is failing. This examination of the reality of the Irish 'war on drugs' endorsed much of Transform's trenchant critique of prohibition. In contemporary Ireland, as in many other countries, drug use and misuse do appear to be 'rising dramatically with drugs cheaper and more available than ever'. In Ireland, as elsewhere, 'policy related harms are now far greater than harms caused by drug use ... and harm reduction initiatives are largely mitigating against harms created or exacerbated by prohibition – primarily prohibition-related crime.'

Chapter 9 confronted the reality that prohibition is remarkably indifferent to these deeply challenging facts. Prohibition has powerful structural, strategic and even emotional advantages, which help erect an almost insurmountable bulwark against countervailing evidence and anti-prohibitionist ideas. Prohibition also has the advantage that it inspires a form of faith, which reinforces its immunity to counterevidence.

Faith in prohibition can be likened to religious faith or to absolutist political faiths, such as Soviet Marxism, because in characterising the world from the perspective of the faithful it both engages deeply with the emotions and offers a strong, prescriptive moral programme for how we ought to behave. But it is also comparable to the kind of scientific paradigm described by Kuhn in his influential work *The Structure of Scientific Revolutions*.[1] According to Kuhn, all scientific thinking and practices operate within theoretical frameworks or paradigms, which give meaning to facts rather than simply arise from facts. These scientific paradigms inevitably involve a significant element of faith.

The prohibitionist articles of faith – that illicit drug use is a rightly criminalised evil and that prohibition can rid the world of this evil – constitute a theory or paradigm, which, in addition to having a normative role, telling us how we ought to act, interprets the facts and in this way dictates how the world is seen. The prohibitionist paradigm provides people with both a worldview and a moral outlook. Consequently, certain ideas are anathema or inconceivable to the prohibitionist. For example, the idea that the state should recognise a human right to use mood-altering substances is an absurdity to the prohibitionist.

In Kuhn's account, scientific paradigms continue to receive the support of the overwhelming majority, in spite of the accumulation of impressive, contradictory evidence, until such time as a tipping point is reached and a revolutionary new paradigm is quite suddenly adopted. The new paradigm sweeps away the old and takes its place as the dominant scientific worldview. For example, the once-widespread belief that the earth is flat and the more recent belief that it is a sphere which the sun orbits, were steadfastly protected by a seemingly diligent and authoritative scientific and religious establishment until suddenly banished by the adoption of radical, alternate theories with a better fit to the accumulating evidence. Of course, theories about the response to illicit drugs are not scientific in the strictest sense since they are not solely descriptive of material or observable reality, but are also strongly prescriptive. However, Kuhn's point is that all scientific paradigms tend to involve an essential component of faith, which strongly influences how we construe and react to social and material reality, and in this way they too shape our moral outlook.

This application of Kuhn's ideas to the prohibitionist ideology has important implications for the discourse on drugs and prohibition.[2] First, it implies that the current dominance of the prohibitionist worldview, its apparent unchallengeability and its secure hold on 'common sense' are no guarantee of its correctness or of its long-term survival. Seemingly secure and well-entrenched ideas can be abandoned with considerable haste.

Second, it is a clear lesson from the history of revolution in ideas that it is necessary to continue to assemble objective evidence and critically analyse received wisdom, however great the odds against change may seem. It is obvious that the prohibitionist worldview is currently a powerful, global phenomenon, upheld and reinforced by a corpus of international law and energetically promoted by the U.S. and the UN. However, one rarely knows when a tipping point will occur and in the interim it is essential to maintain an open mind, question assumptions and challenge myths. It is an important moral and scientific obligation to gather objective evidence, perhaps most importantly evidence that calls the current, dominant worldview into doubt.

While it is necessary to critique prohibition as an idea, prohibition as it actually operates in particular societies and the global legal and ideological system of prohibition, it is also vital to develop and nurture effective non-prohibitionist approaches in single jurisdictions and societies like Ireland. The ultimate target of abolitionists must be the end of the global system of prohibition because no nation can fully succeed in abolishing prohibition within its own borders until the international system of prohibition, which legally binds individual nations, has been dismantled. In other words, the desired tipping point is the transformation of drugs policy at the international rather than the national level because the latter makes little sense and has very limited prospects of success without the former.

A number of developed nations, such as the Netherlands, Portugal, Italy, Spain, Switzerland, Australia and New Zealand, have been at the forefront of experimentation with various forms of decriminalisation and depenalisation.[3] These experiments have focused on the depenalisation of personal possession and use of illicit drugs, including opiates and cocaine, and on diversion of 'inherent' drug crime offenders and, less frequently, non-violent, drug-using property offenders from the criminal justice system into treatment. Of course, the Irish and other systems of methadone maintenance should also be recognised as a form of *de facto* legalisation with critical implications for prohibition. These generally progressive approaches are normally motivated by harm reductionism and premised on a strict bifurcation policy, which permits tolerant approaches to addicts but maintains a harsh law enforcement approach to trafficking and the supply of drugs. This falls far short of the full abolition of prohibition and the acceptance of a right to use drugs that represent the radical revolution of drugs policy advocated in this book and supported by the book's analysis of the failure of the recent Irish system of pragmatic prohibition with strong harm reductionist elements.

In a very few cases, such as the Netherlands, which has legalised the cultivation of cannabis, and New Zealand, which has allowed the manufacture and distribution of BZP,[4] countries have gone beyond the mere decriminalisation of possession and use to something that closely resembles total legalization. Only these latter radical approaches have the real potential to deliver on abolition's promise to sever the link between drugs and organised crime. However, this potential is greatly limited by the fact that only one or two drugs out of many are tolerated, leaving the bulk of the drugs market in criminal hands. In a prohibitionist world, the potential effectiveness of these nations' legalisation experiments is also undermined by the very isolation of nations with progressive and tolerant drug policies, by the inevitable political fragility of these progressive but widely assailed policies and by the fact that such countries become a magnet for drug users and drug traffickers from other countries.[5]

Most of these experiments with decriminalisation and legalisation, whether they remain within the 'cops plus docs' rubric or trespass beyond it into genuinely non-prohibitionist territory, are informative because they provide evidence on the potential benefits of more tolerant and constructive, non-prohibitionist approaches and useful because they actually deliver real benefits in harm reduction for their countries, as is most clearly exemplified in the Netherlands. They also provide evidence which contradicts the dire predictions of prohibitionists that more tolerant approaches will lead to an explosion in drug use.

However, these piecemeal and partial attempts at decriminalisation still operate within both national and international prohibitionist frameworks. At present they still do not fundamentally challenge the global prohibitionist system. In fact, the governments involved find themselves having to contrive convoluted legal explanations to demonstrate continuing commitment to the global prohibitionist order and compliance with international law. As Bewley-Taylor argues,

> Countries committed to a harm-reduction approach to drugs have exploited the latitude which exists within the UN global drug control regime to implement strategies which deviate from the strict prohibition ethos of the conventions. These nations risk pressure being brought to bear through the UN drug control regime, principally by the United States, determined to prevent what it sees as foreign challenges to its domestic 'zero tolerance' approach and its internationalization.[56]

However, in time the evidence of these admittedly very circumscribed and often beleaguered attempts at decriminalisation and legalisation may well make an important contribution to achieving the tipping point at which the human right to use drugs becomes the accepted norm.

The thrust of the abolitionist critique, then, needs to be two-pronged, focusing its attack equally on the ills of prohibition in particular national contexts, such as Ireland, and on prohibitionist ideology and law in the international sphere and especially in the U.S., the progenitor and major sponsor of international prohibition. The implication of the current Kuhnian analysis is that abolitionists should not despair in the face of the current prohibitionist monolith, but, in order to gain the hoped for tipping point, should accumulate objective evidence and arguments, openly articulate and advocate their ideas and build political solidarity with the already strong anti-prohibition movement in the U.S. and elsewhere. Partial abolitionist and harm reductionist initiatives can be encouraged insofar as they reduce harm and therefore support the case for true abolition and the recognition of the right to use drugs.

A third implication of this Kuhnian analysis is that any future revolution in thinking about such a morally sensitive issue as drugs is unlikely to be as dramatic and definitive as the revolution in thinking about an observable phenomenon like the curvature of the earth. However, the recent change in most developed nations in thinking about homosexuality – the adoption of the principle that individuals have a human right to express their sexual orientation – proves the relevance of the Kuhnian paradigm process even to chiefly prescriptive, value-driven issues. The transformation in the treatment of homosexuality demonstrates that a major revolution in the law and social attitudes is possible, even when significant groups in society demur and persist with their outright condemnation.

Finally, it is an inevitable implication of the Kuhnian analysis that all scientific paradigms contain some element of faith. This means that the alternative, abolitionist paradigm on drugs should not attempt to present itself as a purely knowledge-based view with no reliance on beliefs and values. The abolitionist paradigm should admit and accept its own prescriptive, faith- and value-based elements, which primarily focus on the human right to use drugs and on the aspiration to a more constructive relationship between citizen and state. By the same token, abolitionists need not be defensive or apologetic about their values so long as they provide a better fit to the empirical facts and a more effective basis for policy.

The case for abandoning prohibition

This book has surely demonstrated that, while the evidence is overwhelming that prohibition directly and indirectly creates or escalates drug-related harm, there is no neat, all-conquering argument against prohibition. The issues are far too complex and entangled for a single, knock-out blow. It is an incontestable fact that prohibition has signally failed to eliminate illicit drug use or indeed halt its growth and this alone can be regarded as good reason to try an alternative approach. However, the rhetorical, strategic and structural advantages of prohibition continue to underpin its global dominance and make it a powerfully seductive doctrine. These advantages can, one by one, be exposed and rebutted, but, as the previous chapter illustrated, this is a convoluted and protracted task. While it is essential to confront the intricate claims and defences of prohibition and show that they cannot withstand an abolitionist critique nor justify the immense costs of prohibition, this kind of highly nuanced analysis and painstaking, dense argumentation is not going to quickly or easily convince the wider public. What is required to achieve a tipping point, a revolution in thinking, is a bold, inspirational idea to which people can subscribe as a matter of self-evident principle. Only the concept of a human right to use drugs can fulfil this role of providing a meaningful, inspiring and unifying idea which can guide the transition to a fully non-prohibitionist system.

Abolitionists must marshal and deploy the evidence about the costs of prohibition and the gains to be made from abandoning it. However, the ultimate success of the abolitionist case and the arrival of the tipping point will depend on the advocacy of the human right to use drugs, insofar as the rights of others are not thereby infringed. This is the 'one good and right idea' which pithily represents the complexity and moral authority of the anti-prohibition position and, at the same time, is capable of capturing the imagination of large numbers of people. This idea is not a mere rallying slogan, but is pregnant with important implications for how society should respond to drugs. It also clearly ties the drug use issue into the broader discourse on human rights, which is emerging as an increasingly powerful, guiding force behind social policy in developed, democratic countries like Ireland.

The human right to use drugs is a 'good and right idea' not only because it is central to the abolitionist cause, but also because such a right is consistent with self-evidently important libertarian principles, which are strongly valued in Western democracies; because it is derivable from widely accepted, legal and constitutional concepts of individual freedom and human rights; and, perhaps

most importantly, because it recognises the key psychological and physiological realities of the human relationship with mood-altering substances and
accepts that it is futile for the law to struggle against the natural and essentially
unobjectionable grain of human nature.

However, the advocacy of a human right to use drugs, though central to the
abolitionist position and the key to its persuasive success, is inadequate as the
sole basis for an approach to the drugs problem and must be allied with a strong
commitment to actions designed to optimise the potential gains of abolition.
The evidence and analysis in this book do not justify a categorical statement
that the recognition of a human right to use drugs would on its own prevent
all the diverse prohibition-related harms or exploit the opportunities for harm
reduction which such recognition would create. A purely laissez faire, human
rights approach would run a real risk of failing to both end some of the ills of
prohibition and deliver more effective prevention, education and treatment.

Selective criminalisation of illicit drugs and their condemnation as intrinsically immoral and criminally harmful are serious mistakes of prohibition.
Recognition of the right to use drugs is warranted in moral and legal terms and
is in accord with the scientific understanding of human nature. And, indeed,
recognition of the right to use drugs would totally eradicate at least some of
the problems caused by prohibition and substantially reduce others. However,
if abolition is to be effective and justifiable in practical as well as theoretical
terms, if it is to attain its real potential and achieve overall harm-reductive
gains, it is obvious that it must be combined with powerful, harm-reductive
strategies.

Recognition of the right to drug use may be right in principle but an entirely
laissez faire implementation of this right would be irresponsible and would fail
to address the essential, societal tasks of harm prevention and reduction. The
evidence suggests that recognising the right to use drugs would in fact ease the
tasks of harm prevention and reduction and would improve their success rates,
but recognition is only fully justified in the context of a sincere, well-resourced
and energetic commitment to all the non-coercive forms of harm prevention
and reduction, which would become available in the absence of prohibition,
most particularly education.

The concept of a human right to use drugs is the key inspiration and an
essential pillar of the abolitionist cause. But there are two other pillars in the
argument for the abolition of prohibition – the promise of negative gains to
be made by eliminating or substantially diminishing the ills associated with
prohibition and the promise of positive gains to be made by abandoning the
self-contradictory, self-defeating doctrines of prohibition and by changing the
relationship between citizen and state, thereby enhancing the quality of drugs
education, treatment and social relations. The three pillars are interlocking
and interdependent. Harm-reductive action to realise the potential negative
and positive gains of abolition is an essential complement to recognition of
the right to use drugs, but these gains can only be made if the right to use

drugs is fully embraced. There is a tension here; the right to use drugs is to be recognised but harm is to be reduced, often by persuading people to avoid drugs. This tension is resolved by ensuring that harm reduction strategies are always constrained by an overriding obligation to affirm the right to use drugs. The following sections will describe the negative and positive gains to be made from abolition and how they can be achieved within the confines of an over-arching commitment to the right to use drugs so long as the rights of others are not thereby infringed. The real possibility of synergy between the three pillars greatly strengthens the abolitionist argument and increases confidence that a world without prohibition is not only feasible but would also be a better place.

The negative gains

The abolition of prohibition, while by no means a panacea for all drug-related problems, is guaranteed to produce some substantial benefits. The potential gains from eliminating the ills of prohibition are many and diverse. They can be differentiated in terms of the significance of the gain and the confidence we can have that the gain will be either fully or partly realised.

The most important gains are undoubtedly in the area of crime. Many advantages can be confidently anticipated from reversing the criminalisation of selected mood-altering substances. However, this is a complex issue and it is necessary to address separately the potential gains in different areas of crime. In this context, at least four types of crime can be distinguished: 1) 'inherent' drug-related crimes; which are literally created by prohibition; 2) the crimes against humanity and the human rights abuses which are made possible by the global regime of prohibition; 3) drug-related acquisitive crime, which is not necessitated but is seriously aggravated by prohibition; and 4) 'systemic' drug-related crime, for which prohibition is a necessary precondition.

Most certain of all the results of abolition is the total elimination of the crimes created by prohibition – the 'inherent' drug-related crimes. By defini-tion decriminalisation abolishes the crimes of use, possession, trade in and distribution of drugs etc. In Ireland, which is relatively lenient with drug users, the main benefits would be two fold – in avoiding the punishment, stigmatisa-tion and alienation of large numbers of people who use illicit drugs but who are, in the main, otherwise law-abiding, and in freeing up resources for use by law enforcement against more 'legitimate' criminal targets. In countries like the U.S., where a massive, inordinately expensive and socially divisive 'incar-ceration binge' feeds mainly on minor drug offenders from racial minorities, the benefits would be wider and proportionately greater.

The global abolition of prohibition would also be certain to put an end to the senseless disruption of locally socialised forms of drug use in developing and more developed countries and the often brutal and inhumane assaults on the way of life of peasant farmers who produce drug crops. The 'war on drugs' and the economic realities of wealth-creating global prohibition are major influences promoting the corruption, violence and human rights abuses of many regimes in developing nations. Abolition of prohibition would eliminate much of the economic and ideological motive force behind these wrongs, although corruption and human rights abuses would undoubtedly continue for many other reasons. Abolition would also eliminate the 'war on drugs' rationale for international and U.S. collusion with repressive, corrupt and authoritarian regimes and make such collusion far less tolerable to democratic nations. It is reasonable to speculate that an economically viable, open, stable and internationally regulated market in drugs would have a generally stabilising political effect in producer countries, because it would end the current usefulness to drug barons of war, insurrection and other forms of civil chaos in drug-producing regions.

These different 'geopolitical' gains are very significant. In a highly globalised world, the drugs trade- and drugs war-related chaos and oppression in developing nations are by no means remote and irrelevant for small nations like Ireland, which are only peripherally involved in international aspects of the 'war on drugs'. Equally importantly, abolition is the only appropriate way to address the serious, though easily forgotten, moral burden carried by the prohibition system in respect of the harms caused to the ordinary people of third world and developing countries.

The gains to be achieved by abolition in the area of acquisitive drug-related crime are less certain and more limited. Only a small percentage of all users of illicit drugs resort to crime to fund their habit and these are often people who are disposed to criminal choices irrespective of whether or not they use drugs. Moreover, some of the potential gains from abolition have already been made by the provision of methadone maintenance and other interventions which help drug-using offenders to stabilise their lives and avoid crime. Nonetheless, there is an obvious potential for decreasing drug-related acquisitive crime, if abolition can regularise and legitimise access to drugs and thereby undermine the system, which hyper-inflates the price of drugs and greatly enlarges the 'criminal space'.

Certainly, in the case of Ireland, the most important potential gain from abolition is the undermining of serious organised crime. 'Systemic' drug-related crime can in the long run be almost totally eradicated by the abandonment of prohibition. This is not to suggest that all serious, organised crime would be abolished. There would still be many other lucrative areas of operation for ruthless, organised criminals who were willing to use violence. However, if effectively implemented, abolition would deprive criminal gangs of the immensely profitable black market in drugs. The clandestine, negatively glamorous and socially pervasive nature of this black market, supported by many thousands of people who do not regard themselves as victims or criminals, is uniquely dangerous because it is prolifically productive of hardened, ruthless criminals with powerful motivation to resort to intimidation and violence. The past 30 years in Ireland have witnessed a rapid, progressive evolution of organised drug gangs, with each successive generation outdoing the last in recklessness, volatility and callous violence. In the last decade, these gangs have embraced an appalling gun culture, based on the worst models from the drug-ravaged ghettos in the U.S. These developments have impacted widely on the quality of life in Ireland, with pernicious effects reaching far beyond the drug-infested areas and the people involved with drugs. Abolition, by undercutting both the financial and the socio-cultural motivations behind drug trading, confidently promises to eventually dismantle the drugs gang culture. It also promises to more effectively isolate those remaining criminals, who are willing to use violence for personal gain, and greatly shrink their areas of profitable operation.

Another set of ill-effects of prohibition includes the growing punitiveness of the criminal justice system, the hardening of public and political opinion, the rebalancing of criminal procedure so as to erode traditional due process rights, the strengthening to a potentially unhealthy extent of police powers and the increasing indifference of the system and the general public to the inherent injustices of the criminal justice system, especially in its handling of drug-related issues. The emotive 'war on drugs' rhetoric, the bifurcation approach and an unfounded but politically expedient belief in the effectiveness of punishment, in addition to the alarming reality of serious drug-related crime, have played a major role in this unfortunate shift in criminal justice. An important aspect of these changes is that, while they are initially directed at a relatively small number of serious drug criminals, they are subject to a form of creep, whereby they eventually impact on the civil liberties of all citizens and significantly alter the relationship between the police and the ordinary person.

Benefits from abolition in this area are possible but by no means certain. Prohibition and the 'war on drugs' have been the engine behind most of these changes, but it is notoriously difficult to reverse repressive changes to criminal procedure and sentencing legislation, even when these changes have not been proven effective. There are undoubtedly other social, economic and cultural forces driving the shift towards more punitive and repressive attitudes to criminal offending. Abolition would reduce the general political pressure to accede to demands for tougher, more punitive approaches, but a major change in social attitudes would probably be required before the Irish legislature would contemplate a reversal of current trends and the reintroduction of stronger legal safeguards and more restrained punishments.

The capacity of abolition to eliminate the many health and social ills which are partly produced by prohibition, is substantial, but limited. The most significant and achievable, potential gain from abolition is a system of regulation of drugs supply, incorporating effective mechanisms for quality control. There is genuine potential in such a system for a reduction in deaths from overdose and in the deaths and illness which arise from contamination of drugs in the totally unsupervised black market. Prohibition undoubtedly contributes to the spread of serious illness by promoting unsafe and unhygienic forms of drug-taking. Harm reductionism has already curtailed some of these negative effects of prohibition by, for example, making clean syringes and needles more available. However, analysis of the Irish evidence clearly demonstrates that the provision of services and materials, such as clean needles, has had fairly limited success in ending unsafe practices and in lowering the incidence of blood-borne diseases and other health problems amongst drug users. That prohibition remains the guiding legal framework and that the criminal drugs market continues to flourish are clearly major factors limiting the success of harm reductionism in this area.

An understanding of the psychology and sociology of drug experimentation (e.g. the symbolic meaning of drugs, role of curiosity and effects of peer pressure) and of the psychological and behavioural effects of addiction (e.g. the loss of autonomy, distortion of motivation and values, and role of denial processes), provides substantial grounds for scepticism about the prospect of ever fully eliminating risky drug-related behaviours, whether or not the legal framework is prohibitionist.

It is clear that attitudes, values and beliefs and in particular ignorance and recklessness play a crucial role in harmful drug use behaviours. Drug use itself, along with many other factors, shapes the key psychological predispositions. However, prohibition also plays a negative role and has the perverse effect of glorifying and mystifying drug use, granting it immense symbolic importance in the eyes of young people. Prohibition also pushes drug use into dark corners, where ignorance and recklessness flourish. Therefore, although the material provision of harm reduction services or the implementation of an effective quality control system will not prevent all unsafe practices or all overdoses, abolition promises some real gains. Material provision is essential and can be improved further by abolition. Proper quality control of the content of drugs would be of a great benefit and is only possible with abolition.

However, abolition, by creating a whole new set of attitudes around drugs and a far more constructive, less conflicted and furtive climate for education and prevention, could also significantly improve those problems, which are due not to a lack of services or quality control but to avoidable ignorance or unnecessary, reckless disregard of obvious risks. In particular, young people could be more effectively encouraged and persuaded to avoid foolish risks when experimenting with drugs. A more open, tolerant, non-prohibitionist environment, which placed sufficient emphasis on the targeted provision of information on issues like the risk of 'hot shot' overdose, could decrease the prevalence of unsafe practices. Even in the case of established addicts, self-control, self-monitoring and levels of simple prudence could be substantially enhanced.

The positive gains in education, prevention and harm reduction

The total abolition of prohibition would create the Promised Land for harm reductionists, because it would dismantle all prohibitionist barriers to harm reduction. Abolition would put an end to the constant struggles of harm reductionism against prohibition, struggles which prohibition, as the fundamental framework, will always tend to win – as in the current Irish controversy about needle exchange in prisons. Abolition would allow everyone to unite behind the best possible methods of primary prevention, education and treatment without the distraction of the moral and legal problems created by criminalisation.

This is not just a matter of clarifying policy and concentrating strategy on attainable goals, but also of the redirection of vital resources. Globally, hundreds of billions of euro are spent every year waging what appears, on all evidence, to be a futile 'war on drugs'. It has been estimated that 75% of all money spent on drug-related problems is expended on law enforcement and drugs interdiction. In contrast only about 25% is spent on treatment, education and prevention.[7] There is an obvious scandal in continuing to expend enormous economic resources on a system of prohibition, which has failed to lower the prevalence of drug use and may well have contributed to its increase. But it is also clear that great gains could be made, if only a small proportion of the money now spent on law enforcement was transferred to treatment, education and prevention.

The abolition of prohibition also promises a most important benefit by enabling society to shake off the yoke of the intellectual incoherence intrinsic to the current selective forms of prohibition. Incalculable damage is currently caused to the goal of harm reduction by prohibition's inability to fully acknowledge, on the one hand, the differences between less and more dangerous illicit substances and methods of drug use and, on the other, the fundamental similarities between illicit drugs and the ubiquitous, socially regulated or medically prescribed mood-altering substances. Only abolition can dissolve the false dichotomies of prohibition and banish the equivocation, half-truths, and hypocrisies that prohibition trails in its wake. Society will only be able to devise maximally effective preventative and treatment approaches, when it abandons the self-defeating prohibition system, which capriciously condones some substances and demonises others, irrespective of their relative dangerousness. It would clearly be greatly beneficial to shift the focus from the supposed immorality and illegality of using particular substances to the real but widely varying dangers of mood-altering substances – dependence, addiction and the risks to health, personality and economic and social well-being.

Education and prevention would be greatly enhanced by a factual, consistent and less condemnatory approach, which places currently illegal drugs on a similar footing to alcohol. At present the young person's first line of defence for illicit 'soft' drug use is unanswerable. In effect they say: 'you, the older generations and authorities, have your own devastatingly harmful drugs of abuse and we have comparatively innocuous cannabis, ecstasy, and magic mushrooms. It is plainly hypocritical of you to criminalise our use of these substances.' Recognition of the right to use drugs would take the illegality issue out of the equation and compel educators and health promoters to rely on honest, evidence-based information which is far more likely to be persuasive than blanket condemnation and exaggerated fear-mongering. Educators would be free of the current confusions and hypocrisies and fully empowered to promote moderation and safe use as well as abstinence. Young people's current disbelief and openly scornful response to prohibitionist propaganda is a serious problem not only because it facilitates their drug use, but also because it undermines their trust in all information and advice on drugs and drug use, including well-meaning and largely correct public health campaigns.

At present, the self-defeating nature of prohibitionist propaganda works synergistically with prohibitionist law enforcement to promote ignorance and push drug use into dark corners, where for many young people it acquires a glamorous mystique. In the current situation, the gap created by the absence of credible, non-judgmental, plain-speaking tends to be filled by myth-driven countercultures, which greatly increase the allure of drug use for young people, especially those with few other hopeful opportunities in life. Under prohibition, drug use has an enhanced attraction for youth because it is a 'forbidden fruit', which powerfully symbolises maturity, independence and the rejection of mainstream and parental values.[8]

I have argued in Chapter 7 that we should recognise the right to drug use partly because prohibition inevitably tends to challenge the young person's need for autonomy and tends to provoke reactance so that drug use actually becomes more likely. However, abolition could provide an opportunity to use the profoundly human desire for autonomy as a key component in education designed to lower the incidence of addiction and of dangerous forms of drug use. In fact, the tragedy of much drug use resides in the loss of personal control over one's life. If people knew they had a real option to take drugs, that the choice was their personal responsibility, drug use would no longer be a 'forbidden fruit'. Drug-taking would lose much of its symbolic value and negative glamour and would become a more mundane, unemotional, even boring issue, which they would approach with more circumspection and natural prudence. Non-prohibitionist drugs education could exploit this by focusing attention on the specific dangers of drug use for personal autonomy. Raising awareness of how certain drugs and ways of using drugs can subtly seduce people into degrading forms of physical, psychological and economic enslavement could become one of the primary tools of drugs education. In this way abolition could turn the human desire for autonomy from a major factor contributing to susceptibility to drugs into one of the most successful means of harm prevention.

The positive gains for the quality of civilisation and social relations

One of the most important and profound results of successful abolition would be attitudinal change. Change in attitudes, values and beliefs about drugs has the potential to impact dramatically and positively on the quality of social relations throughout society as well as on the behaviour of drug users. The real strength of the abolitionist case derives from the synergies between the three pillars – the recognition of the right to use drugs, the complete or partial elimination of the ill-effects of prohibition and the positive benefits for harm reduction of a logically coherent and unconflicted approach to drugs. Positive synergies can be gained from simultaneously accepting the right to use drugs and abandoning the follies of the prohibitionist system – its intellectual incoherence, its misguided insistence that all illicit drug use is immoral, its ill-placed faith in the power of punishment, its self-defeating approach to harm reduction, its antagonism towards innate aspects of human nature and its utterly false assessment of its own potential. These synergies emerge from the synthesis of a human rights approach and the adoption of a proactive harm reduction approach, based on an informed and honest assessment of both the attractions and dangers of mood-altering substances. The beneficial fruits of managing abolition in this way are to be found in the avoidance of many of the ills of prohibition but also crucially in attitudinal and associated behavioural change. Successful abolition can only emerge from and is clearly dependent on the attitudinal change involved in the acceptance of a basic right to use drugs. The broad effectiveness of abolition will mainly derive from the generation of more informed and more personally responsible attitudes to drugs.

Abolition involves an approach to drugs that prioritises trust and personal responsibility over mistrust and authoritarian discipline. This could be very beneficial, not least because prohibition's malign influence on attitudes to drugs is largely caused by its reliance on coercion and repression in a sphere of life where individual choice inevitably predominates and personal responsibility is desperately needed. As Mark Thornton has written: 'it is human nature that we are willing (at the time of choice) to pay more later to get benefits now. If we are truly worried about time preferences and short time horizons, then the war on drugs is no answer. Prohibition destroys individual responsibility towards drugs and it is individual responsibility and maturity that instil a future orientation where drug abuse and other risky activities are avoided.'[9]

It is easy to underestimate the importance of rather elusive, subjective patterns of thought and feeling like attitudes and perceptions. In fact, as the sociologist, Abrams, points out, 'people's perceptions, however uninformed they may be, are real and people act on the basis of them'.[10] The acclaimed achievements of prohibition, for example in seizing drugs and imprisoning drug dealers, may appear to be far more concrete and practically useful than the promise of attitudinal change offered by a non-prohibitionist system. However, the evidence shows us that the concrete achievements of prohibition do not in the long run impact positively on the drugs culture. Indeed, a major part of prohibition's failure can be attributed to the fact that it engenders unhelpful and distorted attitudes, values and beliefs amongst various actors, such as drug dealers and users. Attitudes and perceptions, however intangible, are actually at the heart of the drugs problem. They are precisely what needs to be changed, if society is to achieve optimal harm reduction.

U.S. policy on handguns is a useful illustration of the potent influence of attitudes not only on behaviour, but also on decisions about how the state should regulate its citizens' behaviour. The parallel is somewhat paradoxical, since the weight of evidence on the handgun issue favours prohibition, while the weight of evidence on the illicit drugs problem favours abandoning prohibition. But the main point is that policy on single pivotal issues, like access to guns or drugs, is able to determine (and in a sense is determined by) a whole constellation of widely shared attitudes, values and beliefs. Policy on drugs prohibition, just like policy on access to firearms, is so crucial that it will inevitably have a pervasive influence on attitudes and behaviour across society.

The U.S. is almost unique amongst developed nations in clinging to a very liberal policy on access to handguns. This policy is directly linked to the extremely high rate of homicide by firearm in the U.S. and the equally high suicide and accidental death by firearm rates. The ready availability of guns also plays a major role in the comparatively high incidence of murderous outrages in schools and workplaces in the U.S. One recent, appalling example is the Virginia Tech Massacre of April 2007, when an aggrieved student with a psychiatric history, who had been able to easily purchase guns and ammunition, killed 32 students and teachers. The U.S. gun lobby is based on a complex set of beliefs, attitudes and values, invoking, amongst other things, the U.S. Constitution, the American notion of liberty, images of the frontier and masculinity, and fear of intruders, predators, rapists and terrorists. All of this makes little sense to Europeans, who can see for themselves the great benefit of restricting access to weapons. Yet pro-gun Americans pour scorn on Europeans for ensuring that 'only felons are armed'. The fact that access to guns saves very few innocent people from harm in the U.S., but contributes greatly to the toll of death and injury, totally escapes their notice. The marked contrast between Europe and the U.S. on this issue relates not only to the physical presence of guns but also to major differences in attitude. In Europe the attitudes which both drive and result from the ban on guns impact positively on the quality of life and the quality of relations between people. The prohibition on guns creates a more civilised as well as a safer society.

In a similar way, the abolition of drugs prohibition promises to create a more civilised society and a generally more informed and responsible attitude towards mood-altering substances. Although one situation is about introducing prohibition and the other about abandoning it, there are deep similarities in terms of the shift in attitudes required to transform the response to guns in the U.S. and to drugs around the world. Both require the kind of courage and vision which would allow people to let go of their fear-driven reliance on comforting, but false convictions. These are, respectively, that providing access to guns will protect innocent people, and that punishing the supply and use of certain drugs will eliminate or alleviate drug-related problems. Both these mistaken convictions favour distrust, threat and coercive action, factors which paradoxically produce counterproductive effects. In contrast, the alternative policies, that is restricting access to guns and abolishing prohibition, would seek to harness the self-fulfilling power of having positive expectations of people. In both cases, the more trusting and less fearful alternative approaches enhance personal responsibility by enabling and requiring self-restraint.

The sharp contrast in quality of life with respect to violence between European countries and the U.S., which can at present be ascribed to their differences on the single policy issue of access to guns, is indicative of the profound difference that abolition could make. At present, under drugs prohibition, deviant forms of social regulation predominate in the drugs culture, encouraging ignorance, impulsive, mindless, reckless and excessive drug use and attachment to isolated, antisocial and criminal subgroups. Legal recognition of the right to use drugs, insofar as it socialises drug use, will empower normal forms of social regulation of drug use, such as social comparison and normative disapproval within family, school, workplace and recreational settings. The drug user whose drug use does not make him or her a pariah is more likely to maintain a positive engagement with society and follow positive role models. This will in turn facilitate reflection, information and understanding and in most cases lead to more moderate drug use and more prosocial lives.

Synthesising the three pillars: the constraints on and conditions for successful abolition

Undoubtedly, the practical problem of managing access to drugs, that is regulating the manufacture, distribution, advertising and sale of drugs, creates the greatest difficulty for anyone promoting an abolitionist approach to drugs.[11] There are many serious dilemmas of drug control which are unavoidable even in a non-prohibitionist system. Most obviously, there is the underlying tension between the requirement to regulate in a harm-reductive manner and the requirement to provide easy enough access to drugs to undermine the black market and effectively end criminal involvement in drugs. This goal is essential to the success of abolition and perhaps the single most significant benefit to be derived from abolition in terms of the elimination of the ill-effects of prohibition. Equally, the substantial advantages of quality control of drugs are dependent on creating a legal market and eliminating the criminal one. A controlled legal market running alongside a substantial, residual black market, which offered cheaper but frequently contaminated drugs, would be a highly undesirable outcome.

Supply of drugs to children, who must be protected because of their ignorance, immaturity and special vulnerability, would certainly still be a matter for
the criminal law. However, access to drugs for adults would have to be quite
liberal. The right to drug use would have to have real substance. Access could
not be made overly restrictive because this would open up opportunities for
criminal involvement. Similarly, government would have to refrain from using
the taxation of drugs primarily as a harm-reductive mechanism. Piling taxes
on drugs and making them exorbitantly expensive would be a clear invita-
tion to criminals to get involved in the trade, even though profits, limited by
competition with the legal market, would be considerably smaller than in the
current, monopolistic black market.

On the other hand, it is easy to overstate the potential problems of allowing
access to drugs. The Dutch experiment, which involves de facto legalisation of
the cultivation as well as distribution of cannabis, the current large-scale Irish
methadone maintenance system and heroin prescription schemes elsewhere,
and the largely unproblematical shops, which, around Ireland and in many
other countries, sell the 'natural' and manmade psychoactive substances (like
BZP) that have somehow escaped prohibition, all bear witness to the real
possibility of sufficient, well-regulated, socialised access.

Writers like Kleiman[12] have even suggested some innovative methods by
which, in a non-prohibitionist system, access could be provided in a usefully
harm-reductive manner without creating demand which could only be met by
criminal involvement in the drugs trade. Kleiman has suggested the possibility
of introducing either a positive or negative licence system for access to drugs.
A positive licence would be available to any adult who had demonstrated a
capacity for safe use, perhaps including attendance at health promotion classes.
A negative licence would be available to any adult, who had not forfeited the
right by violating conditions of eligibility, for example by criminally harming
others through their drug use. Karel[13] has proposed a complex, model legalisation system with a diverse set of graduated regulatory controls, linked to the
relative dangers of different drugs and ways of use, including continuing legal
prohibition in the case of a few particularly dangerous drugs.

At present, harm reductionist provision of syringes and needles is supported
because it has a clearcut preventative rationale within the prohibitionist framework. This provision is, in a sense, forced, reluctant and definitely restricted to
those already caught up in IV use. Under abolition, it would be necessary to
provide equal or even greater access to drug-taking paraphernalia to all adults
and it would be impossible or very difficult to set restrictions aimed at keeping
such equipment out of the hands of the as yet uninitiated. Any other approach
would risk reproducing the unsafe drug use practices caused by strict prohibition, even in a situation where drugs themselves were not prohibited. It is clear
that this open and tolerant approach would require courage, a firm commitment to the right to use drugs and strong belief in the efficacy of education,
information and non-coercive forms of persuasion. Harm reduction without

the shackles of prohibition could be powerfully effective, but its value system would be very distinct from current harm reductionism, which is defined by its relationship with prohibition.

The very real problems surrounding access to and control of drugs have tended to move speculation about abolitionist systems in two directions: 1) towards partial forms of abolition as in the legalisation of cannabis; and 2) towards medicalised systems which, like the methadone maintenance programme, involve prescription of drugs and strict medical control. Neither of these approaches, which fail to bite the bullet of accepting the right to use drugs, satisfies the conditions for successful abolition. Joint consideration of the three interlocking pillars of the case for abolition – the right to use drugs, the need to eliminate the ill-effects of prohibition and the potential gains from a more coherent, morally justifiable and rational approach to drugs in terms of more moderate attitudes, enhanced personal responsibility and more effective prevention – implies that the compromise approaches of partial decriminalisation and medicalisation are totally inadequate. Most obviously they do not respect the human right to use drugs.

By far the strongest campaign for drugs legalisation concentrates uniquely on cannabis. This is understandable because cannabis use is very widespread and involves many people who are otherwise law-abiding. Socialising and decriminalising the drug use of this large group would appear to be preeminently sensible and, politically, the most convenient and palatable step towards abolition. It is also a form of drug use which is relatively harmless in its health and social effects, does not involve IV use, is not strongly addictive and has significant health benefits for people with certain chronic illnesses. The Dutch decriminalisation experiment has already shown the potential of cannabis legalisation to lower use, prevent progression to more serious forms of drug use and separate the cannabis market from the criminal 'hard' drugs market.

However, while cannabis legalisation is a positive demonstration of the benefits of abolition and a useful first step towards the tipping point where the right to use drugs will be recognised, it is clearly insufficient and cannot secure the major gains promised by fully fledged abolition. The continuing prohibition on other drugs ensures the enduring presence of a criminal market and will not end the 'war on drugs'. This means there will be little impact, in both consumer and producer societies, on the pernicious social and health effects of prohibition which are largely concentrated in the 'hard' drugs sector. Moreover, in the absence of a credible, evidence-based system of drugs criminalisation which responds to the real relative potential for harm of different drugs and forms of use, cannabis legalisation cannot resolve the incoherence and self-contradiction of the prohibitionist position. It cannot, therefore, achieve the essential educational and attitudinal gains which are to be derived from an honest and convincing discourse on drugs.

Medical and other health professionals have an essential harm-reductive and therapeutic role in the response to drug problems and particularly addiction. However, the idea that the medical profession, which is itself at fault for the creation of many iatrogenic addictions, could or should police drug use is unworkable. It would be ludicrous to vest powers in doctors to prescribe and control access to the more socialised drugs, such as cannabis, ecstasy, cocaine and psychoactive mushrooms. These powers would be highly questionable from the point of view of medical ethics and would certainly be incompatible with the human right to use drugs. Recognising a right to use drugs is tantamount to recognising the right to self-medicate with mood-altering substances. Furthermore, most individual use of mood-altering substances is neither a serious public health concern nor a significant individual medical issue.

Medical or pharmaceutical control of access would be deeply resented and circumvented in every possible way, ensuring the persistence of a criminal drugs market. Transferring the management of the use of mood-altering substances from law enforcement to doctors would not only be an affront to the autonomy and self-respect of both users and doctors, but would also frequently lead to the creation of new dependency relationships with medical authority which would tend to undermine the user's sense of responsibility for their own choices. It would confer a responsibility on doctors which they would not want and should not have and prevent the kind of informed personal responsibility which only a true abolitionist system could promote.

Current advances in medicine, neuroscience and genetics suggest that in the near-future many better targeted and safer drugs will be available which will enhance various aspects of human performance, such as memory and intelligence, and have powerful mood- and consciousness-altering effects. This is a reminder of the ever-changing face of the 'drugs problem' and of the pivotal importance of informed personal choice and responsibility. Entirely new, exciting and dramatically seductive, manmade drugs will soon be available and widely used and misused. The neuroscientist Michael Gazzaniga is clear about the impotence and inappropriateness of prohibition as a response to these developments. He states: 'the unintended use and misuse of drugs is a constant. Trying to manage it, control it and legislate it will bring nothing but failure and duplicity ... self-regulation of substances will occur; those few who desire altered states will find the drug, and those who don't want to alter their sense of who they are will ignore the availability of the drug. The government should stay out of it, letting our own ethical and moral sense guide us through the new enhancement landscape.'[14]

The current methadone maintenance system demonstrates some of the benefits and possibilities of a non-prohibitionist approach to even serious forms of drug use, but the system is confined to addicted and problematic opiate users and has very clear limits. Medical provision of opiates is strictly controlled and not designed to provide clients with the positive experiences they expect from drug use. This means that a great many of those on maintenance turn to street drugs, undermining the purpose of the intervention and continuing to support the criminal market. Medical supervision of this kind, which is, first and foremost, a form of control and, secondarily, a form of therapy, is inherently compromised and, as the Irish experience clearly indicates, unlikely to provide optimal, long-term, harm-reductive benefits. In short, neither cannabis legalisation nor the medicalisation of access to drugs respects the human right to use drugs. Equally, these approaches will not eliminate the major ills of prohibition nor deliver the preventative benefits of a logically coherent and morally justifiable approach to drugs.

Summary

A revolution in the way we think about drugs, including the abolition of the present global system of prohibition and an end to the 'war on drugs' is a real, though seemingly remote, possibility. This revolution would involve a reversal of official thinking in the U.S., the UN and other international bodies which define and support the international human rights regime. A key element in this revolution would be the adoption by these bodies of the principle that there is a human right to use drugs so long as the rights of others are not infringed by the drug-taking. In order to move opinion towards the tipping point at which such a revolution can occur, a three-pillar approach is required, emphasising the strong moral, legal and scientific basis of the right to use drugs, the devastating costs of prohibition to individual societies and to the global order, and the positive effects of abolition on the quality of social relations, on drugs education and on the prevention and treatment of destructive forms of drug use.

Global abolition is a worthy, if very demanding and difficult, ambition, which offers many significant benefits. Compromises which do not fully respect the right to use drugs, such as partial abolition or medicalisation of drug control, or which depenalise personal possession and use of any or all drugs but maintain prohibition of trafficking and distribution, cannot deliver the major benefits attainable from total abolition. It is impossible to overstate the crucial importance of eliminating criminal involvement in the drugs trade. Wresting the drugs trade from criminal hands is at once a major benefit, which only total abolition can deliver, and an absolutely necessary condition for truly successful abolition. Other considerable benefits, such as a comprehensive system of quality control of drugs, the ending of the detrimental effects of the 'war on drugs' on human rights and criminal justice and the redirection of resources from law enforcement to harm reduction, entirely depend on eliminating criminal control over drugs.

A non-prohibitionist system would require courage, tolerance and equanimity in the face of the drug harms and problems of addiction, which would undoubtedly continue at quite a high level. It would require a willingness to base social policy on drug use on trust and respect for personal responsibility rather than on fear, condemnation and discipline. Abolition, based on a genuine tolerance of drug use, closely allied with an energetic, proactive, but non-coercive approach to harm reduction and the prevention of destructive forms of drug use, could transform societal attitudes and break the highly detrimental hold of the clandestine, criminal drugs counterculture on the minds of young people. Accepting and reinforcing the key and undeniable role of personal choice in the drugs area is the best way to enhance personal responsibility and improve the social and informational context in which choices about drug use are made.

A non-prohibitionist approach to drugs is needed, but abolition will not solve the issues of individuals who by temperament and background are particularly prone to socially disruptive and self-destructive forms of drug use and addiction. Nor will it resolve the problems of social and economic inequality, which make certain disadvantaged and stigmatised communities especially susceptible to drugs problems. These problems demand the vigorous and effective implementation of policies driven by a commitment to identifying, assisting and supporting at risk children and their families and by an urgent and sincere political will to create greater social justice. However, by ending the wasteful and futile 'war on drugs', abolition could promote these more sensible and legitimate policy priorities and could ensure the concentration of financial and human resources on more constructive and hopeful goals.

Prohibition is a virulent, self-inflicted wound. However seductive, 'commonsensical', and inevitable prohibition appears, it is not in fact a necessary evil. Prohibition is not the only, nor the best alternative.

Notes

1 Kuhn, T. (1962) *The Structure of Scientific Revolutions*, Chicago: University of Chicago Press.
2 For a different view of the relevance of Kuhn's ideas to the drugs problem see Shaffer, H. (1986) 'Conceptual crises and the addictions: a philosophy of science perspective', *Journal of Substance Abuse Treatment*, 3, at 285–296.
3 See *Decriminalisation in Europe? Recent Developments in Legal Approaches to Drug Use* (2001) Lisbon: EMCDDA at http://eldd.emcdda.org/databases/eldd_comparative_analyses.cfm. The website http://drugpolicy.org also provides general information on decriminalisation and legalisation approaches around the world.
4 BZP (Benzylpiperazine) has been legal in New Zealand for a number of years but in May 2007 the New Zealand parliament voted to outlaw the drug in December 2007.
5 For an analysis of the difficulties facing the unilateral, progressive drug policies of the Netherlands see Lemmens, P. and Garretsen, H. (1998) 'Unstable pragmatism: Dutch drug policy under national and international pressure', *Addiction*, 93, 2, at 157–162.
6 Bewley-Taylor, D. (2004) 'Harm reduction and the global drug control regime: contemporary problems and future prospects', *Drug and Alcohol Review*, 23, 4, at 483–489.

7 These estimates are cited in Tombs, J. (2002) *Making Sense of Drugs and Crime: Drugs, Crime and Penal Policy*, Edinburgh: a report of the Scottish Consortium on Crime and Criminal Justice.

8 MacCoun, R. (1993) addresses the attraction of the 'forbidden fruit' in the context of a discussion of the deterrent effects of the criminal law in 'Drugs and the law: a psychological analysis of drug prohibition', *Psychological Bulletin*, 113, at 497–512.

9 Thornton, M. (1994) 'The Havard Plan for Drugs', *The Review of Austrian Economics*, 7, 1 at 147–150.

10 Abrams, M. (1973) 'Subjective social indicators', *Social Trends*, 35, 4.

11 Levinson, M. (2002) *The Drug Problem*, Westport CT: Praeger.

12 Kleiman, M. (1992) *Against Excess: Drug Policy for Results*, New York: Basic Books.

13 Karel, R. (1991) 'A model legalization proposal' in (ed. Inciardi, J.) *The Drug Legalization Debate*, Thousand Oaks: Sage.

14 Gazzaniga, M. (2005) *The Ethical Brain*, New York: Dana Press.

Index